UPSTART
TALENTS

UPSTART TALENTS

Rhetoric
and the Career of Reason
in English Romantic Discourse,
1790–1820

James Mulvihill

DELAWARE

Newark: University of Delaware Press

Associated University Presses
2010 Eastpark Boulevard
Cranbury, NJ 08512

The paper used in this publication meets the requirements of the American National Standard for Permanence of Paper for Printed Library Materials Z39.48-1984.

Library of Congress Cataloging-in-Publication Data

Mulvihill, James.
  Upstart talents : rhetoric and the career of reason in English romantic discourse, 1790–1820 / James Mulvihill.
      p. cm.
  Includes bibliographical references and index.
  ISBN 0-87413-848-5 (alk. paper)
  1. Great Britain—Politics and government—1789–1820. 2. Rhetoric—Political aspects—Great Britain—History—19th century. 3. Rhetoric—Political aspects—Great Britain—History—18th century. 4. Politics and literature—Great Britain—History—19th century. 5. Politics and literature—Great Britain—History—18th century. 6. Speeches, addresses, etc., English—History and criticsm. 7. Reason—Political aspects—Great Britain. 8. Cobbett, William, 1763–1835. 9. Romanticism—Great Britain. I. Title.

DA520 .M85 2004
808.53'0941'09034—dc22   2003017179

PRINTED IN THE UNITED STATES OF AMERICA

For my parents,
Neville and Lois Mulvihill

"The upstarts whom good men hate are such as have risen by low and base arts, or who have grown up out of the follies or vices of their particular patrons, or of the government and governing system in general. They may well be denominated mushrooms; for they spring from the rotten part of the state, and the soil that bears them will seldom bear any thing else. Crawling sycophants, labourers in the dirty work of corruption, with all the endless list of jobbers of every description, such as I have seen in America, for instance. Such are the upstarts; men, who, having, as it were, stolen fortunes from the public treasure; that is to say from the labour of the people, become, by the means of those fortunes, the possessors of the land, making slaves of those whom they have already pillaged and impoverished: such are the upstarts, whom every honest and honourable man must hate, and to whose sway he can never submit without impatience."

—William Cobbett,
"Letter V. To the Rt. Hon. William Pitt, On the Causes of the Decline of Great Britain"

Contents

Acknowledgments   11

List of Abbreviations   13

Preface   17

1. Designing Eloquence:
The Rhetorical Context   21

2. Whiggish Energies:
The Ethos of Technical Mastery   64

3. Critical Stratagems:
Anti-Jacobin Imposture and Periodical Reviewing   118

4. Systematic Opposition:
The Case of William Cobbett   161

5. Reason in Extremis:
Narratives of Regressive Rationality   207

Afterword   258

Notes   263

Bibliography   277

Index   285

Acknowledgments

I would like to express my gratitude to those who, in one way or another, helped in the conception and writing of this book. Colleagues from the Department of English at the University of Alberta, Professors Raymond Jones, David Gay, Rick Bowers, and Jo-Ann Wallace, deserve special mention for their kind support. Students in two graduate seminars I taught while this book was being conceived, "William Blake and Mass Culture" and "The Romantic Public Sphere," provided a genial if captive audience for testing some of my ideas. In this connection, I particularly want to thank Rob Summers and Sean Hartigan, both of whom I supervised as Ph.D. students and who also served as research assistants on the project. I also owe the Faculty of Arts at the University of Alberta as well as the Social Sciences and Humanities Research Council of Canada my warm thanks for crucial support in the forms of funding and time. A good deal of the research for this book was done in the Rutherford Library at the University of Alberta and the Robarts Library at the University of Toronto; I would like to thank the staffs at both these fine research libraries for their kind help. I am grateful for the encouragement and interest shown by Professor Donald C. Mell, Chair of the University of Delaware Press, and to the editorial team at the Associated University Presses, in particular Managing Editor Ms. Christine Retz, for their cordial efficiency. I express my warmest gratitude to my wife, Abby, for her unfailing support, sympathy, and encouragement. Passages in three of this book's chapters have been adapted from previously published essays, and I would like to thank the journals in which this material appeared for kindly permitting me to use this material here. Chapter 2 contains material from "Hazlitt on Parliamentary Eloquence," *Prose Studies* 12 (September 1989): 132–46. Parts of chapter 2 and 3 previously appeared in "The Poetics of Authority: Politics and Representation in Hazlitt's Criticism," *Journal of English and Germanic Philology* 101 (October 2002): 540–60. Parts of chapter 5 are adapted from "The History of all Times and Places": William Blake and Historical Representation in *America* and *Europe*," *CLIO* 29 (summer 2000): 373–94; "'Demonic Objectification and Fatal Isolation': Blake and the Culture Industry," *Studies in Romanticism* 38 (winter 1999): 597–620; and "'A Species of Shop'": Peacock and the World of Goods," *Keats-Shelley Journal* 49 (2000): 85–113.

Abbreviations

A-J	*The Anti-Jacobin, or Weekly Examiner. In Two Volumes.* 4th edition (London: J. Wright, 1799)
AJR	*Anti-Jacobin Review and Magazine; or Monthly Political and Literary Censor*
B	William Wordsworth, *The Borderers*, ed. Robert Osborn (Ithaca: Cornell University Press, 1982)
BD	*The Black Dwarf*
CWH	William Hazlitt, *The Complete Works of William Hazlitt*, ed. P. P. Howe, 21 vols. (Toronto: J. M. Dent and Sons, 1930–34)
CPR	*Cobbett's Weekly Political Register*
F	Mary Shelley, *Frankenstein: or The Modern Prometheus, The 1818 Text*, ed. Marilyn Butler (Oxford: Oxford University Press, 1998)
HPR	William Cobbett, *A History of the Protestant Reformation in England and Ireland* (London, 1829)
LE	Thomas Sheridan, *A Course of Lectures on Elocution* (London: A. Millar, R. and J. Dodsley, T. Davies, C. Henderson, J. Wilkie, and E. Dilly, 1762)
LOC	Joseph Priestley, *A Course of Lectures on Oratory and Criticism*, eds. Vincent M. Bevilacqua and Richard Murphy (Carbondale: Southern Illinois University Press, 1965)
LRBL	Hugh Blair, *Lectures on Rhetoric and Belles Lettres*, ed. Harold F. Harding (Carbondale: Southern Illinois University Press, 1965)
PG	William Cobbett, *Paper Against Gold* (New York: John Doyle, 1834)

PL   William Gerard Hamilton, *Parliamentary Logic* (London: C. and R. Baldwin, 1808)

PR   George Campbell, *The Philosophy of Rhetoric*, ed. Lloyd Bitzer (Carbondale: South Illinois University Press, 1963)

R   *The Republican*

RRF   Edmund Burke, *Reflections on the Revolution in France,* ed. L. G. Mitchell, vol. 8 of *The Writings and Speeches of Edmund Burke*, general editor, Paul Langford (Oxford: Clarendon, 1991)

RP   Edmund Burke, *Letters on a Regicide Peace,* ed. R. B. McDowell, vol. 9 of *The Writings and Speeches of Edmund Burke*, general editor, Paul Langford (Oxford: Clarendon, 1991)

S   *The Satirist; or, Monthly Meteor*

TF   Samuel Taylor Coleridge, *The Friend*, ed. Barbara Rooke, vol. 2 of *The Collected Works of Samuel Taylor Coleridge*, ed. Kathleen Coburn (Princeton, N.J.: Princeton University Press, 1969)

WB   *The Complete Poetry and Prose of William Blake*, ed. David V. Erdman (Toronto: Doubleday, 1988)

WJB   Jeremy Bentham, *The Works of Jeremy Bentham*, ed. John Bowring (New York: Russell & Russell, 1962)

WP   William Godwin, *Caleb Williams*, ed. David McCracken (Oxford: Oxford University Press, 1982)

UPSTART
TALENTS

Preface

In a special-forum issue of *Studies in Romanticism* entitled "Romanticism and its Publics," Jon Klancher remarks an historical lacuna where English Romanticism is concerned in Jürgen Habermas's magisterial account of the public sphere.[1] Studies like Klancher's *Making of the English Reading Audiences, 1790–1832* (1987) have at once remedied the omission and challenged the concept, positing not one such sphere but many, and all competing for authority. If the wholly integrated public sphere posited by Habermas has proved too ideal, however, revisionary reconstructions still retain something of an ideal aura. Klancher's use of Bakhtinian dialogism, with its carnivalesque Menippean ethos, celebrates a cultural plurality overrunning the boundaries of the unitary public sphere of his study's counterthesis, and yet such anarchic recontextualizing of the concept leaves intact the idealism at its heart. This revisionary model does not feature a disinherited Romantic public life so much as one locating many heirs to the legacy of Enlightenment. That a faith in enfranchised public discussion survived into the early nineteenth century is evident even amid the fractured cultural reality described by Klancher and others.[2] At the same time, this faith coexisted with profound skepticism. Where radical agitator and playwright Thomas Holcroft could insist that "Surely, this age has more general information, and therefore more virtue, more wisdom, than the past," Sir Robert Peel dismissed public opinion as a "great compound of folly, weakness, prejudice, wrong feeling, right feeling, obstinacy and newspaper paragraphs."[3] If in the *Rights of Man* (1791) Thomas

Paine celebrated what he called "universal conversation,"[4] a public sphere enabling popular dissent, in works like *Reflections on the Revolution in France* (1790) and *Letters on a Regicide Peace* (1796–97) Edmund Burke attacked this Enlightenment ideal as the fabrication of subversive elements among Nonconformists and literary *paradoxeurs*.

What emerges from these positions is a sense of public opinion variously honorific and critical. Holcroft professed a complete Enlightenment faith in the impartial tribunal of public opinion even as government agents provoked Church-and-King mobs into violent demonstrations against prominent reformers like Joseph Priestley in the 1790s. If treason charges were dropped against him by an English court in 1794, he still stood accused in the government-controlled press of using his theatrical expertise to manipulate public opinion, and indeed regretted losing the opportunity to appear in court for perhaps this very reason, among others.[5] Burke, meanwhile, attacked the manners and morals of French revolutionaries by means of the very critique whose subversive uses he condemned in their hands. Later in the revolutionary decade, such methods were employed against rational reform by Tory literati like George Canning and John Hookham Frere in the *Anti-Jacobin* and by these same right-wing operatives in the Ministerial Press during the decades following. Four years after Waterloo, in his preface to *Political Essays* (1819), William Hazlitt represented the war against Bonaparte as a war against Liberty enlisting English libertarianism in the cause of absolute monarchy and thus effecting a "new alliance between kings and people" (*CWH* 7:11). Amidst this deviously orchestrated public campaign, reformers were co-opted to the putatively popular cause, effectively losing their critically reflective function in the public sphere. In 1820, however, these same reformers took up the loyalist weapons of their Tory foes in order to attack a King by defending his estranged Queen.

These and other such rhetorical appropriations call into question the radical/reactionary axis implicit in scholarly discussions of the period. While recent scholarship has reduced a traditionally overdrawn binary of rational reform and reactionary obscurantism to its constituent elements, this study proposes to cut across the left/right poles characterizing discussions of Romantic England by examining the complicated (and sobering) encroachments of the regressive onto the progressive in rhetoric of all political stripes. It begins from the premise that this rhetoric can employ reasoned arguments while also exhibiting irrationalist tendencies not so much supplanting rational discourse as using it in unexpected ways. The materialist emphasis of current cultural studies provides a useful corrective to the grand schemas of intellectual history, but overcompensates by employing only the most nominal generalizations. While revisionist treatments of the "public sphere" have succeeded in breaking the concept down into divers cultural constituencies, this study examines rhetorical assumptions about public discourse common to these constituencies in Romantic England. In the decades following the French Revolution, the reactionary deployment of a subversive cultural critique co-opted Enlightenment notions about free inquiry by means of newly emerging methods of rhetorical persuasion. If liberals like Hazlitt attacked the Ministerial Press and its expedient methods—*"The thing* is hired to soothe or inflame the public mind, as occasion requires" (*CWH* 19:117)—conservative commentators like Burke not only corroborated fears about violent revolution but warned of a greater, because more insidious, moral revolution fomented not by the "great" or the "populace" but by various special interests with a bent for dangerous speculation (*RP* 9:291–92). J. G. A. Pocock has set similar tendencies in seventeenth- and eighteenth-century England within the context of a profound shift in the political culture of this period, portraying a traditionalist rhetoric of propertied independence gradually supplanted by one based on more portable conceptions of power as well as a hedonistic ethic privileging self-interest. A concept like civic virtue was thus reconfigured as a private quality as qualities wholly independent of public morality, such as talent, came to the fore.[6] This study considers the consequences of such a cultural shift for rhetorical practice in Romantic England. It argues that "right feeling" and "wrong feeling," to cite Peel's categories, could be rhetorically exploited by reform and reaction alike to pursue ends that, while putatively different, might result in a similarly regressive issue.

As Don H. Bialostosky and Lawrence Needham note in their introduction to *Rhetorical Traditions and British Romantic Literature*, Romanticism is generally regarded as antirhetorical, even unrhetorical. Where it is considered in terms of rhetoric, as in Paul de Man's *Rhetoric of Romanticism*, these are the terms not of historical tradition but of modern theory. What is needed to supply such omissions, Bialostosky and Needham argue, is "careful attention to the contexts of Romantic literature, leading . . . to an increased awareness of its rhetoricity"[7]—an awareness to which this study hopes to contribute. The following chapters focus on the rhetorical conditioning of rational argument in the public life of Romantic England. An opening chapter starts from the assimilation of empirical philosophy in late eighteenth-century rhetorical theories by which truth validity was reduced to the mere sensation of truth. The latitude imparted by such thinking to rhetorical practice made rhetoric a highly versatile instrument, effectively regularizing fallacy into a rational system of imposture. The second and third chapters examine the exposure and deployment of imposture in parliamentary speaking, public controversy, and periodical reviewing. A fourth chapter on William Cobbett—who, developing his polemical techniques in both the ministerial and reform presses, is the exemplary case— traces in his writings the career of reasoned argument along a rhetorically conditioned bias leading at once away from and towards imposture, while the final chapter examines how the narratives of several well-known Romantic texts run along this same bias. In all these instances, the regressive issue of rhetorically conditioned arguments is the same for either side of a question, liberal or conservative, radical or reactionary.

1
Designing Eloquence:
The Rhetorical Context

> After the young member has reflected upon the
> futility of the opposition to the leading opinions
> of the day, let him observe the changes of the
> arguments employed by their opponents, from the
> beginning of their hostility to the present time.—
> Do the speakers rely upon their former reasons?
> Do they grow strong by the agreement between
> their speculations, and the course of events?
> Do they silence their opponents by referring
> to the former declarations of both? Or rather,
> do they not abandon every position in
> succession, and endeavour to avoid a
> surrender, by temporary evasions?
> —Anonymous, *The Political Primer* (1820)

The career of reason is closely involved in the theory and practice of rhetoric at the end of the eighteenth century. In *Eighteenth-Century British Logic and Rhetoric*, Wilbur Samuel Howell argues that a major shift in thinking about both logic and rhetoric occurred between 1700 and 1800. Howell traces this change to methodologies associated with the emerging New Science of the seventeenth century. Traditional logic of the kind practiced by disciples of Aristotle had consisted in the syllogistic testing of propositions and the dissemination of results to a learned community in terms convincing to such a community, a method effectively combining the functions of inquiry and com-

munication. Its difference from rhetoric was distinct if not absolute. Traditional rhetoric participated in learned inquiry in
order to convey knowledge in more generally accessible terms.
"For all practical purposes," Howell states, "the differences between logic and rhetoric, within the context of the old science,
were derived from the differences between the learned and the
popular audience." If anything, these differences were to widen
with the growing dominance of the New Science. Taken up with
the rigors of observation and experiment, logic claimed solely the
realm of inquiry, its preoccupation with scientific method weak-
ening its traditional role in learned communication. That role
was now adopted by rhetoric with the result that the latter effectively came to be associated with all forms of communication, learned and popular alike.[1] Two centuries later, John Stuart
Mill could definitively state that

> The sole object of Logic is the guidance of one's own thoughts; the
> communication of those thoughts to others falls under the con-
> sideration of Rhetoric, in the large sense in which that art was
> conceived by the ancients; or of the still more extensive art of Ed-
> ucation. Logic takes cognizance of all intellectual operations,
> only as they conduce to our own knowledge, and to our command
> over that knowledge for our own uses. If there were but one ra-
> tional being in the universe, that being might be a perfect logi-
> cian; and the science and art of logic would be the same for that
> one person, as for the whole human race.[2]

The categorical terms of Mill's account, however, overlie a less
certain prospect. Taken out of a social context, logic exists in a
vacuum, its absolute certainty notwithstanding. If rhetoric cannot exist outside such a context, as is implied here, neither can
logic be useful in this context without rhetoric, much less retain
the certainty it would theoretically enjoy in Mill's "Last Man"
scenario.

A motto from Petrarch opening the first number of Samuel
Taylor Coleridge's *The Friend* also considers the possibility of unmediated truth. Taken from "De Vita Solitaria," the passage in
question reflects on the limits of counsel: how far can we legitimately offer light and hope to others? Rather than prescribing
laws, Petrarch promises only "to set forth the Law of my own
Mind"—"which let the man, who shall have approved of it, abide

by; and let him, to whom it shall appear not reasonable, reject it" (*TF* 1:7). If truth here is not necessarily absolute, for all intents it is ideal, the solitary product of one's "own Mind." Acceptance or rejection of this truth is a matter of individual choice, but the fact that it is a truth emerging from isolation ("De Vita Solitaria") implies the possibility of its imperfect communication or reception. In this connection, Coleridge recounts an allegory concerning the fate of truth amid the refractions of life in this world. Toward the close of the golden age, a long absent elder visits his people to deliver a warning received from an oracular voice about a rain that brings madness. He exhorts them to seek shelter from it, but "Confused murmurs succeeded, and wonder, and doubt. Day followed day, and every day brought with it a diminution of the awe impressed" (*TF* 1:8). When the elder returns some time afterward, he discovers that his prophecy was ignored and finds himself surrounded by madmen accusing him of being mad. He then rolls in a puddle, reflecting that "IT IS IN VAIN TO BE SANE IN A WORLD OF MADMEN" (*TF* 1:9). This conclusion only underscores the untenable positions occupied by speaker and listeners alike in the parable.

"Never was a finer Tale for a satire," Coleridge wrote in his notebook of this "Fable of the madning Rain."[3] Possible interpretations are provided in the 1812 and 1818 editions of *The Friend*—"Either says the Sceptic, you are the Blind offering to lead the Blind, or you are talking the language of Sight to those who do not possess the sense of Seeing" (*TF* 1:10)—but these readings beg the question in ways that involve them in the satire. Clearly the elder in the allegory has a truth to communicate and does so in a pointedly rhetorical manner ("the old man moved toward a small eminence, and having ascended it, he thus addressed the hushed and listening company"), just as the argument he presents is simple but logical in its inference ("Go ye therefore . . . retreat to the cavern" [*TF* 1:8]). Only the elder retreats to the cavern, however, and he remains there alone during the rain. As compelling as his truth is, it is compelling only for him. The effect of his speech has been momentary at best and even for that moment it seems not to have been convincing ("confused murmurs succeeded, and wonder, and doubt") and soon recedes ("Day followed day, and every day brought with it a diminution of the awe impressed" [*TF* 1:8]). On a logical

level, acceptance of this message would require agreement with
its opening proposition about the "madning rain," a proposition
drawn from the authority of supernatural revelation. Once accepted, the argument has a certain syllogistic inevitability. What
makes the parable's treatment so nice is the more advanced position implicitly attributed to the listeners, for they simply
cannot be convinced by scholastic syllogizing. Lacking empirical
proof, they have been struck only by the old man's rhetoric, the
effect of which has faded with the absence of further reinforcement until "they could attach no image, no remembered sensations to the threat." What becomes clear is that this golden age
is Enlightenment in provenance. When the elder emerges from
his cavern, he is shocked to find his people regressed to a state
of bedlam from having been "the common children of one great
family, working towards the same aim by reason, even as the
bees in their hives by instinct" (*TF* 1:8–9). Here, then, had been
a Mandevillean utopia, peopled by rational hedonists acknowledging no truth distinct from sensation. For them the prophecy's
fallacious logical premise would be a problem but perhaps not
an insurmountable one. More fatal is the failure of its rhetoric
to convey its truth empirically. The elder has apparently been
away too long from his people, for his epistemology is badly
dated.[4]

But where has this epistemology led? Once the elder has immersed himself in the water of the "madning rain," no one remains to answer. If everyone is mad, does it matter? Questions of
truth validity are moot, however, at least as regards an ancillary
concern in *The Friend* with the problem of communicating truth.[5]
The problem is how to make a truth accessible while not surrendering in the process to the errors that truth seeks to expose.
While *The Friend* is usually distinguished from the earlier
Watchman (1796) for avoiding the topical in favor of philosophy,
it might be more accurate to say that Coleridge shifts his focus in
this work from the topical to the epistemology of the topical, criticizing a popular rhetoric directed more to distraction than exposition. Reading habits fostered by popular periodical writing, for
instance, with its unconnected epigrammatic sentences—a prose
style "purposely invented for persons troubled with the asthma
to read, and for those to comprehend who labour under the more
pitiable asthma of a short-witted intellect"—suggest to Coleridge

how insidious is the reciprocity existing between the age's popular rhetoric and its reception:

> It cannot but be injurious to the human mind never to be called into effort: the habit of receiving pleasure without any exertion of thought, by the mere excitement of curiosity and sensibility, may be justly ranked among the worst effects of habitual novel reading. It is true that these short and unconnected sentences are easily and instantly understood: but it is equally true, that wanting all the cement of thought as well as of style, all the connections, and (if you will forgive so trivial a metaphor) all the *hooks-and-eyes* of the memory, they are as easily forgotten: or rather, it is scarcely possible that they should be remembered. (*TF* 1:20–21)

The "mere excitement of curiosity and sensibility" is an end apparently neglected by the elder in Coleridge's parable, but it occupied the distracted mind of an age in which actors interrupted productions of Shakespeare to score "hits"—effectively stopping a play's action to make the most of a striking line or gesture—and artists described by Blake employed the chiaroscuro technique of sensationally highlighting single details of paintings and engravings at the expense of organic unity.[6] Coleridge by no means underestimates the technical expertise involved in achieving such effects, but he despises and fears the mentality behind them. "It is by the agency of indistinct conceptions, as the counterfeits of the Ideal and Transcendent, that evil and vanity exercise their tyranny on the feelings of man," he states, adding that "The Powers of Darkness are politic if not wise; but surely nothing can be more irrational in the pretended children of Light, than to enlist themselves under the banners of Truth, and yet rest their hopes on an alliance with Delusion" (*TF* 1:37). This passage refers to a specific rhetorical strategy not only employing the skeptical techniques of Enlightenment critique but, more insidiously, pursuing its putative end in truth as well. While the actual end, an appearance of truth achieved through delusion, is by definition an irrational one, the means by which it is achieved is rational, deployed by an intelligence that is "politic if not wise," technically adept if not virtuous.

The Friend exposes the cunning methods of popular rhetoric even as it attempts to rehabilitate a conception of "Truth with-

out alloy and unsophisticated" (*TF* 1:37). In an empirical age,
this is a thankless and likely a vain task, though Coleridge's concern with "the whole question of moral obligation respecting the
communication of Truth, its extent and conditions" (*TF* 1:39), is
productive in establishing a rhetorical norm for his critique. The
frequent target of criticism himself, Coleridge knew of the resources available to the popular controversialist, so that certain
essays in the *The Friend* can be read as critical guides to rhetorical practice in Regency journalism. *The Friend*'s broader aim in
this respect lies in "securing a purity in the principle without
mischief from the practice" (*TF* 1:39), an idealistic premise that
nevertheless suggests how truth may be affected by the circumstances of its transmission. As Coleridge realizes, however—and
he consequently attempts to lay out "the conditions under which
the communication of truth is commanded or forbidden" (*TF*
1:100)—to admit this empirical wild card is to surrender truth's
absolute position to contingency, as his elder has done in the
parable. To say "that virtuous habits may be formed by the very
means by which knowledge is communicated, that men may be
made better, not only in consequence, but *by* the mode and *in* the
process, of instruction" (*TF* 1:103), is to imply that vicious habits
may as easily be formed in this way. It is to describe the dissociation noted in Howell's account of logic and rhetoric in post-Reformation Britain by which rhetoric was becoming an instrument
with no necessary stake in any given truth.

There have always been those who use knowledge for questionable ends. In the parable of the "madning rain," however, the
elder and his people submit to circumstances out of certain conditioned habits of thought. While the elder seems to make a
choice, this choice merely signals resigned acceptance of his
people's hedonism. In *The Friend* and elsewhere, Coleridge
traces this sensationalist philosophy and the mentality it fosters,
at once skeptical and passive, to what in the passage quoted
above he calls "the agency of indistinct conceptions." Perhaps
more than many among his contemporaries, he was aware of how
fallacious arguments can reach the understanding by way of the
feelings to become habitual assumptions (i.e., "even as the Bees
in their hives by Instinct"). To understand this is to be able to

resist such influences—or exploit them. The discipline of rhetoric developing alongside logic since the Reformation was a creature of both instrumental agency and subliminal suggestion, at once tool and medium. Ambivalent associations still surrounding the term "rhetoric" today are the result of this checkered history, a history portraying logic and rhetoric alternately at odds with, and absorbing aspects of, one another until finally settling into occasionally converging paths with rhetoric often on the low road. Yet the last half of the eighteenth century was a remarkable period for British rhetorical theory, a development that needs to be considered alongside the "agency of indistinct conceptions" demonized by Coleridge.

From mid-century onward several important books on rhetoric appeared in addition to numerous popular treatises. The period also saw the establishment of societies devoted to rhetoric. According to one of the co-founders of the Academy of Belles Lettres, Edmund Burke, these clubs sought to inculcate "the more refin'd, elegant, and useful parts of Literature, these seeming the most likely means for attaining the great end in view—the formation of our minds and manners for the functions of a Civil Society."[7] A cultural conservative like Coleridge could find nothing to disagree with in such an end, for Burke only restates the great purpose of classical rhetoric. Howell observes of Cicero, for instance, that "he recognized, as all of us must, that the exchange of ideas between one person and another, or between one generation and another, is at the very center of man's social, political, moral, economic, and cultural life, and that any art which improves man's capacity to exchange ideas is at the very center of all the other arts."[8] It is easy to see how deeply traditionalist works such as Burke's *Reflections on the Revolution in France* (1790) and Coleridge's *On the Constitution of Church and State* (1830) draw on this classical model of cultural transmission. Like so much else in the period, however, rhetorical theory itself was undergoing changes involving the radical rethinking of tradition. These changes resulted not in a recovery of classical rhetoric but in the assimilation of the very intellectual and social pressures distorting rhetorical practice.

The status of rhetoric had been in decline since the Reformation in whose bitter religious controversies it was less a light to philosophy than a polemical weapon.[9] The rise of the New Science with its empirical rigor could only hasten this decline. Arguments against rhetoric typically straiten the definition to mean language conceived to create effect rather than to transmit meaning. Under the powerful impetus of Baconian method, leading figures of seventeenth-century science like Robert Boyle and Thomas Sprat were employing such definitions to portray rhetoric as the enemy of truth, "this vicious abundance of *Phrase,* this trick of *Metaphors,* this volubility of *Tongue,* which makes so great a noise in the World," in Sprat's lurid words.[10] For John Locke, in *An Essay Concerning Human Understanding* (1689), the problem lay with those who *"set their Thoughts more on Words than Things"* and through this dissociation render language imprecise and even illusory. Locke's solution is to distinguish between *"civil use,"* everyday language governed by common convention, and *"Philosophical Use,"* technical terminology designed to convey precise meaning. This solution hardly rehabilitates rhetoric, however. Locke in fact charges that "if we would speak of Things as they are, we must allow, that all the Art of Rhetorick, besides Order and Clearness, all the artificial and figurative application of Words Eloquence hath invented, are for nothing else, but to insinuate wrong *Ideas,* move the Passions, and thereby mislead the judgment; and so indeed are perfect cheats."[11] Rhetoric is thus defined here almost exclusively in its least redeeming sense. The fact that Locke admits as much when he excepts rhetoric that aims at "Order and Clearness"—thereby defining all language usage, both good and bad, as rhetorical[12]— serves only to underline further rhetoric's equivocal nature. Noting this in *Essays on the Intellectual Powers of Man* (1785), Thomas Reid took the more pragmatic position that sciences necessarily employ terms from common usage alongside terms peculiar to their disciplines. Reid makes the case that common words can be better suited to describing mental operations not strictly reducible to logical definition, going so far as to charge that "philosophers ought not to escape censure when they corrupt a language, by using words in a way which the purity of the language will not admit."[13] Reid is no less concerned than Locke about ambiguous language, but he is also skeptical about reason's ability to confine all meaning, a view building on more progressive aspects of Lockean language theory without subscribing to its vestigial referentiality.

Eighteenth-century moral philosophy allows the passions an important, if proportionally declining, role in the progress of civil society. As a subdiscipline of moral philosophy, language theory shared this assumption, moving away from the older referential view of language and positing a primitive natural language— "modulations of the voice, gestures, and features," in Reid's words —from which conventional language arose. In his *Inquiry into the Human Mind on the Principles of Common Sense* (1764), Reid betrays a primitivistic nostalgia for this language of passionate gesticulation, warning that rational discourse comes with a price, for "Artificial signs signify, but they do not express; they speak to the understanding, as algebraical characters may do, but the passions, the affections, and the will, hear them not: these continue dormant and inactive, till we speak to them in the language of nature, to which they are all attention and obedience."[14] For some, language remained all too much in the thralls of passion. As wary of sentiment as Locke, George Berkeley claimed that language in familiar use acts automatically on emotional reflexes "which at first were wont to be produced by the intervention of ideas, that are now quite omitted."[15] Yet an awareness of this emotional element contributed to an understanding of the extra-rational ways by which language communicates meaning. Later eighteenth-century students of aesthetics like Edmund Burke and Lord Kames examined the specific affective properties of language contained in both sound and association, demonstrating (like Longinus before them) that language may be legitimately employed to convey more than discursive sense. Such developments in the theory and criticism of language helped lay the groundwork for a model of rhetoric better adapted to post-Baconian thinking than older classical models. Rhetoricians in the eighteenth century would challenge the notion that to "move the Passions" is "thereby to mislead the judgment," though they would do so at a risk. Where Reid might see a more affective language awakening long dormant passions in the human heart, Coleridge saw a real possibility of regression to conditioned response.

Either could have found his hopes or fears confirmed in Elocutionary doctrine. Largely discredited now, though it became important enough to be called a movement in the nineteenth century, Elocution is related in certain respects to the so-called

New Rhetoric, which was also emerging in the latter half of the eighteenth century. To suggest that Elocution is representative of the New Rhetoric does the latter an injustice. Yet its most influential spokesman, Thomas Sheridan (father of Richard Brinsley Sheridan), is sometimes included among the New Rhetoricians and his ideas exhibit in disarmingly simple relief some implications of New Rhetorical theory. Ciceronian rhetoric listed the functions of rhetoric under five heads, namely, *inventio, dispositio, elocutio, memoria,* and *pronuntiatio,* but modern English rhetoric had been defined ever more narrowly until it seemed to fall exclusively under the sole head of *pronuntiatio* or *actio (elocutio* in classical rhetoric referred to style).[16] The Elocutionary movement, which besides Sheridan included figures like Orator Henley and John Walker, capitalized on this narrowing of rhetoric's province. In *A Course of Lectures on Elocution* (1762), Sheridan sums up Elocution as "the just and graceful management of the voice, countenance, and gesture in speaking" (*LE* 19), a definition that risks relegating what had been a humanistic discipline to the status of a mechanical art. Elocution gets its reputation for quackery from the rote systems with which it is associated in histories of rhetoric,[17] yet it was more than a simple scam, emerging as it did from important historical and demographic factors in eighteenth-century England. H. Lewis Ulman notes a number of compelling reasons for its remarkable popularity. Elocution alone among the five heads of rhetoric remained unappropriated by other disciplines. It responded to a growing educational interest in the vernacular and to the social aspirations of those hindered by regional dialects. It also responded to multiplying opportunities for public speaking in an increasingly democratic society.[18] At a time when Tom Paine celebrated "universal conversation" and William Wordsworth defined the poet as "a man speaking to men,"[19] in its turn the Elocutionary movement promoted the value of speech in a great age of print.

As Sheridan argued, however, the spoken word had to be cultivated if it was not to be supplanted by the printed word. Where traditional rhetorics largely concerned themselves with written discourse, Elocution attempted to get beyond the limitations of the "dead letter" in order to recover the "living voice," a program recalling Reid's primitivistic conjectures about "natural language." In his *Lectures on Elocution* and the earlier *British Education* (1756), Sheridan argues that great cultures like ancient Greece and Rome had vital traditions of oratory, and that in this respect alone Britain falls short of classical civilization despite superior advances elsewhere. All that is required "to render the noblest discoveries in modern philosophy, practically useful to society," therefore, is the cultivation of national eloquence. Once catalyzed by a genuinely rhetorical culture, Britain will be capable of "making a right use of all those blessings, which Providence has showered down with a more liberal hand, on this country, than on any other in the world" (*LE* xii, xiv). This georgic vision of British industry given voice by oratory is taken from the *Lectures* where Sheridan notes much the same split between speculative philosophy and communication that Howell posits between logic and rhetoric in eighteenth-century Britain. Sheridan acknowledges his debt to Locke in the "Introductory Discourse," indicating his affinity with New Rhetorical assimilations of empirical psychology. At the same time, he describes Locke's theories as "concealed knowledge" owing to their abstruse language and their neglect of passion and imagination in favor of an exclusive focus on the workings of reason (*LE* v–vi). It is not wholly true, as Ulman asserts, that Sheridan ignores the work of Hume, Burke, Kames, Addison and others on the relation of passion and imagination to language (*LE* 154–55), but he surely dismisses too easily these writers' thinking on "taste" in order to argue that they mistakenly believe "that by the help of words alone, they can communicate all that passes in their minds" (*LE* x). It is on this point, though—language's power to convey more than mere words allow—that Elocutionary doctrine makes its contribution to modern rhetoric.

That there is more to communication than the rational content of language is surely an idea worth including in any rhetorical theory. For Sheridan the meanings of words are supplemented by emotive elements conveyed in speaking through extrasemantic means. This emphasis on nonverbal persuasion reflects Sheridan's belief that words are independent of written signs and that, because they employ different senses, speech and writing are different languages conveying different kinds of meaning. While they are commonly confounded through habit, they act on us in different ways whether we realize it or not.

When, moreover, Sheridan asserts that "the passions and the fancy have a language of their own, utterly independent of words, by which only their exertions can be manifested and communicated" (*LE* x), he refers not just to nonverbal elements in speaking, such as facial expressions and hand gestures, but to the utterance of words—the different pitches of the voice, its varying emphases, the silences between words. The distinction between written and spoken words is useful, as it opens up possibilities of meaning neglected in a culture of writing and print. Sheridan performs a service by attempting to raise awareness of the ways, good and bad, in which nonsemantic meaning operates on the mind (*LE* xi). At the same time, he underestimates the emotive power of the written word, a circumstance reflected generally in the Elocutionists' confusion of *elocutio* with *pronuntiatio*. The more worrying corollary of Sheridan's emphasis on the emotive is a tendency to discount reason. The question is whether a rhetorical system based only on *pronuntiatio* is adequate to the traditional end of rhetoric, namely, communicating truth. In the context of *inventio*, the discovery of truth, *pronuntiatio* serves a clear purpose as a means of transmission. Alone, it risks becoming an end in itself or worse, clearly an inference of the following passage from the *Lectures* where, having disposed of written language, Sheridan turns his attention to speech: "A just delivery consists in a distinct articulation of words, pronounced in proper tones, suitably varied to the sense, and the emotions of the mind; with due observation of accent; of emphasis, in its several gradations; of rests or pauses of the voice, in proper places and well measured degrees of time; and the whole accompanied with expressive looks, and significant gestures" (*LE* 10). The emphasis on technical presentation in this passage reduces "just delivery" to a matter of facility. Elsewhere it is clear that truth validity is assumed by Sheridan, but no such validity can be guaranteed because Elocution promises only effective expression. Even then, in practice—and Elocution, as understood by the Elocutionists, means exactly that, *actio*, no more, no less—effective means affective. In Lecture 7, for instance, Sheridan cites the case of Methodist preachers, whom he calls "wild orators," to demonstrate that belief may be established through affective means alone, "For were they to read their nonsense from notes, in the same cold, artificial manner, that so many of the clergy deliver rational discourses, it is to be presumed, that there are few of mankind, such ideots, as to become their followers; or who would not prefer sense to nonsense, if they are cloathed in the same garb" (*LE* 128). This case for the efficacy of speech, ironically, implies that the written word might serve as a useful check on the spoken word. Sheridan's understanding of "just delivery," at any rate, implies only the appearance of truth; it carries with it no criteria for establishing the validity of truth claims. Conviction need only be the product of the correct combination of tones and gestures habitually associated with conviction, since "in order to persuade others to the belief of any point, it must first appear, that the person who attempts it is firmly persuaded of it himself" (*LE* 5). To define truth as a sensation, as Sheridan effectively does here, is to confuse means and ends; it is necessarily to elide the distinction between a false and a true impression in the absence of a method for distinguishing the two. While even truth requires a plausible appearance to convince, Sheridan's system, whatever its intent, is set up "to persuade others to the belief *of any point*" (emphasis added).

If Sheridan avoids the worst excesses of Elocutionary doctrine, his system is nevertheless designed to elicit conditioned responses. In "Dissertation 2" of the *Lectures*, he warns against "false knowledge" and blames the press for its "brisk circulation thro' the land" (*LE* 173). That he does so in print, employing analytical methods suited to that medium, is worth noting, for the *Lectures* could be described as a rationally conceived system of nonrational persuasion. Even this system, however, occasionally succumbs to its own irrationalist ends. The fate of argument in Elocution is made clear in Sheridan's "Introductory Discourse." Following an eloquent evocation of the rich rhetorical culture he envisions in a Britain attuned to its own "living voice," he drops these remarks:

> I know there are few capable of tracing a speculation of this sort, thro' all its steps, so as to perceive the justness of the deduction. But I am now little sollicitous about what judgement shall be past upon the theory, since the time is approaching of trying it experimentally. A few sensible effects produced from practice, will carry more conviction to the bulk of mankind, than a thousand speculative arguments. (*LE* xiv)

Portentous indications of an approaching time work the same field of emotional response as the Methodists' "wild orators." More important, Sheridan avoids making a logical case for his system simply by asserting that future demonstrations will provide empirical proof of its effectiveness. Existing in prospect, these "sensible effects" must for the present be taken on faith, offering a proof free of rational intervention.

Sheridan produced his Elocutionary system during the same period that saw the emergence of the New Rhetoric. James Engell asserts that the New Rhetoricians "are, prior to the twentieth century, the most important and cohesive group of critics in English."[20] The New Rhetoric is nevertheless difficult to characterize as a school. Its proponents include Adam Smith (*Lectures on Rhetoric and Belles Lettres*, 1762–63), George Campbell (*The Philosophy of Rhetoric*, 1776), Joseph Priestley (*Lectures on Oratory and Criticism*, 1777), Hugh Blair (*Lectures on Rhetoric and Belles Lettres*, 1783) and James Beattie (*Essays on Poetry and Music as They Affect the Mind*, 1776). Other names might include Sheridan, Thomas Gibbons, Lord Kames, and Robert Lowth. If these latter are more tenuously associated with the New Rhetoric, even its primary proponents are diverse in terms of emphasis and depth; all are committed to preventing the marginalization of rhetoric in a scientific age. Engell and others broadly identify the New Rhetoric with the rise of a critical spirit in eighteenth-century Britain directed to the education of the reading public in matters literary, philosophical, and scientific.[21] More specifically, it is the product of Enlightenment venues like the Aberdeen Philosophical Society, where George Campbell debated Scottish Common-Sense realism and Humean skeptical philosophy, and Warrington Academy where Joseph Priestley gave his *Course of Lectures on Oratory and Criticism*. New Rhetorical theory reflects these origins in its specific application of Enlightenment theories of mind and society to rhetoric. Its privileging of simple rhetorical forms suited to rational discourse distinguishes it from Elocution while at the same time revealing a common ground in shared assumptions about natural language. These assumptions draw equally on reason and emotion for their rationale, emerging from the mixture of essentialist rationality and primitivistic nostalgia that marks Enlightenment cultural theory. Grounding his rhetorical theory in the principles of human nature, then, George Campbell proceeds from the classic Enlightenment premise that "The more that we become acquainted with elementary natures, the more we are ascertained by a general experience of the uniformity of their operations" (*PR* 52). Campbell qualifies his normative terms to stress that they represent conventional rather than absolute criteria—he notes, for instance, "that to which we give the character of purity is the commonest" (*PR* 146)—but designates other qualities, such as passion, as being common not by convention but by nature, "for wherever there are men, learned or ignorant, civilized or barbarous, there are passions; and the greater the difficulty is in affecting these, the more art is requisite" (*PR* 103). Passion is original to human nature, though the latter caveat implies that it may have to be recovered beneath the accretions of civilized life. In his *Lectures on Rhetoric and Belles Lettres*, Hugh Blair puts this case in the generalized cultural terms of Enlightenment speculative history, correlating the state of language with the state of civil society—"In its ancient state, more favorable to poetry and oratory; in its present, to reason and philosophy" (*LRBL* 1:125).

In the middle was rhetoric. Its broader cultural thesis aside, Blair's formulation expresses a sense, the same sense noted at the beginning of this chapter, that rhetoric and logic have parted ways. Elocution not only represents this split in extreme form but capitalizes on it to transform rhetoric into a set of specialized techniques for oral delivery. Sheridan's *Lectures* pay lip service to content along the way, even, in a manner reminiscent of New Rhetoricians, portraying the relation between speech and thought as symbiotic, "for without knowledge, speech would have but little weight; without power of speech, knowledge would have but little value" (*LE* 153), though a phrase like "power of speech" takes in much more than effective public speaking. Theorists of language, indeed, were beginning to view the fundamental ability to use language as inseparable from thought.[22] Sheridan's system, however, makes one independent of the other and privileges effect over logical proof. While the New Rhetoric acknowledges with Sheridan and the Elocutionists the practical importance of effective communication, it attempts to avoid Elocution's irrationalist backsliding, though the danger still lurks in its theories. As Mill would do after him, Blair observes that without rhetoric "Reason would be a solitary, and, in some measure, an unavailing principle," insisting that speech "is the great instrument by which man becomes beneficial to man" (*LRBL* 1:1).

Yet rhetoric still performs an instrumental purpose relative to substantive knowledge in New Rhetorical theory. For this reason, making a case for its primacy requires some qualification. In the following passage from *The Philosophy of Rhetoric*, George Campbell attempts to distinguish logic and rhetoric without reducing rhetoric to handmaid status: "The sole and ultimate end of logic is the eviction of truth; one important end of eloquence, though, as appears from the first chapter, neither the sole, nor always the ultimate, is the conviction of the hearers" (*PR* 33). Campbell refers here to rhetoric both in its specific sense as argument and in what he elsewhere terms its "extensive sense" (xlix), by which he means language pursuing ends other than persuasion—in tragedy and lyric, for instance, where it simply moves the passions. Nevertheless, in argument rhetoric is ancillary to logic. The symbiotic case has some currency among the New Rhetoricians, but for Campbell the relation is at least theoretically an unequal one, for "though he may be an acute logician who is no orator, he will never be a consummate orator who is no logician" (*PR* 61). But this assertion carries the same hypothetical force as Mill's earlier-cited claim about the autonomy of logic. The fact remains that logic needs rhetoric in order to be effective. Campbell thus chooses to elide fundamental distinctions by reducing all to the level plane of utility, arguing that "if the logical art, and the ethical, be useful, eloquence is useful, as it instructs us how these arts must be applied for the conviction and the persuasion of others" (*PR* xlix). Despite such shifts, however, he never once seems to doubt rhetoric's centrality as a discipline. "Nay, without this," he asserts, "the greatest talents, even wisdom itself, lose much of their lustre, and still more of their usefulness" (*PR* xlix). Joseph Priestley makes much the same point in his *Lectures on Oratory and Criticism*, but with a caveat: "It is necessary, likewise, as far as *reasoning* is concerned, that a person be, in some sense, a logician before he be an orator" (*LOC* 3). The caveat concerns "*reasoning*," seeming to suggest that the orator who seeks to persuade by other means need not be a logician. The eminently rational Priestley might object to this possibly sinister construction of his meaning, but in the same passage he repeats the qualification—"it is by the rules of LOGIC that we judge of every thing relating to *arguments*" (*LOC* 3)—before going on to say that "More especially is it of consequence to every orator whose business is with *men*, to be well acquainted with *human nature*; that knowing the passions, prejudices, interests, and views of those he hath to do with, he may know how to address them accordingly" (*LOC* 3–4). Priestley here identifies rhetoric in perhaps its most "extensive sense" as an art of persuasion grounded in human nature—including reason, to be sure, but much more besides, and in proportions not always favoring reason's sovereignty.

The potentially regressive role of passion in eighteenth-century rhetorical theory is an inference of sensationalist philosophy, the epistemological framework employed by New Rhetoricians to take the place of traditional *inventio* in their systems. Invention in the classical sense of discovery has no place in New Rhetorical doctrine. Where Blair attributed invention to natural genius, Priestley and Campbell turned to empirical psychology to explain how ideas are generated and applied.[23] Taking their lead from philosophers like Locke and Hume as well as philosophical critics like Kames, they sought to establish rhetoric as an art based on the science of human nature. Campbell outlines this program in his preface to *The Philosophy of Rhetoric*, proposing to study the mind in order "to disclose its secret movements, tracing its principal channels of perception and action, as near as possible, to their source: and, on the other hand, from the science of human nature, to ascertain with greater precision, the radical principles of that art, whose object it is, by the use of language, to operate on the soul of the hearer, in the way of informing, convincing, pleasing, moving, or persuading" (*PR* xliii). While he hopes to explain rhetoric in the light of epistemology, Campbell does not rule out the possibility that rhetoric has something to offer epistemology by way of its practical concern with human behavior, serving as a kind of applied epistemology. This emphasis has the effect of further orienting rhetoric away from a concern with subject matter per se and toward a concern with the processes, what Campbell terms the "secret movements," of understanding. For Priestley (and to a lesser extent

Campbell), the association of ideas offers the most satisfactory explanation for these processes. Developed by Locke and Hume and elaborated by David Hartley into a full-scale ontology, this principle had already been applied to aesthetics by thinkers like Francis Hutcheson, Alexander Gerard, and Lord Kames, though none had given it the centrality it enjoys in Priestley's system. According to Priestley, rhetoric is a medium of transmission whose function consists "not in finding things with which the mind was wholly unacquainted, but in readily recollecting, and judiciously selecting, what is proper for his [the orator's] purpose, out of the materials with which the mind was previously furnished" (*LOC* 5). But having rejected the notion that rhetorical invention can "discover" knowledge—one of the New Rhetoric's fundamental debts to Baconian method is the distinction between investigation and communication—Priestley needs association to explain how rhetoric manages what the mind already possesses. Thus he does not so much reject the topics of classical *inventio* as offer a psychological rationale for them. In his first lecture, Priestley states that a speaker may expect rhetoric "to assist him in the habit of *recollection*, or to direct him which way to turn his thoughts" (*LOC* 5), suggesting that subject matter serves to give rise to certain rhetorical patterns but is itself extrarhetorical. As Vincent M. Bevilacqua and Richard Murphy point out in their edition of the *Lectures*, "Priestley focused his attention not on the first traditional question of rhetoric—'What may be said on behalf of a cause?'—but on the second—'How may it best be said?'"[24] The topics he treats are therefore not substantive but suggestive in nature, functioning as mnemonic markers devised to stimulate associations in the minds of speaker and listeners alike.

According to Bevilacqua and Murphy, ethical and emotional appeals, formerly essential aspects of rhetorical invention, are relegated by Priestley to ornamental status.[25] This formalist rigor, however, has the effect of putting the emotional on more equal footing with the ethical. Blair reminds us in this connection that "taste," that peculiar quality of sensible perception distinguishing civilized life from Hobbesian savagery, is not a mere deduction of reason but arises intuitively, its impressions affecting philosopher and peasant equally, though it may be refined by reason (*LRBL* 1:16–17). In the same way, passion may supplement reason where more than simple understanding is concerned, for "persuasion" requires emotional engagement. It is thus more complex in nature, prompting Blair to observe that "There are a thousand interesting circumstances suggested by real passion, which no art can imitate, and no refinement can supply. There is obviously a contagion among the passions" (*LRBL* 2:193). Rather than a mind comprising separate, mutually exclusive faculties, New Rhetorical theory conceives one in which the faculties are interrelated and mutually dependent.[26] Argument is no simple matter, then. Campbell asserts that a speaker addressing only the understanding "proposes either to dispel ignorance or to vanquish error" (*PR* 2), a classic application of the enlightenment program to rhetoric. Yet there is a more "complex" kind of persuasion, a persuasion comprising "an artful mixture of that which proposes to convince the judgment, and that which interests the passions" (*PR* 4). As described by Campbell, this form of persuasion ("the argumentative and the pathetic incorporated together" [*PR* 4]) joins logic and emotion in mutually reinforcing combinations:

> Would we not only touch the heart, but win it entirely to co-operate with our views, those affecting lineaments must be so interwoven with our argument, as that, from the passion excited our reasoning may derive importance, and so be fitted for commanding attention; and by the justness of the reasoning, the passion may be more deeply rooted and enforced; and that thus both may be made to conspire in effectuating that persuasion which is the end proposed. For here, if I may adopt the schoolmen's language, we do not argue to gain barely the assent of the understanding, but, which is infinitely more important, the consent of the will. (*PR* 5–6)

In this sequence, emotional appeal entwines itself with argument, which in turn validates emotional appeal with its logical force. But while the argument's "justness" may indeed supplement the emotion, the final effect of the combination does not attain the "justness" of logic, though that may be part of the effect. Its justness, rather, is the sum of the associations carried by emotional appeal and logical force joined together in what Blair vividly terms a "contagion," the "end proposed" necessarily emerging from the complex nature of the means effected. Elsewhere, Campbell warns that "It is not ultimately the justness either of the thought or of the expression, which is the aim of the orator; but it is a certain effect to be produced in the hearers" (*PR* 215), by which he presumably means an effect directed to a given end and to this extent just (like Sheridan's notion of "just delivery"). The "consent of the will" is distinguished by Campbell from a mere "assent of the understanding" on the basis not simply of the nonrational element in the emotional appeal but of a nonrational element in the argument—that is, emotional associations that have come to define a convincing argument in the mind of the hearer. The "end proposed," therefore, involving as it does a mastery of the will by means of heart and mind alike, carries with it at least the possibility of acclamation.

For Priestley, too, reason may carry an unreasonable appeal. "The idea we universally conceive of the excellency of reason," he writes, "of the innumerable advantages of it, and the sense of honor and dignity which from hence attends the consciousness of it, furnish a source of pleasing ideas, which are excited by the perception of the marks of design in human works" (*LOC* 261). While reason's appeal arises from properties integral to reason, habitual associations attached to its "excellency" speak to something very different, which Priestley describes as a sensation "excited" by mere perception. The following passage demonstrates how, when preempted by association, argument becomes "contagion":

> Indeed, prior to our hearing any arguments, we are naturally inclined to suppose, that a strong conviction and persuasion in other persons could not be produced without a *sufficient cause*; from being sensible that a like strong persuasion is founded upon sufficient reasons in ourselves. The ideas of *strong persuasion* and of *truth* being, on this account, intimately associated together, the one will introduce the other, so that whatever manner of address tends to demonstrate that the advocate for any opinion is really convinced of it himself, tends to propagate that conviction. (*LOC* 109)

Thus does *"sufficient cause"* become a stimulus to action rather than a rationale for it. In the same way, a passionate response to rational "design" has the effect of negating reason as a method of discovery. "This is very evident," notes Priestley, "upon the view of a part of any thing the proportions of which are known, as of an animal body, of a regular curve, or polygon, a regular building, a regular garden, or of a consistent set of political, philosophical, or theological principles. With what satisfaction may we often hear persons say, upon seeing part of such an object, or such a scheme, 'You need shew me no more: I see the whole'" (*LOC* 165). A possible result, ironically, the replacement of critical analysis by conditioned response, is an inference of Priestley's argument:

> The first observation I shall make on *the general affections of the passions*, is, that they are engaged, and we feel ourselves interested, in proportion to the *vividness of our ideas* of those objects and circumstances which contribute to excite them. The genuine and proper use of the passions undoubtedly is to rouze men to just and vigorous action upon every emergency, without the slow intervention of reason. It is, moreover, wisely provided, that they should be raised by the immediate view and apprehension of the circumstances proper for their exertion. Being, therefore, blind and mechanical principles, they can only be connected with the view of suitable circumstances; so that, whenever these are presented, whether the passion would, in fact, be useful or not, it cannot fail to be excited, and to rise to its usual height. (*LOC* 79–80)

This passage strangely combines the ethical imperatives of civic humanism with the amoral determinism of sensationalist philosophy. Priestley can speak of "genuine and proper use," "just and vigorous action," even as he educes "blind and mechanical principles" working behind them to preempt rational intervention. In doing so, he risks making moral considerations merely honorific—or worse, for terms like "proper" and "just" may easily become markers of technical facility, as Priestley's reference to "suitable circumstances" does become when viewed as only a stimulus for emotional response.

Associationism carries certain dangers for New Rhetorical doctrine, then. When in the passage above Priestley sees eloquence as engaging the passions through "the *vividness of our ideas* of those objects and circumstances which contribute to excite them," almost like Sheridan he effectively defines conviction as a sensation depending on a complex of elements collateral but not necessarily subordinate to reason. Not the idea, not even the expression of the idea, but the vivid sense of prior associations with the idea is what produces conviction. Where Priestley speaks of "vividness," Campbell says "vivacity" and his model of rhetoric at times reflects a more cultural than epistemological emphasis, but the idea is the same. Campbell is very clear on the necessarily automatic nature of the mental processes involved in the mind's retention and application of experience and of the almost instinctive role of custom in language use. He conceives of three "connexions" governing thought and perception, those existing among things, those existing among words and things, and those existing among words. Conditioning these connections are the unconscious workings of "use" or custom. The connection between words and things, for instance, he regards as purely conventional, for "this is not a natural and necessary, but an artificial and arbitrary connexion" (*PR* 258). If language is conditioned by the connection among words and things, however, logic may be conditioned by the connection among words and other words, so that the mind will immediately accept or reject a given proposition based on the verbal form taken by the proposition—"*Immediately,* that is, even before we have leisure to give that attention to the signs which is necessary in order to form a just conception of the things signified" (*PR* 258). But the justness of a conception is beside the point where mechanical principles are involved. Acknowledging the risk of arbitrary connections in the associationist model, Priestley notes that "all strong passions and emotions are liable to be transferred to indifferent objects, either related to the proper object, or those whose ideas are accidentally present in the mind, at the time that it is under the influence of such emotion or passion" (*LOC* 94). Once again, terms like "proper"—and later in the same passage "*just*" as applied to objects of passion—straddle the line between ethics and technique. More troubling, though, are the random effects produced by the accidental presence of certain ideas in the mind at an inopportune (or opportune?) moment. The fact that such accidents can be anticipated due to the very nature of the principle making them possible must also mean that they can as easily be used to achieve a given end. In this case, a "just" or a "proper" effect would signify only the success with which this end had been achieved.

Such ambiguity is symptomatic of a technical strength in New Rhetorical theory that is also potentially an ethical weakness. What distinguishes New Rhetoricians from the Elocutionists in this respect is their awareness of the problem. Sheridan's only safeguard is his belief that those properly schooled in rhetoric will instantly recognize dissembling in "the least impropriety in tone, look, or gesture" (*LE* 148). New Rhetorical doctrine betrays this sensationalism in its faith in what Lloyd Bitzer calls "the lively idea,"[27] but allows logic a distinct role as the test of truth *prior* to rhetoric's inculcation of conviction. Within rhetoric's uncertain realm, moreover, there is scope for pragmatic discriminations. Recognizing the "capricious and unaccountable" nature of custom, Campbell urges the importance of criticism in regulating "use" (*PR* 152). Yet such a criterion itself depends on use and so is potentially liable to the same manipulation as the accidents of association. Campbell's distinction between what he calls "*reputable custom*" and "*general use*" (*PR* 141–42), good and less good respectively, offers a useful check on vicious usages, but cannot get away from the fact that both kinds of use arise from the same contingent source. An instrument of transmission rather than a method of inquiry, rhetoric selectively transmits received usages, operating in the sphere of public consensus Priestley terms a "*medium of opinion*" (*LOC* 5, 135). According to Campbell, similarly, rhetoric not only speaks *to* a public but *from* it as well, the public being the unconscious arbiter of use: "It is the business of both the speaker and the writer, to accommodate himself to what may be styled the common standard; for there is a common standard, in what regards the faculties of the mind, as well as in what concerns the powers of the body" (*PR* 114). It is unclear whether this "common standard" refers to common usage or a common nature or both; whatever the case, Campbell's rhetorical model assumes certain predictable properties in both. The analogy between mental faculties and bodily powers only reinforces the suspicion that some of these properties are involuntary in nature.

New Rhetorical theory can propose only relative critical checks on seemingly "capricious and unaccountable" effects of automatic causes. That this should be so is inevitable given its rigorous delimiting of what rhetoric may properly claim to be. Within these straitened parameters, truth is either the a priori

product of logic or a provisional category subject to careful definition. In book 2 of *The Philosophy of Rhetoric*, Campbell defines
purity in language as "grammatical truth," a category consisting
in "the conformity of the expression to the sentiment which the
speaker or the writer intends to convey by it." He then distinguishes this kind of truth from "moral truth" ("the conformity of
the sentiment intended to be conveyed, to the sentiment actually
entertained by the speaker or the writer") and "logical truth"
("the conformity of the sentiment to the nature of things"), before
epigrammatically summing up all three: "The opposite to logical
truth is properly error; to moral truth, a lie; to grammatical
truth, a blunder" (*PR* 214–15). These categories decline from the
absolute criterion of logic to the conventional criterion of grammar. In the middle is "moral truth" with its reliance on a
speaker's or writer's real conviction. It is with the two latter
forms of truth, moral and grammatical, governing sincerity and
execution respectively, with which rhetoric is concerned. Depending solely on facility, grammatical truth is morally neutral,
an instrument. The criterion of sincerity, namely, "the conformity
of the sentiment intended to be conveyed, to the sentiment actually entertained by the speaker or the writer," is more problematic. The New Rhetoricians' practical association of sincerity
with truth has an empirical basis. All such a model requires in
practice, notwithstanding ethical caveats not integral to rhetoric, is the appearance of truth, which is to say the sum of sensations associated with conviction. Here, once again, is what
Priestley has to say about conviction: "The ideas of *strong persuasion* and of *truth* being, on this account, intimately associated
together, the one will introduce the other, so that whatever
manner of address tends to demonstrate that the advocate for
any opinion is really convinced of it himself, tends to propagate
that conviction." If conviction is propagated by the appearance of
"strong persuasion," so is the association between truth and its
appearance further reinforced by association's amalgamating
energies. In this way, even genuine conviction may help false
conviction perfect itself through repeated use. As in Coleridge's
parable, the sensation is the message. The respective roles of
conviction and truth in this system are indicated by the operative phrases, "whatever manner of address" and "any opinion."
To allow such latitude is to make rhetoric into a flexible instru-

ment indeed, while perhaps rendering Coleridge's hope of "securing a purity in the principle without mischief from the practice" all the more difficult.

Sensationalist philosophy provides useful explanatory models for rhetorical practice, but has the potential to condition practice once its assumptions are assimilated into theory—as they largely are in the New Rhetoric. Over the past decade, commentators have begun to sift through New Rhetorical influences on English Romanticism, helping us to understand the ways in which Romantic assimilations of eighteenth-century rhetorical theory articulate continuities between Enlightenment and Romantic thinking. Yet the regressive tendencies noted above as implicit in New Rhetorical doctrine remain implicit in Romantic poetics, assiduously teased out though they have been by students of rhetoric like David Sebberson who argues that Wordsworth's preface to *Lyrical Ballads* employs a "rhetoric of technical control" developed by New Rhetorical empiricism. Sebberson uses the demonic model of Enlightenment expounded by Adorno and Horkheimer to argue that "empiricist rhetorical theory" transforms rhetoric into an instrument of domination, so that "The rhetorician need only cast a spell of pre-Socratic darkness to usher in the Enlightenment of scientific method."[28] While drawing on Sebberson's argument, this study regards the New Rhetoric, and for that matter Romantic poetics, less as concluding in what Sebberson calls "a single, overriding expression of ideology" than as tending in that direction—along with other related tendencies, such as the ethos of Whiggism discussed in the next chapter. If the New Rhetoric effects a deliberate break from traditional rhetoric in terms of epistemology, the ethical breach noted by Sebberson is only immanent in the logic of this revision—technical reason in fact exists side by side with civic humanism in New Rhetorical doctrine—acknowledged as an inference somewhat problematic to the theory but not worked out as a fully determined feature of the theory. It thus exists, in effect, as part of the nonverbal argument (which, to be sure, is the argument that counts for Elocutionists). One way to gauge the regressive logic Sebberson detects in rhetorical theory and Romantic poetics is to examine how a sense of rhetorical practice conditioned by sensationalism manifests itself in writings aimed at specific applications. Instrumental logic is far less subtly determined in the latter, which draw not on theory but on practices tangentially emerging from theory.

"Introduce something flattering to the HOUSE.—settle method first" (*PL* 3): thus advises William Gerard Hamilton in *Parliamentary Logic* (1808). In his preface to this volume, Edmond Malone justifies his argument for this book's uniqueness by contrasting its radically pragmatic bent—Jeremy Bentham would find it brazenly cynical—with the typically more rarified nature of rhetorical and logical treatises, "composed by sequestered scholars, unacquainted with the real forms of business, and the actual proceedings and discussions of the House of Commons and Westminster Hall" (*PL* vi). As one might expect in a volume published in posthumous homage, Malone's preface inclines to eulogy, but it nevertheless describes nicely the mentality behind this very curious and curiously exemplary work. What emerges is the portrait of a mind attenuated by long observation and reflection into the narrow embodiment of a method. William Gerard Hamilton (1728?–96) began his forty-year political career with a brilliant maiden speech and then never spoke again in Parliament due to a "nervousness of frame" (*PL* vi). Becoming known as "Single-speech Hamilton," he thereafter devoted himself, in Malone's words, "to the examination and discussion of all the principal questions agitated in Parliament, and of the several topicks and modes of reasoning, by which they were either supported or opposed" (*PL* vi). Never closely associated with any party, he reserved his limited store of conviction for an uncompromising antipathy to parliamentary reform—"he would sooner suffer his right hand to be cut off, than vote for it" (*PL* xxxvii)—while apparently suspending his judgment on all other questions. According to Malone sedulously avoiding either censure or praise of any administration during his long political tenure, he "indeed considered politicks as a kind of game, of which the stake or prize was the Administration of the country" (*PL* xxxv). It is precisely this quality of detachment, however, some might say indifference, that enables Hamilton to detect a peculiar logic immanent in what William Hazlitt would call "the stately significance, and gross familiarity of the dialect of the house of commons" (*CWH* 1:160). Throughout the pithy aphorisms constituting *Parliamentary Logic*, then, Hamilton subjects rhetoric to a rigorous discipline going beyond even his calm neglect of partisan politics, "looking on such occasions," says Malone, "rather to the *object* of each motion, than to the question itself" (*PL* xxxvi).

It is easy to mistake the intent of *Parliamentary Logic*. In his *Book of Fallacies* (1824), in many ways the critical complement to *Parliamentary Logic,* Jeremy Bentham compares Hamilton's book to Swift's droll "Directions to Servants," distinguishing the latter work on the basis of its satire. As no such purpose redeems *Parliamentary Logic*, Bentham can only condemn it as "a sort of school, in which the means of advocating what is a good cause, and the means of advocating what is a bad cause, are brought to view with equal frankness, and inculcated with equal solicitude for success" (*WJB* 2:383). The particular ethos that Bentham detects in Hamilton's premises, "the general predominance of self-regarding over social interest" (*WJB* 2:385), is a subject for the next chapter. It should be noted here, though, that for Bentham *Parliamentary Logic* is the reductio ad absurdum of rhetorical traditions going back to classical antiquity, "teaching with equal complacency and indifference the art of true instruction and the art of deception—the art of producing good effects and the art of producing bad effects" (*WJB* 2:380). If he dismisses it, however, Bentham does not so easily dismiss the method it expounds. His remarks indicate that he regards *Parliamentary Logic* as something more than a treatise on how to succeed in politics, something taking the shape of a theory, however pernicious in its principles.

A first glance at this eccentric work yields little evidence of systematic design. From beginning to end, it consists of aphorisms remarkable for nothing so much as their brazen cynicism. There is no clear order, and repetition abounds. Malone describes it as a collection of "practical axioms" and "parliamentary and forensick wisdom" intended to serve anyone with occasion to speak and argue effectively (*PL* v–vii). Much of this wisdom is proverbial in a narrowly professional sense ("Some argument, some ridicule, some eloquence" [*PL* 15]), while some has almost a Blakean ring, recalling the shrewd artisan rather than the visionary poet ("Grandeur requires room. Contraction streightens. But conciseness strengthens and adjusts the sense" [*PL* 7]). Some voice the stylistic concerns of traditional rhetoric ("Ob-

serve round and clean composition of sentence; sweet falling of
the clause; varying an illustration by figures; weight of matter;
worth of subject; soundness of argument; life of invention; depth
of judgment" [*PL* 26]), while others concern matters of argumentative proof ("Three rules of probability:—what most agreeable
to the nature of things;—what to constant observation, and repeated experience;—what to the attestation of wise and honest
men, and to the concurring testimony of multitudes" [*PL* 12]).
That Hamilton firmly grasps the distinction between rhetoric
and logic in argument, indeed, is evident in his observation that
"Logick handles reason as it is; rhetorick as it is planted in
people's opinion" (*PL* 31). His remark that "There can be but
three causes why a law is made imperfect; want of power, want of
knowledge, and want of inclination, in those who made it" (*PL* 5),
is worthy of Bentham in its sharp pragmatic perceptiveness. In
sum, *Parliamentary Logic* expounds rhetoric as the best and
worst of disciplines. It is a work in which an aphorism noting
that "An epithet of diminution does not alter the principle" may
be directly followed by this advice: "Shew, that the thing asserted, if true, does not affect the question; and then shew that it
is false" (*PL* 19).

But is the author of *Parliamentary Logic* "all theory," as Bentham asserts?[29] If he is, the key lies in his systematic avoidance
of substantive issues, his habit of looking "rather to the *object* of
each motion, than to the question itself." In a lesser politician,
this would merely indicate an eye to the main chance, but Bentham recognizes a system when he sees it, and in Hamilton he
sees the author of a disinterestedly systematic translation of interested practice into theory. His outrage, however—he seems
scarcely to believe anyone could conceive such a work as *Parliamentary Logic*—is a characteristic overstatement of the same
misgivings betrayed by Campbell and Priestley about the vul-
nerability of blind mechanism to arbitrary or corrupt motive. In
Parliamentary Logic, these elements of sensationalist philosophy
exist in almost pure form, unimpeded by the more than vestigial
civic humanism that mitigates philosophic radicalism (and the
New Rhetoric). The conservative taint of Hamilton's aversion to
parliamentary reform only underscores just how free of liberal
scruple is this application of liberal method. Hamilton's Parliament, as Bentham describes it, where "a man takes the one or

the other of the two sides—the side of those in office, if there be room or near prospect of room for him; the side of those by whom office is but in expectancy, if the future contingent presents a more encouraging prospect than the immediately present" (*WJB* 2:385), is surely a disquieting prospect for a philosopher as hedonistically grounded as Bentham. His tendency to take Hamilton to task on ethical matters, then, serves only to distract from the rational underpinnings of Hamilton's system. Throughout *Parliamentary Logic*, commonplace and principle exist side by side. It is one thing simply to advise the speaker to "Consider the particular passion you are to touch" (*PL* 3), for this is merely to employ affective rhetorical strategies going back to Cicero and Demosthenes. The following sequence of reflections, however, is quite another thing:

> Distinction, Amplification, Reflection as a *nexus*.
> What you know, what you do not; what said, what silent; what clear, what doubtful, what contradictory.
> A manifestation of a thing, or a compound of it, not absolutely the thing itself. (*PL* 1)

A progression from the details of rhetorical technique to epistemology is unmistakable over the course of these three assertions. The first and rather gnomic clause seems to put logic, rhetoric, and thought on a par with one another or else simply declines to sort them out, being content to locate them in a nexus where only the obvious fact of their relation is clear. The latter two clauses—all its terms are grammatical fragments but this aphorism in fact opens the book—urge the importance of limiting knowledge to experience. To Hamilton, indeed, experience is the only thing, and he regards argument not as working toward truth or even away from error but as affirming what is known by making it known (even if this requires avoiding or exploiting what is doubtful). His formulation of the more metaphysical question of what *can* be known reveals a radically skeptical and empiricist bent. The world in which rhetoric operates is neither wholly real nor illusory but impressionistic, the mere "manifestation of a thing."

This, then, is what lies behind pragmatic advice to flatter the House but to "settle method first." Indeed, the one naturally follows the other in the applied epistemology expounded in *Parlia-*

mentary Logic. Given the keenly pragmatic cast of Hamilton's mind, it seems inappropriate to assign philosophical labels. Such as it is, however, his intellectual orientation is empirical and nominalist. A profound distrust of generalities, unless used for particular purposes, thus informs assumptions about the nature of language and thought underlying the most pointed of his strategic directives. Rather than a vehicle of transparent meaning, language for Hamilton is a medium made dense by convention. "The secondary meaning which custom has superadded to many words," he advises, "should be distinguished from the particular, common, and primary meaning, and their signification as used by a particular author, age, sect, or party" (*PL* 11). Accordingly, facts employed for or against an argument display the same complex nature, for "A fact may result from a concurrence of traditions, though not resting on the authority of a particular one" (*PL* 16). Such statements, and variations on it recur throughout *Parliamentary Logic*, indicate a mind formed by the English common-law tradition on one hand and, on the other, Lockean empiricism. Even Hamilton's habitual usages betray an empiricist inflection recalling New Rhetorical assimilations of sensationalist psychology. "To define," he explains, "is to state the several simple ideas of which a compound idea consists, in order to explain it" (*PL* 66), an innocuous assertion but revealing in its use of Lockean categories. Similarly, a directive to "Consider what sort of proofs make the greatest impressions on men's minds" (*PL* 25) indicates how fine is the line separating logic and psychology in practice, for rational assent, or rather its form, may easily become a habitual response to the right stimulus. From such passing remarks emerges, if not a fully determined theory of rhetoric, at least the outlines of one based on an empiricist model.

Grounding this sketch of a theory is an associationist premise. All words, all facts, all ideas, all laws are in Hamilton's estimate combinations of many different particulars that have come to be related by chance or custom. Hence this advice to the parliamentary speaker: "Association of ideas from resemblance, and from contrariety. The mention of an event brings into our view another event, similar in its cause, its nature, its circumstances, and its consequences" (*PL* 92–93). To be sure, this is no more than an observation, though one straddling the line between prediction and prescription. As simple observation, it reveals a sensationalist bias when implying that the mind responds automatically and thus predictably to stimuli by means of association. This only gives more point to the prescriptive advice—for instance: "In viewing a subject, consider not only the thing itself, but look likewise to the right and left of it, and by that means associate whatever has a necessary or natural relation to it" (*PL* 92). What Hamilton means by "natural" is anyone's guess given the almost hegemonic ethos of artifice pervading his system. It is difficult to see how it can differ much from a term like "necessary" in the context of his psychological determinism, a sense in which "natural" is sometimes used by Jane Austen.[30] It is more telling that the speaker should be advised, when addressing a given issue, to look to the right and left of the issue, for it is the logic of Parliament, as expounded by Hamilton, to deal with "A manifestation of a thing, or a compound of it, not absolutely the thing itself," which is to say, truth as a sensation. The following advice does not so much discourage a priori reasoning as encourage the bare impression of reasoning inductively: "It is always suspicious, when a hypothesis is first formed, and the arguments are afterwards found out to support it. It should be like experimental philosophy, the *result* of what has offered itself" (*PL* 54–55). The operative word is "like," for the impression is everything. From such a perspective, associations surrounding empirical method are as good as the thing itself—at least in practice.

Parliamentary Logic by no means offers a fully realized theory of rhetoric. From beginning to end, its purpose is practical, at times remarkably cynical. Yet theory supplements practice in this work in ways that leave less doubt about its author's methodology than about his beliefs, political or otherwise. Hamilton would most certainly disavow any sort of theoretical bent less from strategy ("Have a method, but conceal it" [*PL* 14]) than from temperament. There was something of a mannered, even dandyish, reserve in the elderly gentleman who wrote *Parliamentary Logic*. That he is perfectly clear about the implications of what he counsels is never at issue. He knows that "To oppose the argument, and not the question, or the words, and not the intention, is sophistry" (*PL* 12), and he offers several cogent definitions of fallacy, such as "assuming a false principle; stating what is true in a qualified sense, as true in an unconditional one; or ascribing an effect to that which has no efficiency" (*PL* 29). If he can complacently advise that "The best verbal fallacies are those which consist not in the ambiguity of a single word, but in the ambiguous syntaxis of many put together" (*PL* 29), he can also note that "Circumlocution is useful, if you wish to deceive, and not otherwise" (*PL* 73). If he advises the speaker simply to drop inconvenient circumstances or facts from an argument, he adds, "but state clearly to your own mind what is so" (*PL* 18). Perspicacity has its place in Hamilton's system but so has ambiguity, for "It is often possible to state things with such a studied ambiguity, as may admit not only of different, but of almost opposite interpretations" (*PL* 78). While at times his language strays into the morally ambiguous realm occupied by New Rhetorical usages like "just"—his advice, for instance, concerning "the *best* verbal fallacies" (emphasis added)—Hamilton seems less prone than either New Rhetoricians or Elocutionists to elide regressive inferences in his system. Indeed, the only inferences to be made regard Hamilton himself, for the single end proposed by his rhetorical strategies is never in question and may be summed up, simply, as whatever works. Enabling this instrumentally effective and morally versatile methodology is much the same contingent view of truth underlying New Rhetorical doctrine, though in the more straitened world of *Parliamentary Logic* the only truth is grammatical: "Most of the things asserted in argument are true in themselves, but not true in the sense in which they are used: to explain this at large, is one of the first fields of argument" (*PL* 61). For Hamilton there is no expectation that extrarhetorical ethical considerations will constrain what Priestley terms "blind and mechanical principles" in human nature. The only constraint is expedience. Notwithstanding its fragmentary, aphoristic form, *Parliamentary Logic* represents an utterly closed system in which rhetoric is directed to distinct contingent ends. Within this system, conclusive arguments are unlikely, for "the very nature of a disputable question is where some thing plausible, or probable, may be said on both sides; but probabilities are to be balanced" (*PL* 15). Methods employed to gain an advantage, therefore, promise only a relative and temporary advantage that may easily be lost to others employing the same methods: "As there is always a point of light in which a subject may be put to advantage, so there is always another point of light in which it may be shewn differently" (*PL* 63). For Hamilton this is the only absolute.

The Book of Fallacies (1824) is Jeremy Bentham's main contribution to rhetorical theory. It is, he claims, an original of its kind, a systematic study of "the forms, of which such ideas or combinations of ideas as are employable in the character of instruments of deception, are susceptible" (*WJB* 2:379). Like so many of Bentham's works, a version of *The Book of Fallacies* was first published in French by Dumont; much later an English version was compiled and published by Peregrine Bingham. For himself, Bentham reports that he made little progress writing this work until he saw an advertisement announcing the posthumous publication of *Parliamentary Logic*. While he initially feared that Hamilton had preempted his own project, Bentham had only to read this eccentric but very acute little volume to see that it was in fact the latest in a long tradition of rhetorical treatises reducing rhetoric to the instrument of interested ends, good and bad alike: "Dionysius of Halicarnassus, Cicero, and Quintilian, Isaac Voss, and, though last and in bulk least, yet not the least interesting, our own Gerard Hamilton (of whom more will be said,) are of this stamp" (*WJB* 2:380). Reading Hamilton was incisive for Bentham, which may explain an early plan for organizing this work along the lines of parliamentary procedure, treating "fallacies of the *ins*—fallacies of the *outs*—*either-side* fallacies" (*WJB* 2:381). In the end, he opted for the more systematic form of a taxonomy comprising four principal heads: "Fallacies of Authority," by which reasoning is discouraged by the weight of various forms of influence; "Fallacies of Danger," by which discussion is repressed by eliciting fear and alarm; "Fallacies of Delay," which seek to postpone discussion by means of various pretexts; and, finally, "Fallacies of Confusion," the object of which is "to produce, when discussion can no longer be avoided, such confusion in the minds of the hearers as to incapacitate them for forming a correct judgment on the question proposed for deliberation" (*WJB* 2:382). Under these heads are included numerous subdivisions. Starting with what he regards as the most legitimate source of "Authority," for instance, that derived from professional ability, Bentham presents in a descending list

various forms of authority derived from other relative circumstances such as power, opulence, and reputation (*WJB* 2:389).
The most untenable proposition, he argues, while it could not
gain assent resting on itself, will be readily accepted on the basis
of received authority—indeed "the same proposition, extracted
from a page of Blackstone, or from the page or mouth of any
other person to whom the idle and unthinking are in the habit of
unconditionally surrendering their understandings, shall disarm
all opposition" (*WJB* 2:393).

Bentham's quizzing of rhetoric arises from a distrust of language comparable to that of Locke and Berkeley. As a young law
student at Lincoln's Inn he heard William Blackstone deliver the
lectures that would form the basis of *Commentaries on the Laws
of England* (1765–69) only to detect in them what, more than a
decade later in *A Fragment on Government* (1776), he would dismiss as "a string of obscure sophisms" (*WJB* 1:286). At about the
same time, he was attending court proceedings against the
London radical John Wilkes where he was struck by what he
called the *"Grim-gibber"* of the prosecution's rhetoric (*WJB*
10:45). That he had more than a passing interest in the emotion-
ally subversive power of rhetoric, even at this time, may be suggested by the presence of one "Mr. ——— Bentham" among the
list of subscribers appended to the first edition of Sheridan's
Course of Lectures on Elocution in 1762. Like Locke, Bentham
believed that the fundamental inadequacy of language lay in its
sentimentalism. Critical of the use of emotive terms in moral
philosophy, he viewed the writings of a thinker like Mandeville
as an instance of new moral ideas expressed in the archaic terms
of the *littérateur* or satirist. More useful to criticism, he felt,
would be a neutral terminology connoting neither praise nor
blame and purged of sentimentalism. The interrogation of language for ulterior bias, complexes of encoded emotional, political,
moral, and religious content, is thus a salient aspect of his writings on rhetoric. In part 4 of *The Book of Fallacies*, Bentham
argues that certain words possess habitually "eulogistic" or "dyslogistic" (negative) associations, so that their very use in various
connections is enough to elicit unreasoning approval or disap-
proval. For example, the word *"order,"* especially when used
alongside *"social,"* is "in a particular degree adapted to the purpose of a cloak for tyranny" (*WJB* 2:441). Among other such "pas-

sion-kindling appellatives" are "improvement" and "innovation," both meaning the same thing, except that the former has a eulogistic and the latter a dyslogistic cast, and each is used accordingly by politicians (*WJB* 2:438). Under "Fallacies of Danger," then, is listed the subhead of "*The Hobgoblin Argument, or, No Innovation*, in which the hobgoblin in question is *anarchy*; which tremendous spectre has for its forerunner the monster *innovation*." A hot button like this would presumably elicit a visceral response even from Hamilton whose aversion to the hobgoblin of parliamentary reform was apparently his sole unreasoning reflex.[31] Yet the sensationalist epistemology from which such arguments flow is precisely what links Hamilton's and Bentham's respective rhetorical theories, the arguably incidental matter of ethics aside.

The *Book of Fallacies* casts itself in direct opposition to *Parliamentary Logic*. But while Bentham seems to reserve only scorn for Hamilton's work, he implicitly credits it with clarifying his own project, and in fact the relation between *The Book of Fallacies* and *Parliamentary Logic* is less obviously binary than he admits. Hamilton, it is true, does not hesitate to point out to readers the "best" fallacies, insisting only that they be employed with eyes open. Where Bentham rigorously explains the effective framing and execution of verbal fallacies—at much greater length than Hamilton and in characteristically systematic form —he claims a wholly cautionary purpose in doing so. That his own assumptions allow such an unqualified claim is not clear given their sensationalist basis. This much is clear about Hamilton's system, however, that it is at best morally neutral, eschewing or at least disregarding a priori ethical considerations. That it is, at worst, immoral in its designs is a claim Bentham makes by means of the following series of inferences:

> Of a good cause as such—of every cause that is entitled to the appellation of a good cause, it is the characteristic property that it does not stand in need—of a bad cause, of every cause that is justly designated by the appellation of a bad cause, it is the characteristic property that it does stand in need—of assistance of this kind. Not merely indifference as between good and bad, but predilection for what is bad, is therefore the cast of mind betrayed, or rather displayed, by Gerard Hamilton. For the praise of intelligence and active talent—that is, for so much of it as con-

stitutes the difference between what is to be earned by the advocation of good causes only, and that which is to be earned by the
advocation of bad causes likewise—of bad causes in preference to
good ones,—for this species and degree of praise it is, that Gerard
Hamilton was content to forego the merit of probity—of sincerity
as a branch of probity, and take to himself the substance, as well
as the shape and colour of the opposite vice. (*WJB* 2:386)

The proposition that a good cause does not stand in need of a bad
cause to be convincing is valid but does not mean that good is its
own absolute proof, for any cause, good or bad, needs to be put in
terms associated with a good cause. This is no more than Hamilton would happily argue more concisely. Bentham is effectively
arguing from associationist premises, but what is the basis of
his inference that "predilection for what is bad" characterizes
Hamilton?—indeed, that this preference "therefore" characterizes Hamilton? The key to Bentham's argument here seems to lie
in his estimate of the "difference" Hamilton is willing to trade off
between probity and technique in calculating the merits of his
system. Does it then follow, however, that, because this system
treats equally the advocating of good and bad causes, it treats
the advocating of "bad causes in preference to good ones"?

For himself Bentham claims satiric privilege, citing Swift as
precedent. Regarding his own motives, he simply asserts that
"much pains will not be necessary to satisfy the reader that the
object of any instructions which may here be found for the composition of a fallacy, has been, not to promote, but as far as possible to prevent the use of it" (*WJB* 2:383). While Bentham's satiric
bent is real enough (and often overlooked), it cannot explain
away the breach between scruples and tactics opened up by
rhetorical assimilations of empirical psychology. Bentham exposes this breach in Hamilton, who takes it for granted, but his
own system fails to offer any corrective beyond that prescribed
by a civic humanism at odds with a far more integral psychological determinism. The following passage reveals the axe that Bentham, the philosopher, has to grind with Hamilton, the parliamentarian, in this respect:

The notion of the general predominance of self-regarding over
social interest has been held up as a weakness incident to the situation of those whose converse has been more with books than
men. Be it so: look then to those teachers, those men of practical

wisdom, whose converse has been with men at least as much as with books: look in particular to this right honourable, who in the House of Commons had doubled the twenty years' lucubration necessary for, law, who had served almost six apprenticeships, who in that office had served out five complete clerkships;—what says he? Self-regarding interest predominant over social interest?—self-regard predominant? No: but self-regard sole occupant: the universal interest, howsoever talked of, never so much as thought of—right and wrong, objects of avowed indifference. (*WJB* 2:385)

But what does Bentham mean by "social interest," much less "universal interest"? Barring anything like an absolute concept—not likely given his distrust of transcendental universals—he must mean an empirically constructed consensus along the lines of his celebrated "greatest happiness" principle. Grounding this intersubjective norm, however, is surely the same pleasure/pain binary driving "self-regarding interest." This sensationalist premise may not rule out the empirically straitened altruism with which Bentham warns off Hamilton's cynicism, but it hardly makes it inevitable either. His bitter attack on "practical wisdom," moreover, strangely privileges Hamilton's parliamentary sphere as the real laboratory of human nature. If theory does not deduce itself from this scene of practice or, worse, if it deduces itself in all too pure a form, where does this leave Bentham's "social interest"?—as something simply superadded to the Hobbesian savagery so mildly expounded by Hamilton? In order to indict the regressive logic of "practical wisdom," Bentham must implicitly repudiate the inductive logic of his own critical exposure of Hamilton's system.

If *Anarchical Fallacies* (1837?) fails to offer a solution, it does clarify the problem by tracing the regressive potential of rational reform to sensationalist philosophy. This it does, moreover, by analyzing the rhetoric of reform. First published in French by Dumont, *Anarchical Fallacies* is a critical application of Bentham's ideas about rhetoric and fallacy to declarations of rights issued during the French Revolution. The problem, as Bentham formulates it, is that as necessary as the selfish passions are to the existence of the individual, these same passions are the enemies of social peace. At the same time, the logic of abstract rights is premised on such essential entitlements, so that the rhetoric of rational reform, however much it may speak of republican virtue and so on, directs itself to what Bentham calls "the selfish and dissocial passions" (*WJB* 2:497). The result is anarchy in the very language of documents like the Declaration of Rights, published by the French National Assembly in 1791, whose logic Bentham views as being of a piece with its rhetoric, merely "words and propositions of the most unbounded signification, turned loose without any of those exceptions or modifications which are so necessary on every occasion to reduce their import within the compass, not only of right reason, but even of the design in hand" (*WJB* 2:497). What follows is an article by article critique—Bentham candidly admits that he is engaged in verbal criticism, for words are the stuff of this document, "Look to the letter, you find nonsense—look beyond the letter, you find nothing" (*WJB* 2:497)—quizzing the language of the declaration in its minutest particulars. Article 4, for instance, "*Security results from the concurrence of all in securing the rights of each,*" Bentham dismisses as a mere epigram, its "soporific quality" calculated more to put the mind to sleep than to awaken it; Article 5, similarly, relating property rights, is "another definition in the soporific style" (*WJB* 2:526). At the root of these regressive rhetorical lures is the very sensationalism driving Sheridan's Elocutionary system and implicit in New Rhetorical theory:

> Alas! how dependent are opinions upon sound! Who shall break the chains which bind them together? By what force shall the associations between words and ideas be dissolved—associations coeval with the cradle—associations to which every book and every conversation give increased strength? By what authority shall this original vice in the structure of language be corrected? How shall a word which has taken root in the vitals of a language be expelled? By what means shall a word in continual use be deprived of half its signification? The language of plain strong sense is difficult to learn; the language of smooth nonsense is easy and familiar. The one requires a force of attention capable of stemming the tide of usage and example; the other requires nothing but to swim with it. (*WJB* 2:523–24)

Bentham's interrogation of such language is definitive but hardly reassuring with respect to remedies. The result curiously confirms Hamilton's observation that the "best" fallacies arise from ambiguous constructions rather than from the ambiguity of single words. Of the framers of the French Declaration of Rights, Bentham thus concludes that they have failed not simply in their abuse of words "but in undertaking to execute a design which could not be executed at all without this abuse of words" (*WJB* 2:522).

For Bentham a possible solution would be less philosophical or even political than procedural in nature. In his "Essay on Political Tactics" (1837?), he finds at least a provisional rhetorical norm in "publicity," arguing that there "is no reason more constant and more universal than the superintendence of the public" (*WJB* 2:310). Having warned in *The Book of Fallacies* that a sophistical turn in politics at once arises from and gives rise to systems of education suppressing the critical ability to detect fallacies,[32] he here envisions a public life in which all citizens are in the habit of reasoned discussion so that "passions, accustomed to a public struggle, will learn reciprocally to restrain themselves" (*WJB* 2:311). What Bentham would do, then, is open rhetoric up to a sphere wider than the philosopher's study, wider even than Parliament, in order to break its regressive spell. If like *Parliamentary Logic*, "Essay on Political Tactics" is an applied rhetoric assuming the worst of human nature, it applies that unhappy knowledge to systematic reform of parliamentary procedure as compensation for human frailty. This Bentham does always with reference to current practice, where practice fails and where it succeeds, and always with a view to its role in the more comprehensive public life of a state. Discussing the grammatical framing of laws, for instance, he insists on the careful vetting of propositions for "eulogistic or dyslogistic terms" (*WJB* 2:356). Even questions regarding visitors to Parliament— how many should be admitted, whether women should be admitted—are considered in light of how such circumstances will affect the reasonable conduct of proceedings. Bentham in fact decides against admitting large numbers of visitors and against admitting women altogether, suspecting that "the discussion would take a turn more favorable to the excitements of oratory, than to logical proofs" (*WJB* 2:326–27). Such measures seem exclusive given the emphasis on publicity, but for Bentham publicity is not an end in itself but rather a means of disciplining impulses otherwise tending toward the hedonistic anarchy sanctioned by Hamilton. Indeed, if parliamentarians need to be distanced from their passions by strict procedures, the public itself, whose very presence may exacerbate these passions, needs to be distanced from the heat of parliamentary debate by the interventions of print: "The speeches of the orators, which are known to them only through the newspapers, have not the influence of the passionate harangues of a seditious demagogue. They do not read them till after they have passed through a medium which cools them" (*WJB* 2:313). Bentham clearly did not share Sheridan's faith in the "living voice."

Yet such normative provisions serve less to prevent "selfish and dissocial passions" than to diffuse them. As the younger Mill recognized, Bentham was most effective as a critic—"the great *subversive*," Mill calls him[33]—and his skeptical teasing out of verbal fallacies is probably his most important contribution to rhetorical theory. Moreover, despite what over the course of his long career as a reformer was clearly a deep commitment to the social good, his "subversive" method is itself not necessarily conducive to such an end—any more than is Hamilton's necessarily conducive to "bad causes," as Bentham charges.[34] At least an implicit, if negative, virtue of both systems is their skeptical bent, an inevitable product of their empiricism but also a factor in cultivating genuinely critical attitudes. This is clearer in Bentham's case, but Hamilton offers more than ready-made stratagems, for the effective adept of his system must be a keen critic. "Consider," he advises in *Parliamentary Logic*, "if a word has not different significations, and if you may not use it advantageously, sometimes in one sense and sometimes in another; and watch this artifice in others" (*PL* 66). Of another such device he begins, "It is an artifice to be used, (but if used by others to be detected,)" while elsewhere he counsels his reader to "Watch the first setting off, and the manner of stating the question at the outset: *there*, is generally the fraud" (*PL* 67, 32). Hamilton was an acute observer of political tactics and strategy during the forty or more years he sat silent amidst the hurly-burly of parliamentary debate and his is a system as firmly grounded in rational critique as Bentham's. It is also equally subversive in its methods and ethos, despite a reactionary bent directing it to virtually opposite ends, a fact that should not finally surprise, even if it disconcerts—as it clearly did Bentham.

ᵉᔆ   ᵉᔆ   ᵉᔆ

Bentham's unconcealed incredulity suggests that a more impudent performance than *Parliamentary Logic* would be difficult to conceive. Perhaps he was too optimistic. What must have struck him most was Hamilton's peculiar method of representing the most base practice as exemplary. Hamilton is in this respect similar to the fictional Mr. Sarcastic, also a politician and a theorist, in Thomas Love Peacock's second novel, *Melincourt* (1817). "I ascertain the practice of those I talk to," claims Mr. Sarcastic, "and present it to them as from myself, in the shape of theory." To a worldly Reverend, then, he presents himself as a venal cleric, to a corrupt parliamentarian as the epitome of political chicanery.[35] So complete a reversal of practice and theory, of representation and intention, as Mr. Sarcastic effects, however, risks making the means justify the end as technical mastery asserts itself at the expense of conviction. Mr. Sarcastic is such an adept ironist, his meanings being so perfectly double, that when he runs for Parliament in the rotten borough of Onevote he wins the election. His speeches, cleverly constructed of every political commonplace, pass for the real thing and he attains the dubious electoral success he means to condemn. Bentham, try as he might, could not discover in *Parliamentary Logic* even a trace of the irony that at least putatively qualifies Mr. Sarcastic's outrageous theories—not to mention his parliamentary success. Hamilton, it would seem, was most sincere when most cynical. To Bentham's unconcealed astonishment, what might be taken as an ironic mask was evidently the man himself.

Hamilton and Mr. Sarcastic represent a reaction against rhetorical theory paradoxically taking the form of theory, or, rather, many idiosyncratic theories. Their systems take what should be exceptions—the immoral inferences of visceral interest that lurk about Elocutionary and New Rhetorical doctrine, for instance—and make them the rules. In the worldly sphere to which they speak, practical effect takes precedence over ethical intent, so that the latter is relegated to the realm of speculation (where Bentham finds himself in his search for the real William

Gerard Hamilton). The effect of this is to make the line between irony and sincerity at times almost irrelevant. A satiric feature in the radical journal, *The Black Dwarf*, "Tactics for Ministers," for instance, has an obvious polemical purpose, but its advice infers a logic in ministerial practice that could feasibly be applied to good effect by aspirants in the Liverpool administration—for instance: "*Cobbett v. Hunt*—Two sides to the question about them. First, that they are Jacobins and Levellers, and that there is not a pin to choose between them and the Houses of Russell, Cavendish, Howard, Wentworth, Spencer, &c. &c. &c. All of them Jacobins and Atheists alike. (N.B. To get some foolish Country Gentleman to say this)" (29 Feb. 1817: 16). From the other side of the question, an anonymously authored pamphlet entitled *Elements of Opposition* (1803) satirically systematizes political opposition on the basis of observed practice. "As you may feel more resentment against a Minister, than even the present usage of Parliament will allow you to express within the walls," it counsels; "and as it may be of importance to you, on other accounts, to maintain an appearance of candour and moderation in your own language; it will be advisable to get some writer, of a genius calculated to do the courser and more offensive sort of out of door work." Such advice, though ironic—"In order to recommend yourself as a politician, first commit errors, then correct them; then correct your corrections; and then add, that you never advance any thing that is not fact"[36]—is as viable (and venal) as any Hamilton puts forward. *Elements of Opposition* advances preposterous examples of political reasoning that, even as they satirize Whig opposition, amount to the same systematizing of rhetorical imposture that so disturbed Bentham in *Parliamentary Logic*.

In another anonymous work entitled *The Political Primer; or, Road to Public Honours* (1820), the line between political satire and rhetorical system is even harder to distinguish. It is tempting to view *The Political Primer* as pure irony, an exposure of the age's pygmy Machiavellianism, but for the fact that its advice seems sound—for instance, that a young member should give factually substantive speeches and avoid flashiness—if not uplifting. This work pushes what might be called the applied theory of rhetorical practice to its furthest limit, directing its counsel to young university men who have shut for the last time "their classics on ethics" and must now see society as it really is, vices as well as virtues. "All that is here detailed under the form of precept," the author promises, "may soon be observed in action throughout the empire: nothing is invented; and only that which has been actually seen, described." While not strictly a rhetoric, treating other aspects of politics such as advertising and canvassing, *The Political Primer* gives pride of place to the designing eloquence of political rhetoric, "the calculated expression meant to serve a concealed purpose," as in this analysis of a George Canning speech: "It flattered the auditors; was clearly understood by every one of them; and proved invincibly that apparent inertness, and real active power, may co-exist in the same subject: the proof did not require a process of understanding; it struck the mind as light strikes the eye."[37] In these innocuous, if purely cynical, observations is realized the regressive tendency of rhetorical assimilations of sensationalist philosophy over two centuries—its circumventing of reason, its appeal to the senses, its transformation of conviction into sensation. At such a prospect, Coleridge's elder can only surrender his own reason.

2

Whiggish Energies:
The Ethos of Technical Mastery

We have long been deeply interested in your
disinterested plans of self-interest.
—"To the Right-sorrowful, the Lords GREY
and GRENVILLE," The Satirist (1811)

Jeremy Bentham was appalled by the personality behind *Parliamentary Logic* as much as by the book itself. In one respect his estimate of what he calls "the political character of Gerard Hamilton" seems to miss the point; as the previous chapter argues, this is where Hamilton is imputed a preference for bad causes over good. The point, surely, which Bentham acknowledges in almost the same breath, is that it does not matter to Hamilton what causes, good or bad, he supports. Bentham's reasoning is that, as good consists in the opposition to abuse, any position making abuse possible must be opposed to good. He thus says of Hamilton that "it was to the opposing of whatsoever is good in honest eyes, that his powers, such as they were, were bent and pushed with peculiar energy" (*WJB* 2:383–84). Opposition to reform necessarily blocks the correction of abuses by reform, but does not necessarily condone these abuses, though it may. Bentham's critique falters where it seems to credit Hamilton with a coherent, if misguided, morality. Hamilton's reportedly violent antipathy to parliamentary reform may in fact have been his only reliable conviction. It is possible, too, that Bentham would have been anxious to dissociate his own disinterested rationality from Hamilton's. Yet his real estimate of Hamilton turns

64

on disinterestedness, a quality in Hamilton paradoxically put to the service of interest, any interest so long as it secures temporary advantage (for Hamilton there is no other kind). Where Malone's preface to *Parliamentary Logic* notes that Hamilton kept clear of party affiliations, Bentham argues that he was in fact drawn to "that party standing constantly pledged for the protection of abuse in every shape," though Bentham also charges that he was indifferent to questions of right and wrong. The imputation of moral motive (or its lack) aside, however, what party is Bentham speaking of that, pledged to protect abuse, would appeal to so eternally uncommitted a soul as William Gerard Hamilton?—Whigs, Tories? In fact, it could be either, "that party being, of whatever materials composed, the party of the ins." Hamilton, Bentham concludes, "was as ready to side with one party as another; and whatever party he sided with, as ready to say any one thing as any other in support of it" (*WJB* 2:384)— except, apparently, where parliamentary reform was concerned.

While Malone could justly say that Hamilton was not "an ardent party-man," then, it might also be said that he could have been, if circumstances had required it (or made it possible). That he must, in effect, have been one on occasion is probable. Whatever course he took, however, would reflect a tactical choice, arising as it did from a sense of sheer contingency. Bentham's diagnosis of this tendency blames "the general predominance of self-regarding over social interest" in the age (*WJB* 2:385). These are merely two types of interest, representing degrees of the same thing rather than binary opposition, but from the radically empirical and skeptical perspective Bentham shares with the arch-Hobbesian author of *Parliamentary Logic* even degrees are something. While the *Book of Fallacies* anatomizes the abuses of which the empirical mind is capable (and to which in turn it is susceptible), the "Essay on Political Tactics" offers admirably probative remedies to these abuses—precisely because Bentham accepts without reservation the hedonistic epistemology by which Hamilton implicitly rationalizes his cynical counsel. Bentham's "social interest" effectively opposes ethical procedure to venal opportunism, system to anarchy, but never on the basis of anything more categorical than the savagery lurking beneath Hamilton's epigrams. In their different but similarly premised responses to contingency, Bentham and Hamilton might be compared to theorists of Machiavellian power games, their parliamentarians marshalling *virtù* in all its forms in the face of *fortuna*. To be sure, the political realm they describe is at a remove from the nexus of classical and Christian cosmologies through which concepts like "virtue," "fortune," and "corruption" play themselves out in Florentine political thought. Yet empirical contingency—the accidents of association, for instance, demonstrated by Bentham and Hamilton in rational critiques of tradition for purposes of reform and exploitation respectively—might be described as *fortuna* further naturalized, and rationalized, into material necessity.

Bentham in fact observes in *The Book of Fallacies* that "that which Machiavel has been supposed sometimes to aim at, Gerard Hamilton, as often as it occurs to him, does not only aim at, but aim at without disguise" (*WJB* 2:383). Bentham here manages to associate Hamilton with the Machiavellianism of popular tradition while himself not subscribing to this reading. At the very least, he reads Machiavelli ironically—Swift's "Directions to Servants" is cited in this same section—but how seriously he takes Machiavelli as a political thinker is harder to say. In *Official Aptitude Maximized; Expense Minimized* (1830), he speculates that the political state described in Edmund Burke's writings would be run "in the quondam *Venetian* style—a government in which, under the guidance of upstart Machiavelism, titled and confederated imbecility should lord it over king and people" (*WJB* 5:297). This was written during Bentham's later years when he was embittered by the failure of his Panopticon scheme and his writings took the form of monstrous anatomies filled with extravagant invective and fantasy. Even so, he is careful in this passage to read Burke's "upstart Machiavelism" in unmistakably Whiggish terms, as seen from either a Reform or Tory perspective, subjugating to its aristocratic hegemony both "king and people." One could hardly expect, then, that Bentham would embrace Machiavelli as the Classical Republican recently portrayed by Felix Raab and J. G. A. Pocock.[1] Then again, despite his distrust of *littérateurs*, even progressives among them like Mandeville, Bentham often seems to see his dialectical reflection in opponents, which may explain the violence of his reaction to a book like *Parliamentary Logic*. Hamilton's antireformism would not have been nearly so unsettling for Bentham as the distinctly subversive ethos of his rhetorical system. Pocock argues that *The Prince* (*Il Principe*) is not a work of ideology but rather "an analytic study of innovation and its consequences," addressed not to established rulers, certainly not those legitimized by tradition, but to the young prince who, having been the beneficiary of innovation, must now deal with a "delegitimized world" of his own making.[2] *Parliamentary Logic* and *The Political Primer* similarly counsel the political novice. Though of course neither book advocates reforming those abuses its initiates are encouraged to use to their advantage, each is formative of an attitude more prone to exploit than to venerate Old Corruption. "Let us watch the reason of mankind," advises *The Political Primer*, "and adapt our conduct to its dictates" (vi–vii). It could be argued that corruption is part of an immanent "excellence in composition" in the organic state, to quote Burke (*RRF* 8:217). The "peculiar energy" harnessed by Hamilton and *The Political Primer*, however, will hardly direct itself to conserving the excellence of tradition and could even contribute to its subversion. Referring to this ethos in his "Second Letter on a Regicide Peace" (1796), subtitled "On the Genius and Character of the French Revolution as It Regards Other Nations," Burke finds that "its agents were literati, bureaucrats and technocrats, and the form it took was 'energy,' 'talent,' 'a new, a pernicious, a desolating activity'" (*RP* 9: 264–65). While the end of such energies is self-advancement, and tradition one possible means to that end, the necessary consequence is a destabilizing of tradition once detached from its profoundly normative role to become a tool.

The young prince described by Pocock's Machiavelli pits *virtù* against *fortuna* and then attempts to ride out the unpredictable effects by means of this same *virtù*. The latter concept is difficult to define, referring variously to martial prowess, intellectual or artistic skill, even moral virtue.[3] It is associated with the successful negotiation of contingency, though it is not precisely synonymous with either success or a particular skill commanding success. While it may encompass ingenuity, technical expertise, empathy, ruthlessness, decisiveness, prevarication and so on, *virtù* itself consists in the effective marshalling of these or any other means necessary to command success. Elevating the mastery of contingent circumstance to an imperative, it could be termed the art of the provisional. Its most characteristic and problematic trait, therefore, is apparent utter versatility. In her recent book, *Machiavellian Rhetoric from the Counter-Reformation to Milton* (1994), Victoria Khan locates rhetorical usage at the heart of Machiavellian *virtù*, arguing that "Machiavelli should not be chiefly read as a theorist of republicanism but rather as a proponent of a rhetorical politics, one that proceeds topically and dialectically, and that can be used by tyrant and republican alike." According to Khan, republicanism is an inference of the kind of logic that can also make the Machiavellian thinker a dissembler and hypocrite, but while there is a dialectical (and rhetorical) link between the Machiavel and the republican there is no necessary connection. This is both the strength and weakness of what Khan terms Machiavelli's "rhetorical, de-hypostatized *virtù*" in that, by exposing the false consciousness of humanist ethical claims and restoring contingency to its rightful (i.e., realistic) place in human affairs, it puts into question the nature of an eventual outcome—republic or tyranny?[4] Bentham recognized this much in the ruthless sophisms of *Parliamentary Logic*, that the "peculiar energy" of unaligned individuals such as William Gerard Hamilton—who himself drew the line at parliamentary reform—could be bent to virtually any cause. Yet he insisted that Hamilton, and those like Pitt the Younger whom he attacked in the 1790s under the pseudonym of "Anti-Machiavel,"[5] were inclined to bad causes, which is to say, the preservation of Old Corruption. What he failed to acknowledge was the common ground occupied by both reformer and reactionary in a rhetorical realm of probability and appearance.

This ground had been worked for some centuries in religious and political controversy. Whatever questions they disputed, such debates drew on received theological and constitutional topics, some adapted from scholastic casuistry or inherited from the sonorous English common-law tradition, others taken from Machiavellian polity and polemics.[6] Empiricism reoriented even as it helped to explain the rhetorical principles on which they turned. The "peculiar energy" Bentham detects in rhetorical imposture is thus an inference of New Rhetorical and Elocutionary assimilations of sensationalist philosophy. Works like *Parliamentary Logic* make the inference plain, while the more egregious ramifications left implicit in even these cynical guides to practice are exposed by Bentham's critical taxonomy of rhetorical fallacies. There is also the emerging sense of an ethos associated with such systems of rhetorical theory and practice, an ethos or spirit defining a particular kind of civic personality. The various rhetorical systems discussed in the previous chapter all issue in some form of ethos, if only by implication. Thomas Sheridan's Elocutionary system aims at nothing less than a recovery of classical eloquence on a national scale. The most ambitious phase of this program, indeed, would transform a culture of the written word into a culture of the spoken word, effectively reconstituting civic virtue by reconstituting the medium of its transmission and producing a nation of Demostheneses and Ciceros. Sheridan addresses the same cultural concerns as eighteenth-century moral philosophers like Adam Ferguson, who asserts in *An Essay on the History of Civil Society* (1767) that "If virtue be the supreme good, its best and most signal effect is, to communicate and diffuse itself." His rhetorical system, however, is as mechanical as the empirical model of human nature on which it is premised. The national culture he projects would be at once acclamatory and technocratic, its expressions (and impressions) of virtue derived from sensational effect. By contrast, Ferguson's virtuous republic depends on an actively thinking citizenry. Only by retaining their political identities, argues Ferguson, can the people of a modern commercial state resist mechanistic tendencies in economic specialization that replace public spirit with forms of policy. While Sheridan's cultural program has the same worthy aim, his system of rote gestures and intonations privileges form over opinion, an emphasis tending to separate rhetoric from its civic role and make it a specialized technique in its own right. Ferguson goes so far as to claim, in this respect, that "men ceased to be citizens, even to be good poets and orators, in proportion as they came to be distinguished by the profession of these, and other separate crafts."[7]

While offering few practical remedies, eighteenth-century moral philosophy offers insight into the problematic matter of ethos where modern rhetoric is concerned. Like Sheridan, Hugh Blair would recover our primitive eloquence, which he similarly locates in the passions, but his historical perspective tempers the cultural nostalgia informing his rhetorical theories. His account, in the first volume of *Lectures on Rhetoric and Belles Lettres* (1783), of the rise and progress of language describes the typical Enlightenment paradigm, tracing a primitive rhetoric in which passion predominates to a modern rhetoric directed to accurate description rather than powerful expression (*LRBL* 1:97–136). The result involves gain and loss, what is gained being more measurable than what has been lost:

> Thus Language, proceeding from sterility to copiousness, hath, at the same time, proceeded from vivacity to accuracy; from fire and enthusiasm, to coolness and precision. Those characters of early Language, descriptive sound, vehement tones and gestures, figurative style, and inverted arrangement, all hang together, have a mutual influence on each other; and have all gradually given place, to arbitrary sounds, calm pronunciation, simple style, plain arrangement. Language is become, in modern times, more correct, indeed, and accurate; but, however, less striking and animated: In its ancient state, more favourable to poetry and oratory; in its present, to reason and philosophy. (*LRBL* 1:124–25)

Here the original unity of primitive expression, with its organically related tones and gestures, is broken down into the arbitrary relations of rational discourse—more correct and accurate but only, as Campbell would note, within the closed and not necessarily interrelated systems of logic and usage. At the same time, this modern rhetoric might certainly have the technical resources to replicate primitive spontaneity in a rational system such as Sheridan conceives in Elocution. Combined in such a system, the expressive traits isolated in Blair's analysis, "descriptive sound, vehement tones and gestures, figurative style, and inverted arrangement," could "hang together" in a semblance of primitive unity. This, at least, is the ulterior premise of Elocution.

It is also the fundamental fallacy of Elocution and any other system attempting to recover by rational means what is not rational. Blair would likely sympathize with the primitivistic tendency of Sheridan's rhetorical program while having reservations about the system itself. These reservations would manage to reach just past the obvious fact of reason's cooling effects on rhetoric to grasp the possibility that this very coolness, the knowingness and detachment enabled by it, makes possible the counterfeiting of primitive spontaneity. Blair's comparison of two modern writers, the Earl of Shaftesbury and Lord Bolingbroke, favors Bolingbroke's style for its "great impetuosity" over Shaftesbury's more correct but artificial style, while acknowledging Bolingbroke to be "factious" and a demagogue, his reasonings "flimsy and false," even "sophistical in the highest degree" (*LRBL* 1:400). Blair in fact finds Shaftesbury's moral philosophy more profitable to read, notwithstanding the mannered style. This suggests that manner and matter do not hang together in the rhetoric of either writer, that as different as their styles may be, both employ rhetoric as an instrument distinct from whatever opinion it happens to be expressing. Whether vivacious or artificial, neither style emerges organically from the natural expressiveness imputed to primitive speech. Blair considers other writers in whom purity of style and thought more nearly conform to each other, such as Sir William Temple and Joseph Addison, but even in them he finds that a pure style comes at the expense of precision or passion or some other quality. The problem, insofar as it does not originate in the individual writers Blair examines, lies in contradictory assumptions about an original unity in language and the arbitrary nature of its construction. The result is a historical model of rhetorical practice describing a pre- and postlapsarian cultural binary in which, now divided from natural expression, modern rhetoric is subject to every vagary of interest and fashion. Though he defines rhetoric as the authentic expression of passion, Blair is wary of mere demagoguery, unlike Sheridan believing that the ancient Athenians were vulnerable to this abuse (*LRBL* 2:12–13). At the same time, he regrets a tendency in modern civil society, and in Britain in particular, away from passionate expression toward a language "more cool and temperate" and largely directed to rational ends (*LRBL* 2:41). Such observations incorporate themselves into a historical pattern of emerging rationality characteristic of Blair's Enlightenment perspective, but they also raise ethical concerns treated by moral philosophy. As in Ferguson, Whig history exists side by side with civic humanism in Blair who allows for the "cold and sceptical turn of mind" (*LRBL* 2:232) necessarily produced by rational progress even as he argues for a rhetoric capable of sustaining virtue in the public life of modern commercial society.

Rhetoric is only one of many measures of a nation's public life, but it is the primary means by which public life is conducted. At a time when national genius was consciously displaying itself in public art exhibitions, in ballad collections and folklore, and in the recovery of primitive vernaculars like Welsh and Gaelic, specimens of civic eloquence were being published in parliamentary proceedings, newspapers and periodicals, and anthologies of oratory.[8] One such anthology, Thomas Browne's *The British Cicero* (1808), a three-volume compilation of extracts and commentary, is subtitled *A Selection of the most Admired Speeches in the English Language*. Arranged under the heads of popular, parliamentary, and judicial oratory, this work is intended, according to its advertisement, "at once to infuse the spirit of true Eloquence, and the genuine principles of the constitution." Browne's own rhetoric, here and in the commentary accompanying the speeches, is mainly honorific, though he claims an instructive purpose in presenting this collection of speeches in light of the age's "continually increasing number of rhetorical systems." His historical introduction reveals a distinctly Whig bias, tracing the rise and progress of rhetoric in classical antiquity to its acme in post-Reformation Britain, specifically Walpolean England, for it was only then, "after proper checks had been imposed on the abuse of royal authority, and the rights and privileges of the people distinctly ascertained; that the freedom of the press and the still more uncontrolled freedom of speech in parliament gave to British Eloquence that fire, energy, and grandeur for which it has ever since been so justly admired and distinguished." Browne's epistemological assumptions are outlined in a chapter entitled "Of Logic," in which he cites Locke and employs Lockean categories concerning sensations, simple ideas, complex ideas, and association to argue the importance of educating the young in proper rhetorical practice so as to guard against "the deceptions of others, and the still more dangerous sophistry of their own passions." Yet he is confident that the English rhetorical tradition is more than proof against such dangers to civic virtue. His faith remains unshaken even when surveying English forensic oratory—for George Campbell the most problematic category of rhetoric due to "one peculiarity in the lawyer's professional character, which is unfavourable to conviction," which is to say that the lawyer may advocate, with equal skill and apparent zeal, either side of a question. While admitting its necessity, Campbell notes that this versatility must cast doubt on the practitioner's sincerity in other connections: "Surely the barefaced prostitution of his talents . . . in supporting indifferently, as pecuniary considerations determine him, truth or falsehood, justice or injustice, must have a still worse effect on the opinion of his hearers." Browne acknowledges that eloquence may be "prostituted" to base purposes, while dismissing a consequent skepticism about rhetoric as "the language of those cold phlegmatic casuists who cannot feel the divine glow of eloquence."[9]

It is unlikely that Browne counted Campbell among casuists who give rhetoric a bad name (though Campbell finds it difficult to avoid making this charge of lawyers). Given his view of rhetoric—underlying *The British Cicero* is the same coupling of humanistic and empirical assumptions found in New Rhetorical doctrine but without the critical caveats—he may be responding to a dialectical other glimpsed in his own magisterial Whiggism, though anxieties about modern commercial Britain are displaced to classical antiquity. Browne's optimism seems to go hand in hand with a sense, at least where ancient Greece and Rome are concerned, of the necessary correlation of progress and regression. In his introduction, he cites Longinus on the decadence of genius and sublimity, and Tacitus on the corrupt practice of law, ("of all kinds of merchandize the faith of lawyers is the most venal"). He largely dismisses mechanical systems of oratory, and like Ferguson and Blair conceives rhetoric as a vehicle of civic virtue transcending rational interest. His rejection of charges that rhetoric is "merely calculated to interest our passions at the expence of our judgment" notwithstanding, however, Browne walks a fine line not only between reason and passion but reason and calculation as well as passion and sensation in his views on rhetoric. "[W]e must gain the hearts of men, before we can hope to convince their understandings," he argues, and then insists that "we must not leave them cool approvers of our counsels, but hurry them on with irresistible impetuousity:—the glowing words must often be charged with electric fire, to force their way to the inmost recesses of the soul."[10] Does this "irresistible impetuousity" move speaker and listener equally, or is it merely the means by which assent is manipulated? Does the galvanic reference ("electric fire") speak to passionate conviction or conditioned response? Such questions arise relative to modern rhetoric only as they are attributed to the casuistical straw-men of Browne's Whiggish history of ascendant British genius. In the end, Browne's compilation of *"the most Admired Speeches in the English Language"* serves much the same acclamatory purpose as boosterish Academy exhibitions of English art, in this way eliding its own rational Whiggism and so abetting rhetoric's possible declension into unreflecting sensationalism.

No booster of the English trade in art, William Hazlitt was also a keen critic of contemporary English oratory. In 1807, a year before Browne's *British Cicero* appeared, he published his own anthology entitled *The Eloquence of the British Senate; or, Select Specimens from the Speeches of the Most Distinguished Parliamentary Speakers, from the Beginning of the Reign of Charles I. to the Present Time.* More than merely a collection of memorable extracts—and this is equally true of *The British Cicero* and other omnibus showcases of oratory appearing at the time—this two-volume work is "a common-place book of all the principal topics, of the *pros* and *cons* of the different questions, that may be brought into dispute" (*CWH* 1:140). Despite the honorific ring of its subtitle, moreover, *Eloquence of the British Senate* presents in its notes and commentary a critique that extends beyond its selections to encompass habits of thought and expression shaping public life in post-Reformation Britain. The extent to which Hazlitt's criticism generally is conditioned by rhetorical concerns is remarkable considering the greater emphasis placed by commentators on his philosophical bent, though both tendencies are related in ways made clear by New Rhetorical theory. In *Eloquence of the British Senate*, personalities critically educed from individual speeches collectively issue in a composite national ethos, the language of Parliament being coeval in Hazlitt's view with an evolving political identity. Of his purpose in compiling these speeches, Hazlitt points out that "I wished to make it a history, as far as I could, of the progress of the language, of the state of parties at different periods, of the most interesting debates, and in short, an abridged parliamentary history for the time" (*CWH* 1:140).

If for Browne the Walpole administration represents a high point in British rhetoric, in Hazlitt's view this is where it all began to go wrong. The recent Pitt administration serves as his point of reference. *Eloquence of the British Senate* appeared one year after William Pitt's death, and it would have been impossible at this time for any consideration of British Parliament to view the institution, either its history or its prospects, independent of his powerful influence. For better or worse, Pitt was become an institution himself, and this cultish and inevitably revisionary aura would only become more intense in following decades. The fact that Hazlitt appends only a cursory note to his Pitt selection, a maiden speech on economic reform, is possibly a conscious reaction to the beginnings of this posthumous veneration, though Pitt is prominent enough elsewhere in Hazlitt's writings. Yet this omission by faint emphasis is effectively supplied by Pitt's normative, if not salutary, role in Hazlitt's commentary on other figures in *Eloquence of the British Senate*. Hazlitt's estimate of Walpole as a speaker in fact goes against the grain of most comparisons of him with Pitt by stressing their differences as speakers. Employing his typically different criteria for speakers and writers, Hazlitt favors Walpole over Pitt: "The one has the variety, simplicity, and smartness of conversation; the other has all the fulness, the pomp, the premeditated involutions and measured periods of a book, but of a book not written in the best stile" (*CWH* 1:157). Even such marked differences, however, conceal connections evident not in incidentals of style but in an emerging parliamentary ethos. Hazlitt credits Walpole with systematizing parliamentary proceedings, in this way more clearly delineating party differences so that "The combatants on each side, in this political warfare, were regularly drawn up in opposition to each other, and had their several parts assigned them with the greatest exactitude" (*CWH* 1:156). This seems a happy innovation with the potential to infuse a spirit of critical debate into public life. Hazlitt quotes Cowper to note that "'The popular harangue, the tart reply, / The logic, and the wisdom, and the wit,' appeared in all their combined lustre" (*CWH* 1:156). Yet he notes that the effect was to turn the commons into "a regular debating society," over time producing the hollow formalism of the Pitt parliament:

> The effect of this system could not be different from what it has turned out. The house of commons, instead of being the representative and depository of the collective sense of the nation, has

become a theatre for wrangling disputants to declaim in the scene of noisy impertinence and pedantic folly. An empty shew of reason, a set of words has been substituted for the silent operation of general feeling and good sense; and ministers referring every thing to this flimsy standard have been no longer taken up in planning wise measures, but in studying how to defend their blunders. (*CWH* 1:156)

The legislature described here—in Walpole's Parliament "all the common-place topics of political controversy were familiar in the mouths of both parties" (*CWH* 1:156)—recalls the expedient venue variously observed by Hamilton and Bentham. Hazlitt effectively employs Whig history in reverse in this passage to trace a seemingly rational course to its insidious result in Pittite governance.

A separate note appended to Hazlitt's Walpole selection describes a rhetorical practice grounded in purposeful indirection. The speech in question, addressing the Triennial Bill on 13 March 1734, conveys as good an idea of Walpole's speaking talents as any he made, Hazlitt asserts, and so is presumably characteristic of both the speaker and his administration. Hazlitt's note draws attention to a reference in this speech to certain inconveniences of democratic government, noting how Walpole ingeniously disregards parts of the constitution—specifically, those parts designating the House of Commons as a check on other branches of government representing property and power—in order to make the House of Commons answer to "the purposes of all other parts, and in fact to render them unnecessary" (*CWH* 1:374 n). In *Parliamentary Logic*, Hamilton frequently urges just such convenient omissions in argument,[11] but where Hamilton's system speaks to limited tactical ends, Walpole's rhetoric is directed to the reformulation of parliamentary governance itself. This is done on the basis of an incomplete premise, a fallacy. Hazlitt argues that by this means "care has been taken to make sure of the remedy in the first instance, namely by innoculating the patient before the disease was caught, and making the house of commons itself never anything more than the representative of property and power" (*CWH* 1:374 n). It might also be said that the Commons under Walpole is nothing *less* than this, having arrogated to itself the power of the other legislative branches. According to Hazlitt's republican logic, however, it is diminished to exactly the degree it has become the instrument of property and power, its true measure as an institution being its comprehensiveness as a representative body. The contrasting styles Hazlitt describes in Walpole and Pitt—he notes "that the display of controversial dexterity was in Walpole more a trial of wit, and in Pitt more an affair of science" (*CWH* 1:157)—are the least of it, then. Despite their differences, both share an ethos subversive of what in the passage quoted above is designated as "the collective sense of the nation." The methods associated with wit and science alike are analytical; in Wordsworth's words, they murder to dissect. A national ethos may conceivably be exploited by these rational energies, as it is by Blair's Bolingbroke, but not assimilated by them. Hazlitt's estimate of the parliaments of Walpole and Pitt suggests that "the collective sense of the nation" cannot be claimed by the self-aggrandizing rhetoric associated with such an ethos any more than a portion can claim the whole.

Throughout his writings on parliamentary rhetoric, Hazlitt portrays a fundamental binary in the self-representations of the English political character cutting along the lines of change and permanence. These categories are neither mutually exclusive nor strictly reducible to party allegiance or even ideological disposition. Both sides include pragmatists and idealists of either a sentimental or rational nature; either side may appropriate seemingly characteristic techniques of the other. At their most effective, both acknowledge what in his essay "On the Spirit of Partisanship" Hazlitt calls "the difference between the efficient and the inefficient" (*CWH* 17:38–39), their varying degrees of success depending on circumstance and individual character alike.

Eloquence of the British Senate posits a kind of dissociation of sensibility occurring in parliamentary speaking some time after the seventeenth century before hardening into the modernizing ethos of Walpole's Parliament. In his note to a speech by Bulstrode Whitlocke, whom he characterizes as a monument of seventeenth-century learning, Hazlitt observes that men's minds at that time "were stored with facts and images, almost to excess," and yet:

There was a tenacity and firmness in them that kept fast hold of the impressions of things as they were first stamped upon the mind; and "their ideas seemed to lie like substances in the brain." Facts and feelings went hand in hand; the one naturally implied the other; and our ideas, not yet exorcised and squeezed and tortured out of their natural objects, into a subtle essence of pure intellect, did not fly about like ghosts without a body, tossed up and down, or upborne only by the ELEGANT FORMS of words, through the vacuum of abstract reasoning, and sentimental refinement. The understanding was invigorated and nourished with its natural and proper food, the knowledge of things without it; and was not left, like an empty stomach, to prey upon itself, or starve on the meagre scraps of an artificial logic, or windy impertinence of ingenuity self-begotten. What a difference between the grave, clear, solid, laborious stile of the speech here given, and the crude metaphysics, false glitter, and trifling witticism of a modern legal oration! The truth is, that the affectation of philosophy and fine taste has spoiled every thing; and instead of the honest seriousness and simplicity of old English reasoning in law, in politics, in morality, in all the grave concerns in life, we have nothing left but a mixed species of bastard sophistry, got between ignorance and vanity, and generating nothing. (*CWH* 1:147–48)

The key to the traditional style of parliamentary speaking contrasted here with modern eloquence lies in "old English reasoning." By "reasoning" Hazlitt means not abstract rationality but "sense," a "collective sense" in which emotion and intellection grow out of one another, as in the organic fusion of expressive traits that for Blair characterizes primitive speech. Throughout *Eloquence of the British Senate*, Hazlitt cites speakers who reflect this quality in their oratory—John Campbell, for instance, whose speeches "are characterized by a rough, plain, manly spirit of good sense, and a zealous attachment to the welfare of his country," or Henry Booth in whose eloquence Hazlitt remarks "a mixture of local and personal feeling" (*CWH* 1:165, 150). Of Sir John Knight, quoted at full length in his zealous opposition to the naturalization of foreign Protestants, Hazlitt claims that "he is a true Englishman, a perfect islander," arguing further that "downright passion, unconquerable prejudice, and unaffected enthusiasm, are always justifiable; they follow a blind, but sure instinct; they flow from a real cause; they are uniform and consistent with themselves" (*CWH* 1:152, 153). So far does Hazlitt urge this emotionalist strain that in describing the "dull, plodding, headstrong" Charles Pratt (Earl Camden), he argues that "to the generality of mankind, dulness is the natural object of sympathy and admiration; it is the element in which they breath," thus making Pratt "just the man to address those who can only assent, but cannot reason." His very weakness as a reasoner and a debater is paradoxically his strength as a speaker: "The less success a man has in maintaining his point, the more does he shew his steadiness and attachment to his object in persevering in it in spite of opposition; and the proof of fortitude which he thus gives must naturally induce all those of the same sanguine disposition, who have the same zeal and the same imbecility in the defence of truth, to make common cause with him" (*CWH* 1:168–69).

The question of what is properly a nation's "collective sense" is problematic. Hazlitt's historical premise in *Eloquence of the British Senate* requires him to acknowledge historical difference among various periods of English parliamentary eloquence, "the successive changes that have taken place in the minds and characters of Englishmen within the last 200 years" (*CWH* 1:147). At the same time, he regrets these changes to the extent that they have rendered parliament less characteristic as a representative body. Yet his criteria for an authentic parliamentary rhetoric are certainly pragmatic enough. As he describes it in the preface to his *Political Essays* (1819), Parliament is a "mob" governed by "gross and obvious motives" (*CWH* 7:14). Rather than merely exposing political rhetoric as a code for corruption, however, he sketches an epistemology of political persuasion and influence as hard-nosed as Hamilton's, though without the cynicism. It is the successful, and not necessarily corrupt, politician whose practice reflects such assumptions—for example, Walpole's nemesis William Pulteney, the Earl of Bath, whom Hazlitt profiles in *Eloquence of the British Senate*:

> His sentences are short, direct, pointed; yet full and explicit, abounding in repetitions of the same leading phrase or idea, whenever this had a tendency to rivet the impression more strongly in the mind of the hearer, or to prevent the slightest ob-

scurity or doubt. He also knew perfectly well how to avail himself
of the resources contained in the stately significance, and gross
familiarity of the dialect of the house of commons. To talk in the
character of a great parliamentary leader, to assume the sense of
the house, to affect the extensive views and disinterested feelings that belong to a great permanent body, and to descend in a
moment to all the pertness and scurrility, the conceit and self-im-
portance of a factious bully, are among the great arts of parliamentary speaking. (*CWH* 1:160)

Hazlitt does, to be sure, pay attention to the technicalities of Pulteney's style, sentence length, reiteration, and so forth. But he is
more concerned with tracing it to its source in a common medium, a "dialect" that is less a matter of verbal usage than ethos.
Even so, he has no illusions about the nature of this ethos, what
might be called the rhetorical *virtù* displayed by its exemplary
speakers. Pulteney commands a range of parliamentary dialects
enabling him to assume the roles of statesman and bully alike,
and as Hazlitt observes generally of those opposing Walpole's
parliamentary hegemony, "their motives for this were no doubt
various" (*CWH* 1:163). Yet as effectively adapted to contingency
as this rhetoric is, it manages to be more than the sum of its devices, to enter into the "collective sense of the nation" validating
Parliament as a representative body. For this reason, Hazlitt
cautions in an essay "On the Present State of Parliamentary Eloquence" (1820) that talent alone is not enough in opposition, for
there is talent on the other side as well, not to mention influence.
What is required in addition to these qualities is "nothing else
but fixed principle, but naked honesty, but undisguised enthusiasm" (*CWH* 17:9).

Emerging from the vagaries of national sentiment and
adapted to the House, the ethos associated with speakers like
Pulteney serves a normative function for Hazlitt. Opposed to it
are "the insidious encroachments, and undermining influence of
Walpole's administration" (*CWH* 1:163), a memorable instance of
which is Horace Walpole, member for Yarmouth and brother of
Robert. Horace appears to have been almost the equal of his
famous sibling as a speaker and his inferior as a statesman. He
is the very embodiment of a parliamentary Machiavel, characterized both by "a certain ambidexterity of political logic" and "an

habitual readiness in the common-place forms of trivial argument" (*CWH* 1:159). "He had the art to make the question assume at will whatever shape he pleased," notes Hazlitt, "and to make 'the worse appear the better reason'" (*CWH* 1:159). Elsewhere, Hazlitt represents the "insidious encroachments" of the Walpolean ethos in the age of Pitt, and not only in figures associated with Pitt's side of a question. In his essay "On the Present State of Parliamentary Eloquence," appearing in *The London Magazine* in 1820, Hazlitt follows a sketch of the famous Whig member, Samuel Whitbread ("the representative of the spontaneous, unsophisticated sense of the English people" [*CWH* 17:10]), with a profile of George Tierney, another prominent Whig parliamentarian. Tierney was virtually the leader of the Whig opposition against Liverpool but never technically held this post owing to Whig reservations about his unaristocratic origins. Comparing Whitbread and Tierney, Hazlitt judges the latter to be "a better speaker and a cleverer man" while expressing reservations about him as a leader. Hazlitt's brief sketch of Tierney is a study in technical facility apparently empty of convincing conviction:

> He has no quixotic enthusiasm in himself; much less any to spare for his followers. He cares nothing (or seems to care nothing) about a question; but he is impatient of absurdity, and has a thorough contempt for the understandings of his opponents. Sharpened by his spleen, nothing escapes his acuteness. He makes fine sport for the spectators. He takes up Lord Castlereagh's blunders, and Mr. Vanittart's no-meanings; and retorts them on their heads in the finest style of execution imagination. It is like being present on a Shrove-Tuesday, and seeing a set of mischievous unfeeling boys throwing at a brace of cocks, and breaking their shins. Mr. Tierney always brings down his man; but beyond this you feel no confidence in him; you take no interest in his movements but as he is instrumental in annoying other people. He (to all appearance) has no great point to carry himself, and no wish to be thought to have any important principle at stake. (*CWH* 17:10–11)

Tierney seems to epitomize Hamilton's technocratic rhetorician who looks "rather to the *object* of each motion, than to the question itself." Hazlitt is careful to qualify his estimate, but while an impression of conviction is not the same as real conviction, an impression of its absence may be the same in effect as a real absence. If Tierney is too sincere to be a hypocrite, he nevertheless gives the impression of caring less about principle than about gaining his point. Most telling is the imputation of juvenile behavior underlying the Shrove Tuesday reference, the tacit hint of an underdeveloped emotional being. An "unfeeling" strain in both Pitt and Canning in this regard is similarly attributed by Hazlitt to arrested growth. In the end, Tierney is as effective as his stunted affective capacity allows him to be, with the result that the interest of his performance consists solely in "execution." "When Mr. Whitbread got up to speak, you felt an interest in what he was going to say," Hazlitt asserts, "in the success of his arguments: when you hear that Mr. Tierney is on his legs, you feel that you shall be amused with an admirable display of dexterity and talent, but are nearly indifferent as to the result. You look on as at an exhibition of extraordinary skill in fencing or prize-fighting" (*CWH* 17:11).

Combined with other qualities, such ability may speak to reason and assent alike. Devoid of them, it may speak to neither. Another Opposition speaker described in "On the Present State of Parliamentary Eloquence," William Conyngham Plunkett, is not a nice or a deep reasoner, but Hazlitt considers him to be one of the ablest speakers in parliament, for his style answers to his purpose—his speech on the Catholic question, for instance, which while not brilliant was "impregnated with as much thought, imagination and passion as the House would be likely to understand or sympathise with" (*CWH* 17:13–14). The speech nevertheless had a remarkable effect. Hazlitt, who heard it while reporting on Parliament for the *Morning Chronicle*, laments the absence of many like Plunkett in the House: "Nothing but the will is wanting.—The ability, I will venture to say, is there" (*CWH* 17:14). Yet will, which is say its effective expression, means everything in politics and rhetoric alike. For Hazlitt, Sir James Mackintosh is a cautionary instance of ability unsupported by a convincing display of will. Mackintosh's portrait in *The Spirit of the Age* (1825) turns on the tension between his mind, "critical, and not parliamentary" (*CWH* 11:96), and the "phalanx of hostile and inveterate prejudice arrayed against him" in Parliament (*CWH* 11:97). Mackintosh displays the fastidious critical temperament of a rational reformer whose arguments, "with so many *pros* and *cons*, doubts and difficulties," run against the natural grain of party interest (*CWH* 11:97). Mackintosh and Plunkett are both politicians inclining to the progressive side of questions, so that a comparison of them must depend on their efficacy in speaking to these questions, judged by either the measures of traditional affect or modern efficiency. In Plunkett's case, ability and will "hang together" in the manner of the pre-Walpolean ideal that serves as rhetorical norm in *Eloquence of the British Senate*, an ethos joining reason and emotion in indissoluble union. He is, according to the terms of Hazlitt's historical thesis, something of a throwback, though of course his effectiveness is what matters most finally. Unfortunately, Plunkett was sailing back to Ireland when the motion in question was put to the vote so that his speech, having achieved its desired end *as a speech*, evidently failed to achieve the political end of Catholic emancipation. In Mackintosh's case, the progressive ends he pursues are undercut by the very modernity of the means he employs to achieve them, rational argument wholly exclusive of other considerations. In *Lectures on Oratory and Criticism*, Joseph Priestley cautions against nice reasoning in oratory, distinguishing the different mental aptitudes required for writing and speaking—the "nicer discernment" of the author and the "small improprieties" of the orator. The speaker who is too nice in his arguments sacrifices emotional consistency to logical propriety (*LOC* 31). The "critical" method of a speaker like Hazlitt's Mackintosh, consisting "not so much in taking a side, as in stating a question" (*CWH* 17:5), entails just such a sacrifice, for "nothing comes amiss to him that can puzzle or *pose* his hearers; and he lets out all his knowledge indiscriminately, whether it makes for or against him, with deliberate impartiality and scrupulous exactness" (*CWH* 17:6). The discrimination required for speaking to a question in Parliament is no mere matter of logical nicety, for it involves equally nice considerations of bias and sentiment. Reason has a crucial role, but is subordinate to interest. For all his logical rigor, Mackintosh is an undiscriminating speaker because he fails to distinguish his interest from the interests of his opponents. Describing his conduct in questions of the greatest moment, then, Hazlitt observes that, through a too scrupulous regard for impartial reason, "he compromised the argument" (*CWH* 11:96). Even the stolid Earl of Camden, by contrast, manages to carry with him all those who can assent but not reason.

But the unreflecting wisdom speaking through one kind of mind may be put to quite different uses by another. Chapter 6, book 2 of Campbell's *Philosophy of Rhetoric* is devoted to "Perspicacity," a quality Campbell privileges, in an honorific (or pragmatic?) equation of clarity with truth, as an end in itself. In the chapter following, however, Campbell deals not only with the problem of obscurity but also with the possibility of its effective use, asking: "If perspicuity be expedient in convincing us of truth, and persuading us to do right, is not its contrary, obscurity, expedient in effecting the contrary; that is, in convincing us of what is false, and in persuading us to do wrong? And may not either of these effects be the aim of the speaker" (*PR* 273–74)? Within the ethical bounds of his civic humanism, Campbell is able to refute these objections more or less out of hand. By briefly entertaining them, however, he admits an element of instrumentality into the equation whereby there need be no necessary connection between a premise and the means by which it is demonstrated. For William Gerard Hamilton the element ensuring "efficiency" in debate is not loyalty or consistency or any other positive quality, good or bad, but sheer expedience. When counseling obfuscation, then, he advises, "but state clearly to your own mind what is so" (PL 18). In their different ways, the Earl of Camden and Mackintosh fail this critical test of efficiency, because neither has mastered contingency by being sufficiently clear to himself about "what is so." In both cases, the problem involves the relation of premise and demonstration. Camden's traditionalist arguments "address those who can only assent, but cannot reason," leaving both him and his constituency vulnerable to betrayal by the calculated promptings of those who not only *can* reason but whose assent is wholly in the keeping of their reason. Mackintosh's premise, on the other hand, is betrayed by his own reason. The "critical" method he employs is a technique more suited to exposing error than confirming belief, though it may be just as easily employed to reinforce error in that it stands in an instrumental rather than a necessary relation to opinion. While Camden's estimable "imbecility" stands in greatest danger from technique put to such uses from without, Mackintosh's eloquence is sub-

verted from within, betrayed by its own logical nicety. Operating
independent of conviction, this technical ethos is virtually indis-
tinguishable from the contingent circumstances in which it
works, taking extreme form in the mercenary operative Hazlitt
describes in "The Political Automaton: A Modern Character":
"*The thing* is hired to soothe or inflame the public mind, as occasion requires; and succeeds in misleading the ignorant by a voluntary abuse of terms and an unlimited command over the
figures of speech" (*CWH* 19:117).

Where there is rhetoric, however disposed, there is an ethos.
Hazlitt's "Political Automaton" is purely a creature of talent,
but, such as it is, this is a characteristic personality type, expressing a particular ethos in a particular way. It is surely something like this "Modern Character" that Coleridge has in mind in
his essay "On the Origin and Progress of the Sect of Sophists in
Greece" preceding the essays on method in *The Friend*. The term
"SOPHIST," as Coleridge points out, originally signifies "one who
professes the power of making others wise, a wholesale and
retail *dealer* in wisdom—a *wisdom-monger*." While he stresses
that it is in this sense, the retailing of wisdom and not its abuse,
that Plato and Aristotle define "the sophistic character," he adds
that "Their sophisms were indeed its natural products and ac-
companiments, but must yet be distinguished from it, as the
fruits from the tree" (*TF* 1:436). This is a backhanded distinction, as of course the sophism is a necessary inference of the
sophist. One other attribute of the sophists Coleridge notes is
their itinerancy, if anything more troubling to him than the
wisdom mongering. He quotes in this connection a classical authority named Timmus who, while acknowledging the sophists'
accomplishments, fears that "being itinerants from city to city,
loose from all permanent ties of house and home, and every-
where aliens, they shoot wide of the proper aim of man whether
as philosopher or as citizen" (*TF* 1:437). Coleridge points out that
the Sophists emerged during a period when various causes, including military triumphalism, democratic populism, and a rage
for sensational entertainments, were contributing to the corruption of private and public life in fifth-century Athens. To Athenian youth the sophists offered "the arts of persuasion and
temporary impression" as substitutes for an eroding authority of
birth and property by which Solon's institutions inculcated the

"directing motives" of moral discipline. "The loss of this stable and salutary influence," Coleridge suggests, "was to be supplied by the arts of popularity" (*TF* 1:438–39). Regency England is surely glimpsed in the resulting sensualism and nihilism of Athenian culture he describes:

> The restless spirit of republican ambition, engendered by their success in a just war, and by the romantic character of that success, had already formed a close alliance with luxury in its early and most vigorous state, when it acts as an appetite to enkindle, and before it has exhausted and dulled the vital energies by the habit of enjoyment. But this corruption was now to be introduced into the *citadel* of the moral being, and to be openly defended by the very arms and instruments, which had been given for the purpose of preventing or chastising its approach. The understanding was to be corrupted by the perversion of the reason, and the feelings through the medium of the understanding. For this purpose all fixed principles, whether grounded on reason, religion, law, or antiquity, were to be undermined, and then, as now, chiefly by the sophistry of submitting all positions alike, however heterogeneous, to the criterion of the mere understanding, disguising or concealing the fact, that the rules which alone they applied, were abstracted from the objects of the senses, and applicable exclusively to things of quantity and relation. At all events, the minds of men were to be sensualized; and even if the arguments themselves failed, yet the principles so attacked were to be brought into doubt by the mere frequency of hearing *all* things doubted, and the most sacred of all now openly denied, and now insulted by sneer and ridicule. (*TF* 1:439)

For Coleridge, the inference of sophism from philosophy, and a resulting inference of sensation from truth, signals the disappearance of "THE INVISIBLE" in the mental life of a nation. The senses, having served as a means to the ideal, now become ends in themselves, "and taken independently of their representative function, from *words* they become mere empty *sounds,* and differ from *noise* only by exciting expectations which they cannot gratify—fit ingredients of the idolatrous *charm,* the potent Abracadabra, of a sophisticated race, who had sacrificed the religion of faith to the superstition of the senses, a race of animals, in whom the presence of reason is manifested solely by the absence of instinct" (*TF* 1:440). It is in just such a regressed state that Coleridge's elder finds his people in the parable of the "madning Rain" opening *The Friend*.

For Jacques Ellul, reason manifested solely by an absence of instinct typifies the modern technocratic ethos. In *The Technological Society*, Ellul argues that the integration of instrumental reason into the mentality of society is the most profound effect of modern technology. What he terms "Technique" is distinct from ideology in that a given technique may be employed by any ideology in order to gain some end, but is itself neutral, a mere instrument, though of course the habitual use of reason in this way becomes ideology in its own right. As Ellul bluntly puts it, "We no longer live in that primitive epoch in which things were good or bad in themselves. Technique in itself is neither, and can therefore do what it will. It is truly autonomous." The use of technique issues not from a widely held sense of the general good, though of course being autonomous it may do so, but from "special interest"—according to Ellul "the great motive force behind the development of technical consciousness."[12] For Hazlitt the appropriation of political discourse by technique characterizes the political culture of Regency England. He identifies this mentality with what he calls the "Pitt School," whose late namesake exemplifies a sophistical spirit replacing the "collective sense of the nation," certain and concrete, with subtle fallacies. In the rhetorically grounded history of politics Hazlitt elaborates in *Eloquence of the British Senate* and elsewhere, however, Pitt merely finishes what Walpole began, incorporating in himself and his administration a bloodless professionalism superseding the old English parliamentary ethos. In his "Character of Mr. Pitt," published the year of Pitt's death, Hazlitt portrays this remarkable parliamentarian as a wholly rhetorical creature whose sole talent consisted in his "artful use of words, and a certain dexterity of logical arrangement" (*CWH* 7:322). The portrait Hazlitt sketches of Pitt— this is no eulogy—portrays a man whose deficiencies as a human being are what made him as a politician:

> Having no strong feelings, no distinct perceptions, his mind having no link, as it were, to connect it with the world of external nature, every subject presented to him nothing more than a *tabula rasa*, on which he was at liberty to lay whatever colouring of language he pleased; having no general principles, no compre-

hensive views of things, no moral habits of thinking, no system of action, there was nothing to hinder him from pursuing any particular purpose, by any means that offered; having never any plan, he could not be convicted of inconsistency, and his own pride and obstinacy were the only rules of his conduct. (*CWH* 7:322–23).

This political disposition, a kind of neo-Whiggism, reflects the triumph of technique over principle quietly celebrated in *Parliamentary Logic*. Pitt's legacy, indeed, reveals itself more in the absences characteristic of logical fallacy than in a positive influence—as in ministry rhetoric on the agricultural distresses of 1816, for instance, characterized by Hazlitt in the *Examiner* as "an attempt to speak out and say nothing; to oppose something that might be done, and propose something that cannot be done; to direct attention to the subject, and divert it from it; to do something and nothing; and to come to this potent conclusion, that while nothing *is done*, nothing *can be done*" (*CWH* 7:103). In this ambiguous medium, policy is beside the point, or rather it *is* whatever it is said to be at a given moment as technique masters contingency by any means necessary. What is important is that the result signify that difference between "the efficient and the inefficient" so determinative of success in the Pittite ethos.

The Whiggish Court ideology—in the eighteenth century, according to Pocock, "beginning to explore theories of how the diversities of passionate and self-interested action might be manipulated and coordinated"—was the perfect vehicle for the play of instrumental reason. In *The Machiavellian Moment*, Pocock distinguishes two strains of English political thought issuing in characteristic styles of expression. What he calls the "ideology of the Country" depended on the maintenance of propertied independence. To the extent that such a position was becoming increasingly untenable in a speculative commercial economy, the kind of civic ethos around which the country ideology formed itself urged an impractical ideal of virtue grounded in a heroic conception of character. By contrast, the "ideology of the Court" was premised on more portable ideas about wealth, a consequence of which was ready acknowledgment of the view that people were self-interested beings, that virtue was a private

rather than a public quality. These assumptions enabled a latitude greater than that allowed by the Country ideology because
the Court position assumed that policy might operate independent of values. As Pocock notes, however, if the Country ideology
was weakened by a property-based, public conception of virtue, it
discovered its strength in its rhetoric, for "it was endowed with
all the riches of the complex and articulate vocabulary of civic
humanism with which to expound the science and sociology of
virtue." By contrast, the ethical vocabulary of the Court ideology
tended to be thin, lacking as it did a consistent body of principles
or a concept of property grounded in tradition. The conflict, then,
was between civic virtue, with its affective ethos, and "dynamic
virtù," with its effective method; as Pocock nicely puts it, "the
Court ideology could show how to command success, the Country
how to deserve it."[13]

In early nineteenth-century England, Pocock's categories are
still useful, though much refracted. What commentators like Hazlitt were observing was a splintering of these two positions into a
great many positions, often quite different from either of the
originals Pocock describes. The Country ideology is still recogniz-
able in conservative opposition to reform, a reaction that gained
impetus in the early 1790s and that had become seemingly entrenched in the first decades of the nineteenth century. The pragmatic autonomy of the Court position was more easily assimilated by different, even diametrically opposed, interests. One of
these, strangely, was the Country or Tory interest, but even
stranger on the face of it was the adoption of the Court ideology
by Reform. What made the ideology of the Court useful to Reform
of course was its synthesizing ahistorical method, a means easily
detachable from a particular end. The Tory exploitation of this
method was similarly due to its adaptability as a technique distinct from conviction or even a particular rhetoric. According to
Hazlitt, Reform lost on both counts during the Napoleonic Wars,
which is to say that at the same time that its rational reform arguments labored under rhetorical disadvantages outlined by
Pocock in the Court Ideology, it was further undermined by
clever Tory deployments of its traditional libertarian rhetoric.
The dominant theme of Hazlitt's preface to *Political Essays, with
Sketches of Public Characters* (1819) is the complicity of all parties in the late wars. Its opening assertion is less remarkable for

what it says, however ("I am no politician, and still less can I be said to be a party-man: but I have a hatred of tyranny, and a contempt for its tools" [*CWH* 7:7]), than for its deployment of the plain manner Cobbett was transforming into the idiom of English Jacobinism. Its forthright cadences are those of John Bull, but a John Bull sympathetic to Bonaparte and critical of the government's suspension of *Habeas Corpus*. It is not an easy fit, but no stranger than other ventriloquisms in the age's political rhetoric, for John Bull was a strange fabrication at this time, a village bully formed of the broadcloth of English libertarianism drafted by the ministerial press to defend continental monarchy. His bluff honesty was no match for the designing eloquence of those who trampled his liberties and plotted to restore the Bourbons even as they invoked liberty in the war against Napoleon. But John Bull was not the only dupe of the propaganda war, noted Hazlitt, for "the poor Reformers who were taken in to join the cry, because they are as fastidious in their love of liberty as their opponents are inveterate in their devotion to despotism, continue in vain to reproach them [the Tory ministry] with their temporary professions" (*CWH* 7:12–13).

The critical bent Hazlitt isolates in the fractious stance of Reform is not in the first instance an expression of ideology but a method. Tracing its origins in part to the portable and thus autonomous political shifts Pocock identifies in the Court ideology, this method was consolidated in the analytical techniques of philosophic radicalism that independently survived the political program from which they emerged—what in his estimate of Benthamite praxis John Stuart Mill calls "the questioning spirit, the disposition to demand the *why* of everything."[14] In Hazlitt's analysis, the rational reformer is defined by his negative role relative to things-as-they-are rather than by a positive commitment to any *particular* alternative. Reform's love of liberty may be ideologically "fastidious" but it is not constitutively profound, unlike the dedication to tyranny Hazlitt imputes to the Tory, which is "enshrined in traditions, in laws, in usages, in the outward symbols of power, in the very idioms of language" (*CWH* 7:12). The practical consequence of this distinction is very simple: "Speculative opinion leads men different ways, each according to his particular fancy:—it is prejudice or interest that drives before it the herd of mankind. That *which is*, with all its confirmed abuses and 'tickling commodities,' is alone solid and certain: that *which may be* or *ought to be*, has a thousand shapes and colours, according to the eye that sees it, is infinitely variable and evanescent in its effects" (*CWH* 7:13). The Reformer cannot consolidate his own position in nice arguments, though he can bring them to bear on the position of his opponents, forcing the positive Tory hegemony into a dialectic even though he does so at a similar risk to his own position, thus "leaving nothing sufficiently firm or unquestioned in our opinions to withstand the current and bias of inclination" (*CWH* 20:311). If the composed inertia of faith questions nothing, reason questions everything and confirms nothing, even providing the means by which it may be overturned itself. Just as Reform's radical critique infers revolution from the fissures and flaws of civil order, so, Hazlitt argues, Edmund Burke's auspicious elaboration of the traditional state in *Reflections on the Revolution in France*—"extracting the elements of order and the cement of social life from the decomposition of all society" (*CWH* 7:320)—issues from the French Revolution's unsettling critique, subverting the very elements whose subversive analytical techniques it at once appropriates and condemns. Hazlitt's contemporaries (not to mention conservatives today) would have been startled to see such methods imputed to the age's most prominent conservative thinker. But it is just such intellectual contradictions that intrigue Hazlitt here: the deployment of a subversive cultural critique in a reactionary cause.

Burke was himself a Whig, a fact easy to forget in light of his subsequent posthumous adoption by every kind of conservative. William Pitt, who hardly survived Burke long enough to be included among this posterity (though Canning did and could be), considered himself an independent Whig and was as troubled by Burke's *Reflections* as Charles Fox was, calling its arguments "Rhapsodies in which there is much to admire, and nothing to agree with."[15] His Tory administration was willing to exploit alarmist rhetoric when necessary, however. As the Whig party had been in disarray since the breakup of the Rockingham Whigs in 1782, Pitt faced his main opposition in the reputedly radical-leaning Foxite Whigs, while the more conservative Portland Whigs abstained from systematic opposition and even accepted ministry roles just short of coalition. Burke stood largely alone, opposing opposition and ministry alike, effectively subverting

both by taking a counterrevolutionary position diametrically opposed to one and more extreme than the other. Contemporary reaction to the *Reflections* took many forms, extending even to
darkly suggestive psychological analyses of its author, but those
among Burke's readership not preoccupied with gothic sensationalism might have guessed that this purported address to a
young Frenchman was in fact directed to English Whigs. In his
introduction to the recent Oxford edition of the *Reflections*, L. G.
Mitchell suggests that Burke was less concerned with the Reverend Price's radical sermonizing than he was with Charles Fox's
leadership of the Whig party. According to Burke himself, the
counterrevolutionary argument of the *Reflections* was based in
part "on the Idea, that the principles of a new, republican,
frenchified Whiggism was gaining ground in this Country" (*RRF*
8:28–29). Burke feared that Fox's dilatory attitude had allowed
radical elements like Richard Brinsley Sheridan (playwright and
son of celebrated Elocutionist, Thomas) to gain control of the
party. Ambitious Whigs like Sheridan were making known their
sympathy with the aims of the revolution by joining such subver-
sive-sounding organizations as the Revolution Society and the
Friends of the People. While these gestures raised the ire of conservative Whigs, however, party divisions predated events in
France, so that the revolution was likely more a catalyst for sim-
mering resentments. Certainly, it was seized on by Sheridan as
an opportunity to raise his profile in the Whig party. To some
Whigs, indeed, it seemed that the *Reflections* was provoked not
by Price's sermon of November 1789 but by Burke's debate about
French affairs with Sheridan in February 1790.[16] The phenomenon of Whiggism, at any rate, was more than capable of taking
in even such sharp differences as these, notwithstanding a revolution in France.

A letter published in Cobbett's *Political Register* in 1820 questions some statistics cited in a previous issue, objecting: "The
statement about Whigs and *Tories* is nonsense; for, where are
there *now* any *Tories*?" (*CPR* 7 Oct. 1820: 818). Cobbett's correspondent (if this is not in fact Cobbett himself, disenfranchised
Tory that he was) seems to suggest that these days everyone is a
Whig, even the Tories. Though no party man, William Gerard
Hamilton held appointments as a Lord of Trade under the Duke
of Devonshire and as Chief Secretary to the Lord Lieutenant of

2 / WHIGGISH ENERGIES

Ireland under the Duke of Newcastle, both Whig administra-
tions. His passionate opposition to reform and his expedient,
even subversive, philosophy in other respects are alternately rec-
oncilable to Country and Court Whiggism, and either attitude
would have commended him to or estranged him from one or
another of the Whig factions. Burke, who served as Hamilton's
personal secretary in Ireland from 1761 to 1764,[17] thus found
himself among the same opposing interests and principles that
his old patron had negotiated so suavely but with so little real
distinction. As Pocock points out, only a regime that possessed
the "liberal flexibility" of Whiggism even at its most oligarchic—
expressing itself in "rhetorics that ranged from the ancient constitution to the Wealth of Nations"—could have sustained the
complicated ethos of modernity Burke both exemplified and opposed.[18]

Attitudes towards Whigs on the part of Tories and Reformers
in this period combine contempt and distrust. At times, they are
dismissed outright as a spent force in party politics, or at best as
merely a party of "outs" who would rule like Tories once in office.
The radical *Black Dwarf* charges that "The Whigs, with all their
talent, with all their *wealth* and *respectability*, are now only political cyphers," and that "an *insipid whig* is quite as *useless*, as a
determined Tory is *mischievous*" (*BD* 19 Apr. 1820: 507). Yet descriptions of Whigs as "*insipid,*" as "political cyphers," may suggest a certain transparency, even purposeful transparency when
combined with the typical concession to "*talent.*" *A Short Reply to
a Short Defence of the Whigs* (1819), published under the cava-
lierish pseudonym of Carolus Candidus, responds to a Whig
apologia by Lord Erskine, pointing out that "We are, my Lord, by
experience, too familiar with the *moderating sophistry* of the
Whigs, to suffer ourselves to be again deceived." The pamphlet
goes on to assert that "A retrospective view of the principles and
practice of this Faction, must teach every reflective mind, that
the term Whig, as applied to the present party, can never *be used
but as a reproach*, and in that sense the Political History of our
Parliament justifies its application."[19] This kind of historical
thesis—Hazlitt puts forward one like it in *Eloquence of the
British Senate*—is typical in attacks on Whig principles. Even
while furiously indicting Lord Liverpool's long-lived Tory administration for parliamentary abuses, for instance, a lead editorial

in *The Republican* pauses long enough to trace the problem to Walpole, "who in the reign of the First of the present Family, was a most violent Whig, and advanced himself by his boldness and abilities to the office of Prime Minister, completely systematized this mode of corruption" (*R* 21 Jan. 1829: 38). Of the Pitt government's wartime popularity, the *Black Dwarf* asserts that "Supported by this infatuation, Mr. Pitt took his measures for the completion of that system of *governing by corruption*, which Walpole had ushered into the cabinet of the House of Brunswick." (*BD* 3 Sept. 1817: 497). Thirty years later, one year before the final extinction of the Whig party in 1852, Walpole is still being excoriated in conservative polemics as "that minister, who first reduced corruption to a science and openly proclaimed that 'every man had his price.'"[20] Carolus Candidus reaches back even beyond Walpole to discover the original sin of Whiggism in the Glorious Revolution, exposing the Whigs' putative sympathy to reform—a position revived by Rockingham in the 1760s and then by Fox in the 1790s—as a ruse to create a stalking-horse in popular dissent. "With this party, a set of men distinguished for talent, but without public principle," Candidus argues, "exalted by rank, but debased by their corrupt designs, adopting the appellation of patriots, but strangers to the dictates of honest feeling, have connected themselves and are confounded in the mass."[21] This strangely suggests a conspiracy within a conspiracy, first the grand historical conspiracy that is Whiggism and then its infiltration in turn by elements displaying all the stereotypical traits of—Whigs. This is no more than Burke had feared of the party of Fox three decades before, though by the end of the Regency party lines were more clearly defined even if party policies could be as flexible as required.

The charges brought by Carolus Candidus against the Whigs speak largely to rhetorical practice. Much as Hazlitt (and Browne, more honorifically) educes a history of parliament from the evolving body of political topics and commonplaces constituting its rhetoric, he grounds his attack on the Whigs in a critique of their rhetorical self-representations since the Glorious Revolution, exposing their affectation of a patriotism devoid of "honest feeling" as the product of talent without principle. In this, and this only, they have been utterly consistent, and "a greater mixture of duplicity, falsehood, and sophistry never was

presented for public indignation to scoff at, from the commencement of the party to the present time."[22] Whig rhetoric at this
time, indeed, is virtually identified with deception. An article in
the *Black Dwarf* entitled "The Edinburgh Review to become the
Advocate of Universal Suffrage: What Wonder Next?" marvels at
what appears to be a sincere Whig position on a fundamental
reform issue (*"honesty* seems to have got the better of *expediency,*
and we find language and sentiments that really seem to have
been copied from the BLACK DWARF"), but warns that "men
can use language very foreign to their hearts," and in fact finally
finds that the *Edinburgh* writer's position rings hollow. "When
your object is to *perplex a subject,* and not to explain it," he decides, *"write a great deal.* Go about it, and about it, and about it;
but take care you never touch upon any essential" (*BD* 17 Feb.
1819: 148, 150). Another number of the *Black Dwarf* complains
that "We cannot take up a piece of *whig policy* in the present day,
without detecting the *patchwork* of its composition," while in yet
another number an essay starkly entitled "WHIGGISM *versus*
HUMANITY" traces the emotional insincerity of Whig rhetoric
to Locke's tabula rasa, calling Whigs "sheets of blank paper until
some *respectable* knave is moved to make an impression upon
them" (*BD* 2 Aug. 1820: 178). In "The Base and Ignorant Whigs,"
Cobbett's Weekly Political Register asserts that the English
people now see through the Whigs and "are disgusted with their
cant about expediency, and despise their mean evasions of fundamental principles" (*CPR* 5 Aug. 1820: 181–82). Perhaps hoping
for a speaker of William Plunkett's caliber, Carlile's *Republican*
predicts that "The energy of an individual in the present corrupt
state of the parliament will weigh more to the public weal than
all the florid speeches of those who are called Whigs" (*R* 17 Mar.
1820: 291).

What makes Whig rhetoric so flexible is its ability to mediate
permanence and change. Hazlitt's term for this quality in *The
Spirit of the Age* is *"Modern Antique"* (*CWH* 11:60), a seeming
paradox but native to the Whig idiom. Submerged beneath virulent attacks on Whigs as "political cyphers," on the *"patchwork"* of
Whig policy, are the outlines of a characteristic ethos. Nicholas
Phillipson describes a Whig rhetoric emerging during the reigns
of Queen Anne and the early Hanoverians incorporating in itself
"tensions between ancient constitutionalism and modern Whig-

gery, between the claims of ancient and modern prudence."
Speaking to Country, Court, and Exchange alike, it could be employed to equal effect by junto Whigs, opposition Whigs, Tories,
Tory/Jacobites, and so on.[23] It helped to consolidate Walpole's
modernism even as it helped to articulate opposition to Walpole
by figures like Bolingbroke. The latter's rhetoric, indeed, is a
classic instance of a Tory appropriation of Whig constitutionalism, profoundly traditional in style and substance but, as Blair
implies, Whiggishly subversive in method and aims. The account
Phillipson gives of Bolingbroke's ability to reject exploded conceptions of feudal authority while simultaneously drawing on
"the true old English spirit, which prevailed in the days of our fa-
thers" (232–33), corroborates Blair's critical estimate of Bolingbroke. In this account, Bolingbroke manages to harness Jacobite
passion to the cool control of policy. The patriot king becomes
Machiavelli's innovating Prince as the good old cause is transformed into a rational program of subversion directed against
ministerial corruption. Pocock can only reflect in his well-known
essay on Whiggism that "what so outspoken a deist as Bolingbroke had been doing at the head of an Anglican party in Anne's
reign is a question that seems to transcend any answer (however
justified) in terms of political duplicity."[24] The answer lies in
Pocock's own emphasis on the *varieties* of Whiggism and their
adaptability to contingent circumstance. A pamphlet published
in 1773 entitled *A Dissertation on the Rise, Progress, Views,
Strength, Interests and Characters, of the Two Parties of the
Whigs and Tories* distinguishes the parties broadly on the basis
of characteristic temperament or ethos. Where the Tories are
known by their "impetuous passion," the Whigs are moderates,
insipid by policy, though a small Republican Whig faction, a
Commonwealth survival, is as headlong as the most violent of
Tories. The writer concedes that there are moderate Tories who
remain stubbornly loyal to their party, but notes that "the moderate Whig and Tory form almost the same party, under the
common appellation of Whig."[25] This suggests hegemony, if not
necessarily ascendancy, and even the most bitter of the Whigs'
foes, whether conservative or radical, tend to view Whig sophis-
tries as entrenched and systematic.

The Pittites were heirs to both Walpole and Walpole's opponents, systematizing ministerial control under the rhetorical

cloak of Country opposition. An instance of how complex was the idiom of neo-Whiggish politics in a post-Pittite age is suggested by Hazlitt during the spy controversy of 1817–18. In a series of articles "On the Spy-System" in the *Morning Chronicle*, he notes a speech given in the House of Commons by Lord Castlereagh defending the Home Office's domestic use of spies and asks:

> What will John Bull, who has been crammed these twenty-five years with the draff and husks of concrete prejudices, unsifted, unbolted, in their rawest state, say to the analytical distinctions, to the refined *police*-morality of the Noble Lord? We might consider his harangue on the public services and private virtues of spies and informers, according to the utility-doctrine of modern philosophy, as forming an era in the history of English loyalty and Parliamentary pliability. (*CWH* 7:210)

The Government spies in question, Cassels and Oliver, were purportedly involved in fomenting as well as reporting seditious activity. This is bad enough, but the Government's co-optation of revolutionary subversion apparently extended into Parliament itself, for in defending the actions of his spies, Hazlitt claims, Castlereagh "mingled with his usual stock of political common places, some lively moral paradoxes, after a new French pattern" (*CWH* 7:208). Castlereagh was responding to opposition objections to the use of such continental tactics, countering that, by making these charges, the opposition "attack all that is valuable in our institutions" ("The Opposition and 'The Courier'" [*CWH* 7:216]). Brazenly conceived in the face of "English loyalty," Castlereagh's arguments sanction rogues like Cassels and Oliver so that, as Hazlitt observes, "to be a *cat's paw* is to be virtuous— is to be moral—is to be pious—is to be loyal—is to be a patriot— is to be what Castles *is*, and Castlereagh *approves*" (*CWH* 7:210). "English loyalty" is used here not as a guide, certainly not as a foil, but as a screen for policy. Beyond its own use of paradox for shock value, Hazlitt's critical representation of Castlereagh's rhetorical strategy reveals how subversive critical methods ("analytical distinctions," "the utility-doctrine of modern philosophy") could be employed not to subvert established authority but, paradoxically, to affirm it through the subversion of traditional concepts like "English loyalty" and "public service." Though he has no wish to expose the now merely honorific significance of these concepts, Castlereagh nevertheless exploits it for his own interested purposes. The Mandeville reference ("public services and private virtues") further underlines this unlikely alliance of rational subversion and civic humanism.

Castlereagh, to be sure, was neither the speaker for new French paradoxes nor Old English sentiment. Hazlitt is more likely inferring here a general ministerial ethos in the Liverpool administration both post-Pittite and neo-Whiggish in nature. A satiric piece in the *Black Dwarf*, entitled "Tactics for Ministers," could be modeled after the how-to genre of *Parliamentary Logic* and *The Political Primer*, offering ready-made arguments and tactical advice like the following: "Trap for the young ones of Opposition—Rash declarations—Canning to be ready to spring the mine and pounce upon them" (*BD* 29 Feb. 1817: 16). Indeed, if there was any minister in the Liverpool administration perfectly suited to such tactics it was George Canning, president of the Pitt Club and Castlereagh's rival for the Pitt mantle. An article in the *Black Dwarf* entitled "Candid Reasons for Believing a Moderate Reformer, Either Madman, Fool, or Knave—From the confessions of Mr. Canning, Mr. Tierney, and Others" clearly opts for "Knave" where Canning is concerned, locating this quality squarely in Canning's rhetoric: "All his harangues are as contemptible in matter, as they are dangerous in effect. He is a quibbler, but a quibbler from *intent*, not accident. His object is to pervert, and confuse" (*BD* 24 May 1820: 703). In an article attacking a speech in which Canning had defended the repressive Six Acts, *Cobbett's Weekly Political Register* notes Canning's deployment of a fallacy of the type detected by Hazlitt in Walpole's veiled attack on parliamentary democracy in his Triennial Bill speech: "Having, by these preliminary tricks, prepared your audience for what was to follow, you proceed to a defence of the *Six Acts*, as you pretend; but, you content yourself with what you deem a defence of *one out of the six*" (*CPR* 8 Apr. 1820: 250). In his essay "On the Present State of Parliamentary Eloquence," Hazlitt reflects that Canning requires an essay by himself. "If I were compelled to characterise Mr. Canning's style by a single trait," he nevertheless ventures, "I should say that he is a mere *parodist* in verse or prose, in reasoning or in wit. He transposes arguments as he does images, and makes sophistry of the one, and burlesque of the other" (*CWH* 17:19). Hazlitt is undoubtedly thinking of the contributor to the long-defunct *Anti-Jacobin* as much as the government minister but this passage suggests that the two are not unrelated. As for Canning's reasoning, Hazlitt observes the same habitual deployment of fallacy by omission noted by Cobbett above, for "Mr. Canning, I apprehend, never answered a speech: he answers, or affects to answer some observation in a speech, and then manufactures a long *tirade*" (*CWH* 17:19). Hazlitt's Canning is even something of a trickster—not an uncommon characterization of Canning in the radical press[26]—turning earnest to jest and making a mockery of principle: "Hence his gravest reasonings have very much the air of concealed irony; and it might sometimes be suspected that, by his partial, loose, and unguarded sophisms, he meant to abandon the very cause he professes to magnify and extol" (*CWH* 17:20).[27]

An anonymous pamphlet published in 1818 makes a speech delivered by Canning in Liverpool the occasion for a harsh antiministerialist attack. Taking the form of an open letter, the pamphlet presents its subject as a study in rhetorical imposture, its ironic references to "merits" and "value" revealing the inverse relation of principle and talent in Canning's speech, for the merit of this performance points to talents bent to the sacrifice of virtue to raw expedience. To draw Canning's attention to "the very different modes, but equal excellence, of Lord Castlereagh's and your eloquence" seems hardly to praise him as a speaker, though the "difference" between Castlereagh and Canning speaks to their respective abilities only. Castlereagh was re-nowned for his inept performances, while Canning is here (and elsewhere) credited with a kind of eloquence. That Canning's "excellence" as an orator is the equal of Castlereagh's speaks to something completely different again—which is to say, his moral excellence, something disposed of early in the pamphlet in reflections on whether there is anyone "so degraded, and abandoned, as not to feel that any connexion with you would be yet deeper infamy." Yet the pamphlet does credit Canning, if not with virtue, then with a *virtù* that may see its way past principle to an ulterior end made possible by such shifts. "You display," observes the pamphleteer, "more splendid examples than ever of that natural facility (which I suppose you improved in the House of Commons, by your early habits of speaking against time in the service of the minister) of uttering a rhapsody of sentences without a single distinct idea in your own mind, or exciting one in your hearers." That such indirection is described as "facility" suggests that Canning's indeterminacy as a speaker ("Will you never learn, Sir, that metaphors are not the major and minor of a syllogism, and a simile the conclusion") serves a distinct purpose. Canning's assumptions about the people's "respectful forbearance" to king and lords, for example, that they regard them merely as temporary evils to be eradicated by parliamentary reform, are dismissed as a base libel on Englishmen even as a nice logical inversion is noted "that turns their very virtues into crimes." Another instance is more equivocal—like the ministerialist press the radical press wished to regard its foes as at once dangerous and incompetent—suggesting as it does that even a technically inept rhetorical performance may serve a deliberate object: "If you have any meaning in this mob of metaphors, it is, that England is indebted for escape from the power of France to some secret virtue in her constitution, under its present practice. In the fury of inspiration, you confound a moral with a physical cause; and I fear without so much as a single precedent of poetical license to support you." The physical cause referred to here is England's insular geographical position, but mere facts are beside the point where the loyalist sentiment being appealed to in this fallacious reasoning is concerned. The pamphleteer's response to such tactics is to expose in Canning's portrayal of himself as a defender of traditional English values a more subversive purpose:

> All the profligate and abandoned who pant for the fall of the country, that they may build their fortunes with its ruins, look to you for the consummation of their only hope. Your determined perseverance in the present corrupt system of government opens to them a bright prospect of the violation of the signal patience of the people. They foresee in the desperate struggle of the country against slavery, that confusion of the political elements which wrecks all that is good and great in the state, and produces the misery in which they exult, and the destruction in which they prosper.

If Hazlitt's Burke extrapolates the traditional state from its breakdown in France, the pamphleteer's Canning has brought that same state to the verge of breakdown in England by means of rhetorical transmutations of corruption into civic virtue. In this dubious achievement, the pamphleteer claims, Canning is in fact exemplary: "For yourself, Sir, you are peculiar to the present age; and it would be the highest negative injustice to your contemporaries to limit their enjoyment, by letting them remain in ignorance of your full value."[28]

A rhetoric at once "contemptible" and "dangerous," one that turns on cleverly deployed fallacies, does not immediately suggest the homely candor of a Country ideology, whether Tory or Old Whig (though Cobbett thought he detected in Canning's more gothic speeches a *"young Burke"* [*CPR* 8 Apr. 1820: 275]). Even so, as a politician Canning could speak to the virulently reactionary Toryism associated with rural boroughmongers even as he enjoyed a reputation for liberalism—his support for Catholic emancipation, for instance—rare among others of the Liverpool administration.[29] The young Canning in fact briefly considered a career as a Whig. Lacking aristocratic connections, however, he had little chance for advancement in a Whig oligarchy, assuming the Whigs were to regain office,[30] and in any case a party boasting the likes of Sheridan was already crowded with the kind of talent he had to offer. Accordingly, he became Pitt's protégé, prompting Lady Holland to observe that "Principle, I believe, did not sway him much."[31] (One of the *Black Dwarf*'s cross-readings—a regular feature in which newspaper columns were scanned horizontally for humorous readings—runs: "To let, during the summer season,—the abilities of Mr. Canning" [*BD* 23 July 1817: 416].) What, despite his anti-Radical views, distinguished Canning from ultra-Tories was his Whiglike penchant for expedient solutions, though again his resentment of what he called "the Great Monopolising Whig corporation"[32] put him on common ground with radicals he so harshly attacked at other times. Lady Holland could even speculate that "He is, in his heart, the veriest Jacobin there is, and would, if he were not in power, manifest his principles in a most dangerous, innovating opposition."[33] What Canning's shrewdest observer remarked in him was not ideological but temperamental inclination. In policy Canning was as consistent in his opposition to reform as the author of *Parliamentary Logic*. His methods, subversive tactics brilliantly put to the service of a reactionary cause in the *Anti-Jacobin* and latterly transposed to Tory governance under Liverpool, are a subject for the next chapter. The "dangerous, innovating" temperament sensed by Lady Holland in the erstwhile Whig protégé, however, combined with an virulent antireform position adopted for sheer expedience, makes Canning the ultimate expression of Whig technical mastery, not least because he was a Tory.

But then, it was against a particular breed of politician, whether Tory, Whig or Radical, that Burke warned in the *Reflections* and elsewhere. Whether he spoke of the Reverend Price's anarchistic zeal ("It is not for the diffusion of truth, but for the spreading of contradiction" [*RRF* 8:62–63]) or unnamed "Machiavelian politicians" who saw in the French Revolution an opportunity for purposeful mischief at home, Burke feared a revolt of talent against property (*RP* 9:241). If he acknowledged the powerful eloquence of the revolutionary leaders, he warned in the *Reflections* that "eloquence may exist without a proportionable degree of wisdom" (*RRF* 8:215). Talent independent of property was capable of anything, he believed, unfixed as it was by permanent interests. Lady Holland recognized such restless talents in Canning who, she claimed, "abhors titles, and the aristocracy of hereditary nobility; the lowness of his own extraction first made him envy, then wish to destroy, those whom chance had raised above him."[34] Among the landed boroughmongers of the Tory party Canning's highly portable talents had ample scope to work, in the process rendering Canning himself a somewhat ambiguous figure. In an article simply entitled "George Canning," the *Black Dwarf* attempts to trace Canning "from *what he was* to *what he is*, through the various *disguises*, of affected modesty, false honor, and deceptive talent," finally asking: "In which of his many characters will this right honourable supporter of every political abuse appear most captivating?" (*BD* 18 Mar. 1818: 161). The answer, it seems, would depend on *fortuna*. If former acquaintances at Holland House knew Canning to be capable of "a most dangerous, innovating opposition," contingency directed his characteristic *virtù* to an equally subversive defense of the established order. "Had he never found patronage," Peter Dixon suggests, "disappointment might have driven him to Radicalism. As it was, he remained essentially a defender of a status quo which provided him, perhaps fortuitously, with the opportunities he sought."[35] It was such surprising (and purposeful) disjunctions between talent and temperament, between party and principle, that made a man like Canning so cautionary to friends and foes alike.[36] That he might have been exemplary—embodying a particular quality in the age termed by Jeremy Bentham "upstart Machiavelism"—is a possibility emerging from the stresses to which public life in the Regency was frequently subject.

◦ʂ ◦ʂ ◦ʂ

One such stress was the Caroline Affair of 1820–21, an occasion when rhetoric, logic, and principle were as hardly used as they have ever been in full public view. In 1820, following the death of George III, Caroline of Brunswick landed in England to assume her duties as queen consort to George IV, her long-estranged husband. Caroline had lived on the continent since 1814 following two widely publicized investigations in 1806 and 1813–14 into charges concerning illicit relations. Neither investigation was successful but Caroline was persuaded to quit England in exchange for an annuity of £35,000. Sensational reports suggested that she was leading an extravagant life abroad, among other things taking on an Italian valet named Bergami with whom she was alleged to be involved sexually. Determined to divorce his wife but himself lacking the credibility to proceed in ecclesiastical court, George IV pressured a reluctant Liverpool administration to bring against his wife a "Bill of Pains and Penalties," a parliamentary act for punishing someone without resort to a legal trial. By this means the queen was effectively put on trial as the bill was debated in the House of Lords. The scandal that ensued was short-lived but remarkably intense, ending with the withdrawal of the bill in November of 1820 and the queen's exoneration. Enjoying a brief triumph, Caroline died the following August.

This chapter concludes by briefly considering the Caroline Affair as a notable public exercise in rhetorical imposture. Recent commentary has shifted attention from the official event to the popular sensation it generated, a remarkable outpouring of feeling both affectionate and hostile, manifesting itself in addresses to the queen by various groups, broadsides, lampoons, melodrama, popular assemblies, and even riots.[37] Anna Clarke credits it with enabling radicals "to draw upon the vitality of plebeian popular literature in order to create a new political language," one more suited to the realities of democratic public life than the rhetoric of constitutional politics.[38] Cultural history has succeeded in recovering a popular context for this episode without which our understanding of it would be restricted to the legal/political maneuverings of plaintiff and defendant. While such readings of the affair have proven corrective, however, they in turn risk insulating it from rhetorically articulated debates wholly accessible to Hazlitt's "collective sense of the nation." To imagine that the "peculiar energy" Bentham noted in Pittite governance was restricted to elite venues is to discount the *virtù* displayed in Reform tactics. His infamous reference to a "swinish multitude" notwithstanding—widely misquoted by the radical press to great effect—Edmund Burke both respected and feared the disenfranchised mind. His alarmed sense of new energies and new talents, "a new, a pernicious, a desolating activity" threatening public life, issued from his fear of what might be termed itinerant reason—whether in the popular assemblies of revolutionary France, the enthusiastic transports of dissenting chapels, or the polite society of Holland House. As his old patron Hamilton knew, to speak "rather to the *object* of each motion, than to the question itself," is to cut across lines of class, party, and conviction alike.

A pamphlet entitled *From the Queen's Answers to Various Addresses Presented to Her* (1821) suggests just this—of reformers who rallied to the queen's cause. These "'wicked panders' to revolutionary ambition," the pamphlet charges, have made Caroline "the instrument of effecting THEIR OWN *criminal designs*, (for *her*, she may be assured, they care not a pin),—which criminal designs COULD ONLY be effected by the TOTAL OVERTHROW of all the political, the civil, the ecclesiastical establishments of the country." Written from a pro-ministerial position, this pamphlet takes a rhetorical view of the affair, purporting to catch the public mood by excerpting and commenting on public addresses presented to the queen and her published answers. As the Tory pamphleteer surmises, the latter were written by radical polemicists on behalf of the unfortunate queen whom he imagines "under the pernicious influence, and by the evil advice, of wicked counsellors." He is thus careful to attack not Caroline herself but rather her rhetorical exploitation by radicals for whom he claims the object of violent reform is more central than the question of her case. His method consists in quizzing the rhetoric of the various answers written in Her Majesty's name. He observes of the "Answer to Aylsbury," for instance, that "The fallacy of this mode of reasoning is exposed in the observation upon the Queen's answer to the address from St. Leonard's, Shoreditch, page 35," and of the "Answer to Chipping Sodbury" that "Incitement to revolution is apparent in *every line* of it." Of another of the Answers, he finds that "The concluding paragraph is very artful and insidious, but well calculated to make its impression,—and to further the wicked objects of those who dictated it." Like Bentham in *The Book of Fallacies*, he hunts out "dyslogistic" associations in the very language of the "Answers" calculated to elicit unreasoning responses. The Bill of Pains and Penalties, he argues, is an act normally used in cases of divorce and the loss of status accruing to divorce: "Whence then arises all the unfounded slander—all the vehement clamour against this Bill? It is from its unfortunate *name*, and its *name* alone. The popular feelings have run away with the *sound* (as is generally the case in political matters) wholly regardless of the *substance*." With respect to demands for further clarification of charges brought against the queen, he wonders what Her Majesty would have made "more *plain*, more *filthy*, more DISGUSTING," noting that "There is the same fallacy in this reasoning, as in that with regard to the Bill of Pains and Penalties. The exercise of a moment's reflection will be sufficient to convince us of the fallacy of both." At the same time, it is clear that in rebutting "topics of inflammation calculated to operate upon the pubic mind, in the generation of sedition and treason, and to work them up to the overturn of the *temporal establishments*, and the constitution of the *state*," the pamphleteer himself has an object beyond the royal divorce. Addressing the "fallacious impression," promulgated by the queen's advocates, "that THE LIBERTIES OF THE NATION are involved in the ISSUE OF HER INDIVIDUAL CAUSE," he employs rhetorical hot buttons equally calculated to elicit visceral responses from the same readers he urges to use "sound, good, common sense." Even, for instance, as he criticizes a lead article in the *Old Times* drawing parallels between the queen's landing in England and that of Henry VII, he evokes more recent events across the channel to suggest that her arrival is calculated "to set the country in a blaze of civil war—and to 'hurry us out of the highway of heaven, into all the vices, crimes, horrors, and miseries of the French Revolution.'"[39] The "*extreme art*" he detects in the rhetoric of the queen's public defense, then, in his opinion merely a screen for sedition, he does not himself scruple to use to attack Reform—also through the person of the queen.

Attacks like this on "Her Majesty's evil counsellors" can be traced to Renaissance humanist debates about "good counsel," a doctrine whereby active citizens display virtue through responsible counsel to their ruler. "By curbing human passions and mitigating misjudgements, 'good counsel' stood between order and chaos," writes John Guy. "By instructing rulers who would otherwise become tyrants or near-tyrants in the ways of virtue and honesty, it was the touchstone of government."[40] A failure of virtue in government, then, might be traced to the failure of counsel—most ominously, bad counsel. While the concept of good or bad counsel could be, and undoubtedly was, expanded to cover many forms of political discussion, including dissent, the Caroline Affair seems exemplary in this respect. Here were two sovereign figures in conflict being advised and represented by others in terms potentially affecting the political stability of a state. Charges of bad counsel were rife on both sides. For their part, radicals were critical of the advice being given to both king and queen, though they reserved their harshest criticism for the ministerial faction. A pamphlet by one Charles Phillips, for instance, entitled *The Queen's Case Stated* and "Dedicated to the Memory of Anna Boleyn, the Martyr'd Consort of Henry the Eighth," addresses itself to the king, absolving him of evil intent personally and warning him against the false counsel of "wily sycophants and slanderers, who have persuaded you of what they know to be false, in the base hope that it may turn out to be profitable."[41] Phillips uses arguments similar to those of the pro-ministerial author of *The Queen's Answers*, but this time it is the king who is the instrument of counselors who pursue other, unspecified, ends under the screen of his action against the queen. Other such addresses to king and queen alike in the radical press commonly warn one or the other against self-serving advisors, excepting the radicals themselves. "Her Majesty knows too well the trickery and intrigues of the Whigs to place any confidence in the councils of place-hunting rogues," an article in *The*

Republican asserts; "they are not her friends, and only want to use her as a cat's-paw" (*R* 17 Nov. 1820: 405–6). As for good or bad counsel, it must have been difficult to see where the advantage of King, Queen, or country lay in the midst of so many arguments pursuing so many objects. To an outside observer like Princess Leiven, wife of the Russian ambassador in London, the case seemed purely a matter of political intrigue with scant principle involved. "They are no more concerned with the Queen now than with me," she said of the various parties.[42]

The anomalous, if not bizarre, nature of this affair led to some strange crossovers in the disputants' rhetoric. While Caroline came to be styled by Reformers as a radical figure—and was attacked as such by the King's faction—Reformers necessarily found themselves speaking a royalist idiom as they defended their Queen from her enemies and portrayed their ministerial opponents as dangerous innovators. "The language of radicalism in 1820 was pure monarchical apologetic," points out Thomas Laqueur. "Even if its proponents did not believe what they said—and clearly at some level they did not—the important fact is that they were, nonetheless, enmeshed in a royalist discourse." If they did not believe what they said, of course, it was because they were republicans dedicated to radical democratization, though they understood well enough the powerful appeal of royalist rhetoric to their popular audience and almost certainly felt it themselves. Laqueur traces the chivalric impulse behind radical advocacy for Caroline to Burke's famous apostrophe to Marie Antoinette in the *Reflections*, though he is not sure the allusion was a conscious one.[43] In fact, radical polemicists were well aware of the rhetorical game they were playing and of their appropriation of perhaps the most famous passage of Tory royalist rhetoric to be written by a Whig. In a "Letter to Alderman Wood"—portrayed by the radical press as an ardent champion of the Queen, Wood was characterized by others as an "enlightened mountebank"[44]—*Cobbett's Weekly Political Register* explicitly draws on Burkean apostrophe to mobilize popular support for Caroline:

> If thousands of swords ought to have flown from their scabbards to avenge the insult offered to the Queen of France, what ought to be the feelings of the people of England, at the insult offered to their Queen at St. Omers? However, the age of chivalry is not

wholly gone. The spirit of that age is still left in England, but it appears to live only in the breasts of the people; that people, which have been charged with a want of loyalty, with a want of reverence for the Throne, with a want of attachment to Kings and Queens; and who now are charged with factiousness and sedition, because they set up an unanimous shout of "GOD SAVE THE QUEEN!" (*CPR* 17 June 1820: 1021)

As unshaken in his fealty is the pamphleteer of *The King's Treatment of the Queen shortly stated to the People of England* (1820), who insists that "Yes, the many virtues of our country, have not yet retired. 'Ten thousand swords shall leap from their scabbards to avenge even a look that may threaten her with insult.' "[45] The *Black Dwarf* observes that the spirit of chivalry eulogized by "the apostate Burke" may have receded but is not extinct; rather "it has abandoned the prostituted temple of title and nobility, and has found for itself a pure asylum in the hearts of the lowly, the abused peasantry of our country" (*BD* 14 June 1820: 807).

Burke's original apostrophe, ostensibly a candid appeal to right-thinking Englishmen, also served a less forthright purpose in attempting to subvert the radicalization of the Whig party by Fox and Sheridan. While speaking from a diametrically opposed ideological position, Caroline's radical supporters were using the same rhetoric to achieve a very different end in parliamentary reform. A corollary of this radical royalist program were attacks questioning the loyalty of government ministers, undertaken, moreover, with an ironic deliberation that left no doubt about their purely tactical nature. It was a strategy that exposed the hypocrisy of ministerialist attacks on the Queen even as it masked a more radically subversive object under the cloak of loyalty. "These pretended enemies of revolution, are smoothing the way for its introduction," charges the *Black Dwarf*; "and while they would alarm the titled and wealthy by a display of the excesses committed in France, instead of leaving them as a beacon to avoid similar guilt, they are attempting to put in practice the theory of that revolution." Adopting the manner of Burkean jeremiad, the writer warns that while, unlike the French, the ministry proposes to rid itself of only part of the royal family, England may come to regret the precedent: "They propose to send away the QUEEN! Who shall insure the country that they will not ultimately propose to send away the KING?" (14 June 1820: 805, 804). To Castlereagh's charges that the Queen is being used as a "handle" for revolution, *Cobbett's Weekly Political Register* thus simply replies that "If, however, there are dangers of revolution, whom has your Majesty to thank but this very CASTLEREAGH and his colleagues?" (*CPR* 29 July 1820: 100, 102–3). Such ironic inversions of the ministerial position had the effect of co-opting attempts by wily ministers like Canning to have it both ways. Hence the *Examiner*'s impatience with "the sudden, exclusive, and useless sensibility of Mr. CANNING, who cries out 'How chivalrous I *could* shew myself in this instance,' and 'what an affectionate incapable creature I am!' "[46] Due to alleged past intimacies with the queen, Canning had to tread carefully and ultimately left England while the Affair played itself out. In its early stages, however, he managed to play the chivalric card while tacitly aligning himself with the anti-Caroline faction under the pretext of urging impartiality. Cobbett's "A Letter to Mr. Canning" exposes these tactics while betraying some ingenious polemical shifts of its own:

> You are professing the best wishes for the Queen. You are professing an anxious desire that she may come white as snow out of the inquiry. You are describing and extolling her Majesty's numerous excellent qualities. You are expressing your *"ardent affection"* for her. And just at that very time, while you are doing this, this favourite Courier; this Courier which has been the channel of your attacks upon the people, is loading her Majesty with every species of calumny. (*CPR* 8 July 1820: 1193–95)

Here Cobbett imputes double-timing to Canning by implicitly identifying the people with Caroline (and Canning with his "favourite" *Courier*), so that to praise one while the *Courier* attacks the other is to betray both. Thus Canning's Burkean turn ("expressing your *'ardent affection'* for her") is preempted at the same time that, through a convoluted but likely accurate line of reasoning, Canning is tacitly accused of libeling the queen from the other side of his mouth via the ministerial press. When, after his public professions of fealty, Canning abruptly departed the country, the *Examiner* concluded: "This was the cant of insincerity. It was his business as a man, to defend her quite as much as he did before; but as a Minister, he found it inconvenient; therefore he describes her as a woman of all others who ought to be defended, and leaves her. This again is the cant of over-cunning, committing itself."[47]

That similar charges might in turn be made of pro-Caroline reformers like Cobbett was beside the point only for those who could assent but not reason. Since Pitt, the governing Tories had become adept at working up public feeling with neo-Burkean rhetoric designed to bypass rational assent while appealing directly to visceral English prejudices and loyalties. If, as Hazlitt noted, Reformers had been sandbagged by this strategy during the wars, they were considerably wiser to the regressive uses of rhetoric when the Caroline Affair fell into their laps. An article appearing in an 1817 number of the *Black Dwarf*, "Change of Public Opinion," announces that Reason has prevailed since the impostures practiced by Pitt during the wars: "At that period, by a species of public infatuation, a considerable majority of the people was induced to believe the unaccountable paradoxes, *that to crush liberty abroad* was the *only possible means of preserving it at home*" (*BD* 3 Sept. 1817: 497). Yet even as they took this line, reformers exploited rhetorical strategies that might be rationally conceived but that in fact appealed to the very feelings they had formerly sought to bypass with rational arguments. Responding to putative government concern about leveling associations in 1817, for instance, the *Black Dwarf* asserts that the real danger to English property is posed by the government itself—"the ministers are the *real Spenceans*" (*BD* 5 Mar. 1817: 90). In its regularly featured "Cross Readings in a Newspaper," then, the *Black Dwarf* detects this announcement: "A true bill for treason and conspiracy has been found against—all the Cabinet Ministers" (*BD* 2 July 1817: 361). If the seditious nature of this program had not been made clear enough by charges of Jacobinism leveled at ministerialists, radical polemicists detected subversive energies operating even in the moral campaign against Caroline being waged in rural England by William Wilberforce and the Vice Society. Drawing on the same classical defenses of property against itinerant reason made by cultural conservatives like Burke and Coleridge, for instance, *The Republican* terms moral crusaders against the queen like Wilberforce "itinerant orators," thus implying both the sophistical and subversive nature of their arguments (*R* 6 Sept. 1820: 46). Such charges, however lightly made, had the tacit rhetorical effect of numbering the Tories among the forces of innovation threatening tradition. During the Caroline Affair, then, charges that the ministerialist faction was fomenting revolution by threatening the very basis of English liberty, its constitutional monarchy, shifted the rhetorical advantages of the Country Whig ideology to the proponents of rational reform. Canning himself must have half-admired the impudence of reformers using rhetoric normally associated with Tory boroughmasters: "What a Jacobin crew have we now for masters!" (*BD* 14 June 1820: 807).

No one understood the limits of argument better than a neo-Tory radical like William Cobbett. His reservations about Caroline's advocate, Henry Brougham, extended beyond simple anti-Whig sentiment, common enough among the Queen's radical supporters, to astute questions about how defense arguments were playing in the court of public opinion where verdicts might be rendered on extrarational grounds. A close analysis in the *Political Register* of a speech in which Brougham noted the English public's appetite for royal scandal, to which he claimed the press was *"pandering,"* does not, as one might expect, question the validity of Brougham's arguments or even the propriety of his language; rather, it wonders about the advisability of awakening, by means of inadvertently suggestive rhetoric, memories of past investigations hardly helpful to the queen's case:

> Having made use of these expressions, having resorted to this mode of *defending* his royal client, he need not, in words, have called our recollection to the year 1809, when the discussions were going on with regard to the corruptions of which *Mrs. Clarke* was the agent; he need not, to all the rest of what he said, have added this allusion and given rise to this association of ideas, so manifestly disadvantageous to his royal client: he need not have carried us back by precise words to the year 1809; for the train of argument, so degrading to the cause of the royal lady whose defence had been placed in his hands; the train of argument, which he now resorted to, was precisely the train of argument resorted to upon that occasion. Eloquent as is his abuse of the press and of the public, strong as is his picture of the pandering disposition of the one and of the voracious, foul and disloyal appetite of the other, that picture really contains not one single

trait or tint which will not be found in the speeches of the injudi-
cious, not to say treacherous *"defenders"* of his Royal Highness
the Duke of York. (*CPR* 10 June 1820: 919–20)

These kinds of observations, directed more to involuntary reactions provoked by arguments than to rational responses, occur
throughout the *Political Register*'s analysis of the Caroline
Affair. While he claimed initial surprise that Caroline's prosecutors should be making assertions that could not be proved, Cobbett was aware that effective arguments—effective in achieving
their ends if not honest in their means—might be mounted in the
absence of rational proofs, for "when we consider, that *re-action*
was the object of the charge; when we consider that the charge
was intended to turn the tide of public opinion and to lay reason
asleep; than our surprise ceases and we can account for the monstrous falsehoods stated in that charge" (*CPR* 2 Sept. 1820: 433).
Notwithstanding patently ingenuous attempts by Canning to
urge Tory gentlemen to keep their minds *"like blank sheets of
paper"* (*CPR* 8 July 1820: 1193–95), Cobbett realized how decisive a role was played by emotional association in seemingly rational arguments through what might be termed their rhetorical
half-life. Such psychological tactics were available to all parties,
moreover, and might work for or against any of them. Those who
appeared as the prosecutors of the Queen had also been the prosecutors of the radicals, for instance, so that the vindication of one
might vindicate the other. Cobbett knew that the Queen's enemies among the Tory boroughmasters feared that their enmity
toward radicals and Queen alike, both now associated with each
other in the popular mind, must contend not only with arguments but with "Her Majesty's *gracious, affable, unaffected* and
winning manners and *deportment!*" In the context of Caroline's
radicalization by the reform press, then, *"popular Royalty"* (*CPR*
29 July 1820: 78–79, 79) and popular dissent might both take on
new associations in the minds of those seeing "a great deal of
merit in the elegance of the Queen's person as well as in the gra-
ciousness of her Manners" (*CPR* 8 July 1820: 1218).

Beyond the person of the Queen, moreover, there were other
equally volatile topics that polemicists like Cobbett could employ
in their rhetoric—the infamous Green Bags, for instance. Figuring sensationally in the government's psychological war against

dissent, these highly charged legal props, ostensibly containing damning evidence against the queen, displayed prominently but suggestively withheld, could serve the purposes of either Caroline's prosecutors or her advocates. Cobbett's strategy consisted in calling attention to the prosecution strategy with respect to the Green Bags even as he exploited their potent associative power in his own strategy:

> If the Queen had consented to go abroad, the bags were not to be opened; but since she would not consent to that, they were to be opened! This speaks volumes to the nation. It at once clearly shows what was the great object of the threat at St. Omers and of the bags in London. It is impossible to remove from the public mind the impression which it is calculated to imprint upon it, and which it has imprinted upon it. We are told that the bags contain most horrible accusations; yet, all these were to be sunk for ever, and we, out of our labour, were to give a princely income to the person against whom these accusations were preferred, if that person would but consent to go and live out of the country! (*CPR* 1 July 1820: 1120–21)

There was, in addition, the matter of these Green Bags' employment by these same prosecutors against radical defendants, a circumstance similarly impressed on collective memory. "The people have not so soon forgotten the *Green Bags* of 1817," Cobbett reminded everyone, including the people. "They had not so soon forgotten, that those Bags and their contents, formed the pretext for sending into dungeons a great number of men" (*CPR* 1 July 1820: 1110). If *The Republican* concluded that amidst all this government chicanery there was no longer any need to argue the radical case ("A mere statement of facts is now become the only duty of republicanism" [R 25 August 1820: 614-5]), Cobbett found that it didn't hurt to repeat some of those facts over and over again:

> The contents of the bag have been characterised by Mr. Brougham; but the public did not stand in need of even that. The charges being *in a Bag*: that was enough for the public. Their being submitted to a committee selected by the ministers; and that committee being a secret one; these circumstances were not necessary to enable the public to make up their minds as to the

contents of the Bag. The bare circumstances of the charges having been brought in a bag, together with her Majesty's frank and
heroic conduct, was quite enough to make the public come to a
conclusion upon the matter. (*CPR* 1 July 1820: 1125)

While perhaps not the result of reasoned argument, as Cobbett
well knew, this conclusion might effectively supply the place of
one.

If there was a question in this affair overlooked in the pursuit
of an object, it surely related to the queen herself. To be sure,
after earlier investigations, Caroline herself was no stranger to
interested strategy. Yet at one time or another she was a means
employed by Tories, Whigs, and Reformers for one end or another, as Canning noted when he remarked in the Commons that
"Faction marked her for its own."[48] As a debate over "good counsel," then, the Caroline Affair concerned issues that went beyond
the tawdry circumstances of the affair itself, even if they spoke to
more general tendencies in public life hardly more salutary. The
month following the queen's virtual exoneration, Hunt's *Examiner* considered what the lingering effects of the controversy
were likely to be and spoke of something it termed a "crisis" in
public opinion. It would be strange if a publication with the *Examiner*'s radical sympathies did not view such a crisis as favorable to reform, and of course the writer of this article does, but its
assertion that "Sophistry will not always pass current" is based
on a thesis about public attention in times of crisis that has no
necessary relation to particular party positions:

> There are periods of popular excitement (and the present we
> take to be one), when attempts to maintain that this Island is a
> "free, happy, and prosperous country," are treated as an assertion
> that black is white—as insults, in short, to the common sense of
> mankind. Suffering sharpens the intellect amazingly, and on
> that principle alone might we account for the state of feeling we
> are describing; but when to that is added the appeals made by
> this affair of the QUEEN to so many sympathies of the human
> mind, it would be astonishing indeed if the public sensitiveness
> was not now at a most unusual height.[49]

Yet radical opposition during the Caroline Affair made ample use
of "black is white" arguments in rallying loyal Englishmen to

defend their queen against levelers and Jacobins in the Liverpool ministry—in the cause of reform. If anything, such charges were bound to undermine confidence in the management of public opinion by interested parties on either side of a question. More telling possibly than even the ethos of technique characterizing political debate in a post-Pittite age was the belief that such an expedient spirit controlled public life, regardless of incidentals like party conviction.

Attacks on the queen's prosecutors and advocates alike by the radical press seemed calculated to produce cynicism about civic life generally. "The Lord Chancellor's treaty between God and his conscience begins to be understood," charged the *Black Dwarf*. "He has made his speech against the Queen; or to speak more properly, he has made his speech to preserve his place; for a more self-interested piece of legal sophistry never disgraced the head of a Crown-lawyer before" (*BD* 8 Nov. 1820: 658). Observing that, with notable exceptions like Alderman Wood, no men of talent were willing to step forward on behalf of their queen, Cobbett could only lament, with Burke thirty years before, that "Miserable indeed is that state of society when, in such a case, men are under the sway of cold calculation!" (*CPR* 29 July 1820: 82–83). In an article on the hearings in the House of Lords, Cobbett focuses not only on the logic of the prosecution case but on the sincerity of the solicitor-general's professed wish that the queen be fully and clearly exonerated. "To suppose that the present ministry could remain in power after such an acquittal is impossible; and, therefore, to believe you sincere in this wish," he points out, "we must first believe that you most anxiously, most sincerely, most devoutly, and from the *bottom of your heart*, wish to be turned out of office, and to see blasted forever all hope of obtaining those emoluments and honours which were the naturally expected reward of that political apostasy, which no man ever falls into without being actuated by a motive sufficient to overcome all the ordinary feelings of our nature." On the contrary, Cobbett can only conclude that the prosecution wishes to ruin the queen at any cost (*CPR* 16 Sept. 1820: 558–59). The motives of even the Queen's defenders, most conspicuously her official counsel (and Whig M.P.) Henry Brougham, are similarly called into question. Brougham clearly felt that the queen's best interests would not be served by presenting her to the Lords as a radical, and radicals never forgave him for this (or acknowledged their own motives for wishing him to do so). To *The Republican*, Brougham was no better than the prosecutors: "He has displayed so much equivocation, such an inexcusable anxiety for place and profit, like Gifford and Copley, we consider his principles not to be virtue proof against prostitution" (*R* 16 June 1820: 253–54). The character of Brougham promulgated in the radical press is the epitome of Whig caricature, particularly in *The Republican* for whom his opening speech on the Queen's behalf proved only "that Mr. Brougham's object is to play a sure game, whichever side might triumph over the other" (*R* 13 Oct. 1820: 221–22). If, however, *The Republican* concluded that "Mr. Brougham is a man of unbounded talent, we wish we could add the word *honesty* to it" (*R* 13 Oct. 1820: 223), it detected the same doubtful Whiggish abilities in one of Mr. Brougham's legal adversaries, Sir John Copley, who along with another minister out of cabinet, Sir Robert Gifford, was prosecuting the case. Copley was in fact an erstwhile Whig who, according to *The Republican,* had immediately removed a portrait of Fox from his office before taking up his ministerial appointment—but then, *The Republican* reflected in an open letter to Copley, "Whiggism is a species of easy virtue" (*R* 11 Nov. 1820: 361–62).

Still smarting from Pitt's brilliant manipulations of national sentiment during the late wars, reformers took up the rhetorical weapons of their enemies in the Caroline Affair. That this tactic was effective is clear. Whether reformers managed to maintain "a purity in the principle without mischief from the practice," to quote Coleridge once again, is another question. Hunt, in *The Examiner*, believed the Caroline Affair had succeeded somehow in freeing popular opinion from the spell of Pittite sophism. To William Hazlitt, it was not clear who was wise to whom after this episode:

> There was the cant of loyalty, the cant of gallantry, and the cant of freedom mixed together in delightful and inextricable confusion. She was a Queen—all the loyal and well-bred bowed to the name; she was a wife—all the women took the alarm; she was at variance with the lawful sovereign—all the free and independent Electors of Westminster and London were up in arms. . . . Though a daughter of the Duke of Brunswick, though a grand-daughter

of George III., yet because she was separated from her husband, she must be hand-and-glove with the people, the wretched, helpless, doating, credulous, meddlesome people, who are always ready to lick the hands, not just then raised to shed their blood or rivet on their chains. There was here an idol to pull down and an idol to set up. There was an imperial title and meretricious frontispiece to the spurious volume of Liberty. (*CWH* 20:136).

In the midst of it all, Hazlitt noted, an English subject named Bruce was sent to Botany Bay for speaking to another man convicted of treason—"and no notice was taken of it" (*CWH* 20:136).

3

Critical Stratagems:
Anti-Jacobin Imposture
and Periodical Reviewing

> We have no doubt that every candid man, on
> reading the preceding, which is substantially true
> in all its parts, will see the erroneousness of the
> Reviewer's reasonings, the latter part of which are
> an odd compound of assertion and syllogism.
>
> —"Strictures on an Article"
> *Blackwood's Edinburgh Magazine* (1817)

In August 1820 Lord Castlereagh reportedly read aloud to Parliament passages from Carlile's radical journal *The Republican*. The passages in question criticized the queen's trial. An open letter to Castlereagh in *The Republican* the following week remarked the attention it was receiving in the Lower House, calling the foreign secretary's notice a *"puff direct"* (R 4 Aug. 1820: 505) before going on to criticize his speech. The reference to puffing, literary endorsement by flattery, places radical writer and government minister in symbiotic relation to one another, each puffing or criticizing the other and thereby pursuing his own advantage. The conceit is developed at some length in the *Republican* piece even to the point of suggesting an analogy between politicians and reviewers:

> Your lordship is a most excellent reviewer, you hit on just such
> passages for comment, as I should have pointed out to you if you
> had asked my advice, and consulted my wishes, and in return,

my lord, when it becomes your lot to *stand prostrate, to turn your back on yourself*, or become a *contrast to yourself*, I will remember what you have done for me in this instance, and if I cannot use sufficient influence to get you employed as a critic and a reviewer of books, in an established magazine or review, I will certainly, out of my high consideration for your Lordship, start one myself, for the very purpose. The world is thoroughly satiated with your political and diplomatic talent, you have risen to the acme of splendour in each of these pursuits, and as satiety is apt to glut, and to create a dislike to the continuation of a sameness however beneficial, this new project of mine will still continue your lordship as the pole of attraction, if not as a politician and a diplomatist, yet as the first of critics and of literary characters. (*R* 4 Aug. 1820: 505–6)

Castlereagh's proficiency as a reviewer, of course, says no more for his moral character than do his political abilities. In this respect, then as now, politicians and journalists enjoyed no respective advantages. As he certainly realizes, the *Republican* writer is handling a double-edged blade, damning both professions for their expedient subjection of means to ends. If parliamentary speakers and periodical reviewers are on a par ethically, this passage implies that they practice similar crafts. While as a minister his lordship will only repeat his old tricks, as a critic he might continue to use these same tricks in a new line.

Perhaps William Hazlitt had this relationship between politics and the press in mind when he complained in the *Edinburgh Review* of the age's unprecedented "manufacture of newspapers and parliamentary speeches" (*CWH* 16:20). Elsewhere, in *Political Essays*, clearly alarmed by such hegemonic alliances, he asserts that "we neither consider Lord Castlereagh as the Constitution, nor *The Courier* as the Country" (*CWH* 7:216). Castlereagh was well-known as both a poor speaker and an adept politician, arguably among the age's most effective parliamentarians. Much of the attention he received in the opposition press focused on his considerable political influence and his not inconsiderable rhetorical liabilities, the latter including eccentric coinages and fallacious logic—though some critics saw some reason in the illogic. Among the Castlereaghisms noted in the *Republican*'s open letter is an instance of syllogistic reasoning similar to the ethical inversions that, three years before, Hazlitt had noted in Castlereagh's specious defense of domestic spying: "According to your idiom, that is the well regulated mind which supports the abuses and corruptions amidst which you thrive and flourish, and agreeable to that idiom, to write the truth and expose those abuses and corruptions, is licentiousness" (*R* 4 Aug. 1820: 513). More telling, however, is his lordship's resort to quoting out of context. One of the passages he reportedly read to parliament is singled out in turn by the *Republican* writer— reviewing the reviewer was a common critical strategy, employed to particular effect by the anti-Jacobin press—as not bearing on the question of the queen's trial but instead serving to associate the *Republican* with other, unpopular views. The *Republican* writer assumes the role of injured author when he objects: "What had this last paragraph or the distinct observations on religion to do with the case of the Queen? Nothing. But it was adopted by your lordship for the worst and most paltry of purposes" (*R* 4 Aug. 1820: 517–18). The religious card was played by government and press alike at a time when it was becoming increasingly difficult to get juries and readerships to swallow trumped up sedition charges. Blasphemy could still be relied on get a rise out of loyal Englishmen who might revere their church more than their government. In an attack on ministerial press coverage of the trial of two men convicted and sentenced to death for wounding a police officer, *Cobbett's Weekly Political Register* detects such a strategy not in the prosecution case but in press coverage of the trial. The case did not involve either sedition or murder, though Cobbett suggests that it became involved with both crimes by means of its devious representation in the ministerial press. That what should properly have been a matter of aggravated assault had become a capital case Cobbett attributes in part to the Tory *Courier*, his paragraph by paragraph critique of that paper's coverage of the affair turning on an exposure of what today would be called press spin. In the course of its analysis, Cobbett notes the devices employed by the ministerial paper: use of inaccurate terms like "*murderers* and *assassins*" to describe defendants charged with assault; vague deferrals to "*unquestionable*" authority; and, finally, dubious allegations about the religious beliefs of one of the condemned men. He then employs quotations from the *Courier* to demonstrate that the latter charge is made persuasive not through argument and evidence but through suggestive rhetoric, for "they assume that MAGGE-NIS was an *infidel*; that that made him *wicked*; that that made him kill Birch, or, at least, *shoot him*; and then they rush, without more ceremony, to this conclusion, that infidels are *always* ready 'to sport with the lives and PROPERTY of their fellow-men'" (*CPR* May 13 1820: 637, 658–59, 670).

These tactics were effective, if questionable. As the previous chapter shows, William Cobbett was himself in a position to appreciate the rhetorical adroitness behind such outcomes. Lord Castlereagh knew something about imposture too, notwithstanding a reputation for clumsy rhetoric, for the *Republican* commentary is serious enough about tricks commonly employed by reviewers and politicians. To speak of Castlereagh's excellence in either capacity, moreover, is to judge technical proficiency alone. If anything, the evident skill with which Castlereagh has selected "passages for comment," the very ones the *Republican* writer claims he would select in the minister's place, demonstrates his expedient disregard for valid argument and proof. But then, as George Campbell candidly admits, pointedly distinguishing rhetoric and logic, "It is not ultimately the justness either of the thought or of the expression, which is the aim of the orator; but it is a certain effect to be produced in the hearers" (*PR* 215). Yet Campbell applies this caveat to orators only. While the *Republican*'s reviewing analogy is facetious, it speaks to a more serious problem in political rhetoric and periodical criticism alike, a problem originating in the unholy symbiosis Hazlitt alludes to in troubled references to "newspapers and parliamentary speeches."

A critic himself, Hazlitt believed his contemporaries to be at once too critical and too uncritical in their thinking. The paradox is only apparent, for uncritical tendencies in an age of periodical criticism could take the form of a culture dependent on critical mediation to the point of enervation. In *Lectures on the Age of Elizabeth* (1820), Hazlitt nostalgically harkens back to the age of Sidney when "those middle men, the critics, were not known. The author and reader came into immediate contact, and seemed never tired of each other's company." Readers today, by contrast, are "fastidious and dissipated," critical by proxy (*CWH* 6:319). Elsewhere, Hazlitt concedes that critics perform a necessary function, but regrets the loss of a formerly unmediated connection between reader and author as "authors in proportion to their numbers become not formidable, but despicable" (*CWH* 8:215). Readers are separated from literature first by its sheer quantity and then by the very machinery of critical mediation that has emerged to synthesize it. Having overwhelmed the primary literature it explicates—Hazlitt speculates in an essay "On Modern Comedy" that Shakespeare himself would be overcome by the present day's "dense atmosphere of logic and criticism" (*CWH* 4:14)—it is almost inevitable that criticism should begin to acculturate readers to its own conventions. The effect is to weaken critical thinking itself while making the idiom of criticism virtually second nature, so that "every one becomes a critic who can read." "An author is no longer tried by his peers," Hazlitt observes. "A species of universal suffrage is introduced in letters, which is only applicable to politics. The good old Latin style of our forefathers, if it concealed the dullness of the writer, at least was a barrier against the impertinence, flippancy, and ignorance of the reader" (*CWH* 4:83). This "impertinence," a result of retaining the form of critical reception while neglecting its function, may explain what Hazlitt means by the age's "critical" attitude. When he observes that "the prevailing style of conversation is not *personal*, but critical and analytical" (*CWH* 4:12), he is speaking not of a fundamental critical orientation so much as shallow formalism. This is the basis for unfavorable comparisons of modern political rhetoric ("critical, and not parliamentary") with the eloquence of an older tradition—as exemplified by a Lord Chatham who, speaking to established feeling and belief, "did not stay to dispute about words, about nice distinctions, about trifling forms" (*CWH* 7:298).

A result of the Walpolean parliamentary ethos treated in the previous chapter, at least as this ethos is characterized in anti-Whig polemics, was the dissociation of thought and feeling in political rhetoric. This division of mind from heart enabled each to exploit the other and, in the process, made both potentially independent of ethics. Hazlitt's (and, in the previous chapter, Blair's) strictures on modern rhetoric, with its "nice distinctions" and "trifling forms," seem to suggest that reason has utterly supplanted passion in rhetoric, but it should be noted that reason pays a price as well—at a cost involving the very role of logic in argument. While George Canning could be accused of many rhetorical abuses, including demagoguery when it suited his purpose, he was also capable of the kind of close reasoning that characterizes the modern rhetorical ethos for Hazlitt and Blair. Yet unlike James Mackintosh, whose hapless rationality often worked against his own and his party's interests, Canning does not seem ever to have allowed reason to get the better of self-interest, notwithstanding his studied impartiality in the Caroline Affair. The *Black Dwarf*'s observation, that "He is a quibbler, but a quibbler from *intent*, not accident. His object is to pervert, and confuse" (*BD* 24 May 1820: 703), notes a critical strain in Canning's rhetoric while casting doubt on his motives, effectively accusing him of demagoguery, quibbling and all. Yet if the object is confusion is not the logic misapplied, if it is even really logic? Perhaps Canning employs only the form of logic in order to achieve ends more in keeping with the affective persuasion traditionally distinguishing rhetoric from logic. To be sure, what to a rational reformer is confusion, a perversion of the truth, might to the conservative mind be the affirmation of traditional beliefs praised by Hazlitt in Chatham's eloquence: "The business of an orator is not to convince, but persuade; not to inform, but to rouse the mind; to build upon the habitual prejudices of mankind, (for reason of itself will do nothing,) and to add feeling to prejudice, and action to feeling" (*CWH* 7:298). There is also, pace Earl Camden, "imbecility in the defence of truth," carrying with it those who can assent but not reason. Canning, as characterized by the *Black Dwarf* anyway, is neither a Chatham nor a Camden, though his rhetoric may aim at ends similar to theirs. These ends would be at odds, however, with the putative logic he employs. In the same way, the form of critical reception appealed to by this logic would be at odds with an uncritical assent to what he is really speaking to in his audience. Whether or not the end justifies this means, the *Black Dwarf* article suggests that either logic or rhetoric is misused by Canning, perhaps both.

Campbell's insistence that the end of oratory concerns the "effect" produced would seem to allow some latitude even to logical quibbling. For Campbell, criticism and grammar are the ministers of "use" or convention and as such should not presume to impose absolute standards. This is not to deny them their roles in regulating or even supplementing rhetoric. Campbell sees a supplemental role in forensic rhetoric, for instance, where

"critical explications of dark and ambiguous statutes, quotations
of precedents sometimes contradictory, and comments on jarring
decisions and reports, often necessarily consume the great part
of the speaker's time." Such "nice and hypercritical" rhetoric is
too specialized to command the attention of any but specialists,
however, though questions concerning justice and natural rights
allow scope for eloquence (*PR* 104). Priestley cites pulpit oratory
as a case where rhetoric employs critical analysis, its practitioners "ascertaining the meaning of every passage they quote with
all possible accuracy" (*LOC* 63). While Campbell holds rhetoric
to be subject to "use," he disagrees with Priestley's view that the
best forms of speech will in time naturally establish themselves
(*PR* 161). Reluctant to discount an element of the perverse that
may encourage usages neither simple nor agreeable, he reserves
a place in rhetorical practice for rational censure. It is criticism,
he argues, that serves "to suppress every unlicensed term, and to
stigmatize every improper idiom," and so defend against rhetoric's abuses (*PR* 152). For Campbell, criticism and rhetoric ide-
ally stand in complementary relation to one another, but there is
a suggestion that each has the potential to encroach on the
other:

> In some instances *custom* may very properly be checked by *criti-
> cism,* which hath a sort of negative, and though not the censorian
> power of instant degradation, the privilege of remonstrating, and
> by means of this, when used discreetly, of bringing what is bad
> into disrepute, and so cancelling it gradually; but which hath no
> positive right to establish any thing. Her power too is like that of
> eloquence; she operates on us purely by persuasion, depending
> for success on the solidity, or at least the speciousness of her ar-
> guments; whereas custom hath an unaccountable and irresist-
> ible influence over us, an influence which is prior to persuasion,
> and independent of it, nay, sometimes even in contradiction to it.
> Of different modes of expression, that which comes to be favoured
> by general practice may be denominated best, because estab-
> lished; but it cannot always be said with truth, that it is estab-
> lished because best. (*PR* 160–61)

The limits set to criticism here, its purely negative agency, recall
Hazlitt on the limits of rational reform. This is no more than criticism needs to be in order to check abuse. The difficulty lies not in

differences between rhetoric and criticism but similarities. If "use" is independent of persuasion, criticism and rhetoric both exert their powers wholly by that means, depending for success on either the validity or "speciousness" of their respective methods. It is possible that each may employ the other in order to persuade, even to the point of assuming the other's function and distorting rhetorical and critical practice alike.

It could be objected that criticism is itself a form of rhetoric, and should therefore not be viewed as being distinct from rhetoric in the way that logic is distinct. While logic may be universally valid, however, its effective expression will depend on a correct observance of rhetorical decorum. This in itself suggests a critical reflex by which the statement of a logical idea is judged on the basis of its conformity not only with logical but conventional criteria as well. At the same time, if criticism may judge a sound logical proposition to have been poorly conveyed according to contingent standards of usage, it may also detect logical fallacy in rhetorically effective expression and explain such dubious success on the same grounds. Even if criticism is viewed as a branch of rhetoric, then, it can be provisionally distinguished from other forms of rhetoric by its reflexive function. While it judges according to convention, and in doing so relies on conventional means for its own effectiveness as rhetoric, within this contingent realm of "use" it serves as a kind of practical reason mediating logic and eloquence. To push it too far in either direction is to compromise its effectiveness or its validity. While the "critical" style of speaking Hazlitt associates with Sir James Mackintosh sacrifices effectiveness for validity, the critical rhetoric affected by Castlereagh and Canning involves an entirely different kind of compromise, its object being to pervert and confuse meaning under the guise of critical explication. The fact that "real" critics in *The Republican* and the *Black Dwarf* are on to the politicians may simply mean that criticism is doing its job. Yet techniques like strategic quotation are, as the *Republican* writer admits, part of the periodical reviewer's rhetorical stock-in-trade, so that perhaps the fellowship ironically suggested by Castlereagh's *"puff direct"* betrays a troubling mutual recognition by reviewer and politician. While a distinction between criticism and rhetoric may be provisional at best, encroachments of the kind remarked here suggest how uncertain was the line dividing political demagoguery and periodical reviewing in an age of "newspapers and parliamentary speeches."

One explanation for this situation is given in an 1822 *Blackwood's* essay entitled "Rise, Progress, Decline, and Fall of the Edinburgh Review." According to this account, literature was ruled by a benign if rigid neoclassical oligarchy prior to 1789 only to be overthrown by "a race of literary democrats, as vulgar, as presumptuous, and as ignorant as their political brethren." The causal relation of this coup d'état in letters to the political revolution is not made clear, but there is no mistaking the view that politics and letters alike had been invaded by "new elements" bent on subverting tradition. Burke is credited with first recognizing this emerging alliance of literary and political Jacobinism and so establishing what might be called an anti-Jacobin critique. For three decades after his death, indeed, Burke was the posthumous Whig patron of the Tory ministerialist press. His portrayal in the *Blackwood's* article borders on hagiography:

> Against these rash and innovative demagogues, a Whig of that revolution, by which the liberties of England were secured, in other words, a Tory of that revolution which threatened them and those of all Europe with abolition—Mr. Burke was the first who effectually raised his voice. With the irrepressible enthusiasm of the hermit Peter rousing Christendom to the dangers of the rising deluge of Saracanic devastation; he demonstrated the necessity of raising ramparts and barriers to protect philosophy from the ravagers who were making such dreadful inroads on the most sacred and venerable recesses of the vineyard; but only indirectly, and chiefly with reference to the effects which the ravage produced on political institutions. (671)

This translation of Burke into a Tory ignores his isolation from Whigs and Tories alike during the revolutionary decade. The author of the *Reflections* had no more reason to think Pitt's Tories more reliable, or less reluctant, allies than the Foxites, though immediately after his death he proved useful enough to the talented young founders of the ultra-Tory *Anti-Jacobin*. Whether or not he would have appreciated the discipleship of such as Canning, Frere, et al., he might have recognized them and other ambitious anti-Jacobins as a necessary inference of Jacobin philosophy, "this weapon," as he called it in the *Reflections*, that "will snap short, unfaithful to the hand that employs it" (*RRF* 8:272), as necessary in their way as Napoleon.

Burke's critique proved inestimably useful to Tory critics of New School poetics, though even a reform-minded critic like Hazlitt employs it in his famous discussion of the Lake poets in *Lectures on the English Poets* (1818).[1] The *Blackwood's* writer is correct in noting that Burke does not address literature per se except as it has contributed to a general revolution of political and social values associated with what Burke termed "literary caballers, and intriguing philosophers" (*RRF* 8:61). But Burke does not so much treat the role of letters during the 1790s "indirectly" as synthetically, viewing it as part of an emerging politicization of society he fears will irrevocably transform European culture into something both more refined and more barbaric than anything yet conceived by the political projectors he so despises. Throughout the *Reflections*, then, a special terminology is employed according to which those whom Burke calls "Your literary men, and your politicians" come to refer exclusively to such projectors in England and France, "the whole clan of the enlightened among us" (*RRF* 8:138–39). Expedient and ruthless, speculative and sophistical, these subversive elements—writers and politicians alike—share a form of rhetorical *virtù* similar to that expounded by Burke's old patron Hamilton. "Their attachment to their country itself," Burke says of them, "is only so far as it agrees with some of their fleeting projects; it begins and ends with that scheme of polity which falls in with their momentary opinion" (*RRF* 8:138–39). Burke's account of how men of letters became "political Men of Letters" extends back to the decline of Louis XIV's powerful hold over French culture, one effect of which was the decline of literary influence under his successors. The subsequent radicalization of letters—a reaction out of all proportion, Burke claims, to "the desultory and faint persecution carried on against them, more from compliance with form and decency than with serious resentment" (*RRF* 8:161)—compensated for the loss of court patronage by means of an exclusive incorporation among writers themselves, leading to the founding of the academies and eventually the production of the Encyclopedia. Zealous proponents of "innovation," these political *littéra-*

teurs directed their talents wholly to the destruction of tradition, first targeting religion, "with a degree of zeal which hitherto had been discovered only in the propagators of some system of piety" (*RRF* 8:161), before going on to attack established government. An emerging popular press enabled them to circulate these views widely. "The writers of these papers indeed," Burke notes in "Thoughts on French Affairs" (1791), "for the greater part, are either unknown or in contempt, but they are like a battery in which the stroke of any one ball produces no great effect, but the amount of continual repetition is decisive." The galvanic reference and the sensationalist emphasis on "continual repetition" describe a rhetorical strategy that, materially extended through the press, aims at automatic stimulus on a mass scale—a logical, if extreme, inference of New Rhetorical and Elocutionary assimilations of empirical psychology. As Burke observes, again in "Thoughts on French Affairs," "The little catechism of the Rights of Men is soon learned; and the inferences are in the passions."[2]

If, as the *Blackwood's* article notes, he does not treat literature as such in the *Reflections*, Burke critiques the intellectual hegemony he claims its practitioners, whom he calls "a sort of demagogues" (*RRF* 8:162), have created through rhetorical imposture. Their influence, he charges, is supported by both zeal and opportunism, exerting itself through whatever means are required to achieve its destructive ends, whether reason or deception:

> I will venture to say that this narrow, exclusive spirit has not been less prejudicial to literature and to taste, than to morals and true philosophy. These Atheistical fathers have a bigotry of their own; and they have learnt to talk against monks with the spirit of a monk. But in some things they are men of the world. The resources of intrigue are called in to supply the defects of argument and wit. To this system of literary monopoly was joined an unremitting industry to blacken and discredit in every way, and by every means, all those who did not hold to their faction. To those who have observed the spirit of their conduct, it has long been clear that nothing was wanted but the power of carrying the intolerance of the tongue and of the pen into a persecution which would strike at property, liberty, and life. (*RRF* 8:161)

Such power, Burke argues, now threatens the security of France through a potent new alliance of literary and political interests.

If writers have become political, politicians have become literary, adopting in their proceedings the radical skepticism of *paradoxeurs*. "Your legislators," Burke remarks to his French correspondent in *Reflections*, "seem to have taken their opinions of all professions, ranks, and offices, from the declamations and buffooneries of satirists; who would themselves be astonished if they were held to the letter of their own descriptions" (*RRF* 8:218–90). Observations like this recall the confounding of rhetorical *virtù* with civic virtue detected by Jeremy Bentham in writers as various as William Gerard Hamilton and constitutional framers in revolutionary France. In the *Book of Fallacies*, Bentham traces the troubling elision of necessity and opportunity he detects in Hamilton to its origins in rhetorical fallacy. Beyond even the tactical coups of Hamilton's aspiring young Machiavels, Hazlitt shows how Walpole could deploy fallacy to distort parliamentary governance itself. In Burke's (and Bentham's) view, however, revolutionary France is the grand demonstration of rhetorical imposture, its legislators making their equation of rhetoric with polity a basis for government: "As to the rest, the paradoxes of eloquent writers, brought forth purely as a sport of fancy, to try their talents, to rouze attention, and excite surprize, are taken up by these gentlemen, not in the spirit of the original authors, as means of cultivating their taste and improving their style. These paradoxes become with them serious grounds of action, upon which they proceed in regulating the most important concerns of the state" (*RRF* 8:218–19). In his "Remarks on the Policy of the Allies" (1793), Burke marvels that so complete a revolution in France should have been effected by men of letters, "not as subordinate instruments and trumpeters of sedition, but as the chief contrivers and managers, and in a short time as the open administrators and sovereign Rulers."[3]

What Burke found alarming in this prospect, then, was the necessary prominence in government of a certain kind of literary character. Hazlitt's characterization of him in *Political Essays* not as a great politician or a profound philosopher but as "an acute and accomplished man of letters—an ingenious political essayist" (*CWH* 7:227) suggests that Burke would recognize a literary turn in politics when he saw it. "Fourth Letter on the Regicide Peace" (1795) is an extended analysis in which he reviews Lord Auckland's pamphlet, *Some Remarks on the Apparent Cir-*

cumstances of the War in the Fourth Week of October (1795), a
work he describes as "Jacobinism sublimed and exalted into most
pure and perfect essence" (*RP* 9:52). Familiar with the tempta-
tions faced by the clever reviewer, he resolves not to judge Aukland's work on the basis of "detached paragraphs" but to refer the
parts he examines to the whole, though he finds that "Examining
it part by part, it seems almost every where to contradict itself."
"His march is mostly oblique, and his doctrine rather in the way
of insinuation than of dogmatick assertion," he asserts of Aukland. "It is not only fugitive in its duration, but is slippery, in the
extreme, whilst it lasts" (*RP* 9:49). What disturbs him more than
Aukland's equivocal rhetoric, however, is the uniformly skeptical
turn of mind this rhetoric displays, the fact that "the Author expresses his sentiments only as doubts" (*RP* 9:58). Such observations reserve for criticism a role supplemental to statecraft. To do
otherwise, Burke believes, would be to subordinate the necessarily positive embodiment of national sentiment in government to
the purely negative energies of critical analysis. Hazlitt, in some
respects the most reluctant of Burkeans, notes the dangers of critique in an essay on "The Spirit of Controversy" in which he portrays civil society as the perpetual site of a kind of Comtean
dialectic of organic and critical impulses: "As faith is the prop and
cement that upholds society by opposing fixed principles as a barrier against the inroads of passion, so reason is the *menstruum*
which dissolves it by leaving nothing sufficiently firm or unquestioned in our opinions to withstand the current and bias of inclination" (*CWH* 2:311). The "chaotic mass" of revolutionary France
from which Hazlitt's Burke extracts the elements of civil order is
the logical outcome of an ungoverned critical impulse. This, the
murderously dissective power of autonomous critique, is for
Burke the progeny of what in the *Reflections* he terms "total revolution" (*RRF* 8:154). While he suggests that Aukland's skepticism is only apparent—tracing it to Berkelean philosophy, "for a
good while a fashionable mode of composition" (*RP* 9:59)—the
fact that such a stance has presented itself as the motive for revolution and war is reason not to dismiss it outright, fallacy or not.
The wry observation that "In this doubt there is much decision"
(*RP* 9:58–59) at once rejects the proposition that a nation could
wage a war of skepticism and takes seriously the rhetoric arguing that it could. The most prescient inference in the *Reflections*

concerns not only the impending terror but the rational form this terror might take. This false consciousness has become, Burke fears, a "complexional disposition" (*RRF* 8:218–19) in revolutionary society, rather like the critical formalism Hazlitt detects in Regency readers. The fact that such an attitude operates as a conditioned reflex does not render criticism ineffective so much as indiscriminate. If even as much authority as is necessary to maintain order in a state may be subverted by the disposition to question everything, then no authority, not even that of the revolution, is secure from this double-edged critique. Addressing the heavy hand of revolutionary authority, then, Burke claims that the "coin of sophistic reason" has circulated so widely in France that even peasants can cite revolutionary doctrine against its own authors when they resort to prescriptive measures. "You lay down metaphysic propositions which infer universal consequences," he points out, "and then you attempt to limit logic by despotism" (*RRF* 8:270–71).

That critique and coercion might be rhetorically combined, however fallaciously, is for Burke the cautionary lesson of literary Jacobinism. As late as 1823 in the *Edinburgh Review*, Hazlitt detected a quality he termed "Literary Jacobinism" in Landor's *Imaginary Conversations*, defining it as "that despotism of the mind, which only emancipates itself from authority and prejudice, to grow impatient of every thing like an appearance of opposition, and to domineer over and dictate its sudden, crude, violent, and varying opinions, to the rest of the world" (*CWH* 16:243). Whether Burke's prescience as an "ingenious political essayist" extended to the unexpected forms this tendency would soon take is hard to say, though he would have understood Hazlitt's use of the term. In the years immediately after his death, ideological lines between Jacobin and anti-Jacobin were so strongly drawn that it is easy to miss a distinctly Jacobinical ethos—in Burke's influential sense—informing ministerialist press tactics. The nature of the war being waged against revolutionary France suggests the extent to which the agenda was being set by a rhetorical sensationalism very different from "the collective sense of the nation" eulogized in works like *Eloquence of the British Senate*, not to mention Burke's *Reflections*.

The Peninsular campaign of 1808–9 is a case in point, revealing the conflicting imperatives of battlefield and home front faced by the English government. Radical commentators like William Cobbett accused ministerialist papers of misrepresenting the true state of affairs in Spain, even claiming that dispatches written by Sir John Moore, the general in charge of the campaign, were being selectively excerpted in the ministerial press in order to mislead readers. "But, there is no measure to the deception, the falsehoods, the lies, the frauds, that are practised upon this gullible nation," Cobbett charges. "—'*Extracts*'! Why extracts? Why did you not give us the *whole* of Sir John Moore's dispatches?" (*CPR* 14 Jan. 1809: 42). Truth is usually the first casualty of war, but the form taken by this propaganda strategy was also distinctly literary in character. Employing the kind of reviewing practices ascribed by the *Republican* to Castlereagh, the English government was using the press to give its own policies a "puff direct." In his *Life of Napoleon*, Hazlitt suggests that the unfortunate General Moore had more to deal with than the editing of his dispatches as he contemplated his army's situation. While advance was perilous, Moore knew that the English public at home was catalyzed by the cause of Spanish liberty:

> He consulted Mr. Frere, the British minister and a sort of itinerant camp-critic and writer of dispatches (of the Canning school) who advised him to proceed by all means and risk every thing for the chance of succouring Madrid. Mr. Frere was a wit, a courtier, and an enthusiast in the cause of Spanish liberty; for he saw with what a different eye courts and cabinets must regard that liberty or will of the people which consisted in their determination to have no will of their own, but to leave all power in the hands of kings and priests, and that other sort of liberty which France had tried to obtain, of having a will of her own and taking some of the supreme power out of the hands of those that held it. One of these two kinds of patriotism or liberty, which was both courtly and popular, was the finest opening and handle in the world for overturning the other which had never been courtly and had ceased to be popular. (*CPR* 14:342)

Moore, "who was not of the Canning school," declined to take up this challenge. John Hookham Frere had been in the late 1790s an associate of George Canning's on *The Anti-Jacobin, or Weekly Examiner*, and his advice to Moore seems more like editorial

policy than military strategy. Hazlitt clearly sees in the activities
of this "itinerant camp-critic" the application of ministerial press
techniques to government policy. From Frere's witty perspective,
"that liberty or will of the people which consisted in their deter-
mination to have no will of their own" is an exploitable paradox.
His technique consists in critically educing and rhetorically de-
ploying this false consciousness on behalf of the ministerial program. As Sir John must have realized to his dismay, he and the
Minister were fighting different wars.

Such instances suggest a government-sponsored press as subversive in its methods as any spies hired by the Home Office. In
"The Periodical Press," published in an 1823 number of the *Edinburgh Review*, Hazlitt credits the right-wing *Anti-Jacobin*
(1797–98), among whose chief contributors was George Canning,
with establishing the "Ministerial Press," a powerful machine directed to subverting what Hazlitt and other reform-minded writers viewed as the necessarily liberal tendency of intellectual
suffrage. Realizing that "reason was against them," the *Anti-Jacobin* reviewers decided that "they should be against reason,"
Hazlitt argues (*CWH* 16:234). But this was no instinctive turning to "the collective sense of the nation," for it issued from, and
at least putatively appealed to, the same critical perspective as
Castlereagh's and Frere's cynical manipulations of paradox. The
ministerial strategy was deliberate and rational, employing critical subversion solely as a technique, a means directed against
the end it was originally conceived to attain: "Knowledge, writing, the press was found to be the great engine that governed
public opinion; and the scheme therefore was, to make it recoil
upon itself, and act in a retrograde direction to its natural one"
(*CWH* 16:233–34).

It would be a mistake to dismiss the anti-Jacobin press of the
1790s as merely an expression of Tory reaction. While it certainly
appealed to such sentiments, it also subsumed other views not as
easily reconciled with right-wing alarmism. In *Jane Austen and
the War of Ideas*, Marilyn Butler argues that anti-Jacobinism
was part of a general reaction against literary and philosophical
sentimentalism during the revolutionary decade, a sentimentalism associated with progressive social views since the mid eigh-

teenth century. That the lines were not as clearly defined as this might suggest, however, is evident in her caveat that even progressives at this time were becoming critical of sentimentalism. Butler suggests that Burke deliberately drove his opponents—Paine, Priestley, and Mackintosh among them—to "a sometimes exaggerated posture of rationality" in their response to the *Reflections*. The latter, accordingly, she reads as an effort to reappropriate sentiment for conservatives while demonstrating its abuse by rational reform. The *Reflections* is, she asserts, "a typical sentimental performance" in its enlisting of affective rhetoric to make a case for tradition, but its critique of unfettered reason is also directed against unfettered emotion—that is, the selfish passions sanctioned by skeptical philosophies of mind with their hedonist models of human nature. In Burke's critique, the regressive logic of such thinking "is cunningly worked out with the full range of sentimental effects."[4] Butler has shown elsewhere that binary sets like reason/passion, classical/romantic cannot be sorted out along clear-cut ideological lines in this period.[5] If the Romantic sensibility exposed by the *Anti-Jacobin* in literary Jacobinism was, as she notes, the pervasive tenor of Burke's famous conservative tract—and of the neo-Burkean strain in the *Anti-Jacobin* itself—so did critical energies detected by Burke in the revolutionary ethos also condition its dialectical other in English anti-Jacobinism.

Journals with the designation "anti-Jacobin" in their titles emerged in the late 1790s as part of the counterrevolutionary reaction in Pitt's England. They included *The Anti-Jacobin, or Weekly Examiner*, which ran from 1797 to 1798 and is best known for parodies of New School verse and drama written by prominent Tories like Canning, Frere, and apparently even Pitt, and *The Anti-Jacobin Review and Magazine*, which considered itself in some sense a successor to its shorter-lived and more famous namesake, running from 1798 to 1821 under various other titles like *The Anti-Jacobin Review and Protestant Advocate*. Another such journal was *The Satirist; or, Monthly Meteor*, which ran from 1807 to 1814 and which also portrayed itself as successor to the original *Anti-Jacobin*. A subtitle sometimes appearing on the banner of the *Anti-Jacobin Review*—*Monthly Political and Literary Censor*—points to the critical focus of these journals, not so much a double focus as one conflating politics and letters in a single over-arching preoccupation with detecting and exposing subversion in English public life. That this might itself involve subversive methods is inevitable given what amounts to an Enlightenment program of bringing error to light, even if this was ultimately in the service of Church and King. Despite their reactionary agenda, anti-Jacobin critics tend at times to conduct themselves like reformers pitted against powerful vested interests—much like French philosophes whose opposition against the ancien régime Burke dismisses as a deliberate overreaction to "desultory and faint persecution" by Louis IV's successors.

Anti-Jacobin criticism bears the equivocal impress of its rhetorical provenance in Burkean critique and jeremiad. The historical narrative of benightenment by enlightenment sketched by Burke, his account in the *Reflections* of the rise and entrenchment of literary Jacobinism, is brought to a grand consummation by anti-Jacobin critics in the late 1790s (and latterly by their Regency successors in journals like *Blackwood's*). In the preface to its third volume, the *Anti-Jacobin Review and Magazine* describes a period, before its establishment, of liberal domination by journals like the *Analytical Review* and *Monthly Review* "when the literary world was subjected to the intolerable tyranny of those arbitrary Sovereigns, exempt from all control, whose decisions were irrevocable, and whose fiat was law" (*AJR* 1799: vii). In their "Prospectus," indeed, its editors had claimed that "criticism has long been monopolized by men who, favouring the views of the French *economists* and other *philosophists* of modern times, have facilitated the propagation of principles, subversive of social order, and, consequently, destructive of social happiness" (*AJR* 1798: 4). A later issue sees signs of light, however, in a vigorous conservative press poised to bring down the Jacobin hegemony, "having torn a part of the empire of literature from the monopolizing hands of dissention" (*AJR* May 1800: 89). This assertion, that the Jacobins have lost their hold on English letters, is factually true to the extent that such a hegemony had not been exaggerated in the first place, though it was so often repeated by anti-Jacobin writers that it became something of a critical commonplace. Butler points out that anti-Jacobin satire was in fact more popular than the works it satirized, publications like *The Rolliad* (1784), Gifford's *Baviad* (1791) and *Mae-*

viad (1795), Mathias's *Pursuits of Literature* (1794), and *Poetry of The Anti-Jacobin Review* (1799) going into numerous editions.[6] If the alarm sounded by Burke's *Reflections* seemed an overreaction in 1790, and was later viewed as either prescient or self-fulfilling, perhaps the putative threat of literary Jacobinism was partly a product of the reaction it provoked from conservative critics. To liberals and reformers, the Tory renaissance for which the anti-Jacobin press was taking credit might have seemed more like reactionary retrenchment.

To unaligned observers, if there were any, it might have seemed strangely like Whig history. The idea of overthrowing an empire ruled by "dissention" catches the paradox inherent in anti-Jacobin rhetoric, its portrayal of conservative reaction as a program of enlightenment. On the one hand, anti-Jacobins make a point of displaying their Burkean credentials. In his "Prospectus" to the original *Anti-Jacobin*, Canning embraces "*partiality* and *prejudice*," wholly disavowing "that spirit of liberal indifference, of diffused and comprehensive philanthropy, which distinguishes the candid character of the present age." In a particularly disingenuous confession of faith, he asserts that "We have not arrived (to our shame, perhaps, we avow it) at that wild and unshackled freedom of thought, which rejects all habit, all wisdom of former times, all restraints of ancient usage, and of local attachment; and which judges upon each subject, whether of politics or morals, as it arises, by lights entirely its own, without reference to recognized principle, or established practice" (*A-J* 1:3–4). In a similar vein, the "Prospectus" to the later *Anti-Jacobin Review and Magazine* pledges its solidarity with "all who are of the opinion, that a rage for innovation is no symptom of political wisdom, and that the overthrow of establishments is a dangerous experiment, deserving rather of punishment than of praise" (*AJR* 1798: 6). Such views are not surprising, given the pronounced counterrevolutionary stance of these journals. No more surprising is an apparent hostility to social paradigms based on progressive enlightenment. Amid the hostilities of war, one would be hard-pressed to find evidence that an Enlightenment had ever occurred in England, so exclusively is it identified by anti-Jacobins with what the first issue of *The Satirist* denigrates as "the ethics of France." Set against Enlightenment thinking, "the new school of philosophy," is English patriotism. Rather in Canning's vein, then, *The Satirist* confesses that "We are still old-fashioned as to love our *kindred* better than our kind; and, in spite of the refinements of modern feeling, have the boldness to exclaim, 'England, with all thy faults, we love thee still'" (*S* 1 Oct. 1807: 4). The result is a stance, still current today among conservatives (perhaps originating with Burke) that paradoxically combines defensive anti-intellectualism with intellectual superiority. In its "Weekly Examiner" section, then, the original *Anti-Jacobin* scoffs at "the intolerable stupidity of those Scribblers who, in the Jacobinical Prints, assume the style of superior intelligence, and impudently attempt to convince the world that it lay immersed in ignorance till they kindly undertook the province of enlightening it" (*A-J* 18 Dec. 1797: 183). Paradigms are more easily opposed than escaped from, however. No matter how reactionary its aims, a revisionary program directed to exposing imposture and correcting error might legitimately be suspected of Enlightenment tendencies. A lead essay in the *Anti-Jacobin*, indeed, fears that literary Jacobinism has been most effective in its influence on "the less enlightened part of the Nation"—those who can assent but not reason, presumably— blaming the apathy of those who should have known better but allowed error to pass without contradiction (*A-J* 9 July 1798: 619). The anti-Jacobin press not only credited itself with assuming such a corrective role, but was claiming victory by the end of the 1790s. The following passage in the *Anti-Jacobin Review and Magazine*, from a letter to the editor by one Clericus, announces the triumph of reaction in terms that would not be out of place in Hume's account of the Reformation:

> At length the Anti-Jacobin appeared, formed upon a more direct and comprehensive system of detection and defence: the mischief was increasing, and means of energetic investigation and positive conviction became indispensable.—These the talents and opportunities of the authors of the Anti-Jacobin could amply supply: superior intelligence and extensive information stamped its pages with incontrovertible authority.—The Reviews of opposition became the objects of its deserved reprehension, and their falsehoods, their misrepresentations, their partialities, were exposed to the public eye. (*AJR* May 1799: 80)

Tracing public life from Jacobin imposture to enlightened Toryism, narratives like this reveal the triumphant outlines of Whig
history.

The phrase "detection and defence" sums up the paradoxical
alliance of enlightenment and reaction that characterizes the
anti-Jacobin program. Canning's "Prospectus" to the original
Anti-Jacobin conveys an attitude that could only be described as
ministerialist opposition to opposition:

> Novelty indeed We have to announce. For what so new in the pre-
> sent state of the daily and weekly PRESS (We speak generally,
> though there are undoubtedly exceptions which we may have oc-
> casion to point out hereafter) as THE TRUTH. To this object
> alone it is that Our labours are dedicated. It is the constant vio-
> lation, the disguise, the reversion of the Truth, whether in narra-
> tive or in argument, that will form the principal subject of our
> WEEKLY EXAMINATION: and it is by diligent and faithful dis-
> charge of this duty,—by detecting falsehood,—and rectifying
> error,—by correcting misrepresentation, and exposing and
> chastising malignity,—that we hope to deserve the reception
> which We solicit, and to obtain not only the approbation of the
> Country to our attempt, but its thanks for the motives which
> have given birth to it. (*A-J* 1: 2)

The reference to novelty is meant to be taken ironically, for it is
the meretricious novelty of Jacobinical thinking that the *Anti-
Jacobin* will subject to "WEEKLY EXAMINATION." Burke exposes a similar literary voguishness in Aukland's pamphlet,
observing that writers of the new school value novelty over
durable merit even if their productions last no longer than "the
painted silks and cottons of the season." "Every thing is new," he
notes, "and according to the fashionable phrase, revolutionary"
(*RP* 9:45–46). Yet Burke's anti-Jacobin protégés implicitly make
novelty part of their appeal to a readership sated with the novel-
ties of literary Jacobinism. Their rigor in the exposure of error,
their championing of "TRUTH," even if it is a truth emerging by
"reversion"—reaction by any other name—exploits the ethos of
innovation it opposes. In effect, talent contests an authority it reveals to be subversion while the form of innovation is employed
on behalf of permanence. "They are always best opposed by the
arms which they themselves furnish," assert the *Anti-Jacobin*'s

editors of their opponents. "Jacobinism shines by its own light" (*A-J* 22 Jan. 1798: 371–72 n).

This strategy is so often remarked in the *Anti-Jacobin*'s verse parodies that its use in anti-Jacobin criticism—*The Satirist* heads an exposure of Cobbett's writings with the motto: "Out of thine own mouth will I convict thee" (*S* 1 Jan. 1811: 30)—is often overlooked. In fact, the greater part of the original *Anti-Jacobin* is devoted to criticism, famous satiric performances like "The Rovers" and "The New Morality" appearing in a semiregular "Poetry" section. In addition to regular reviews and notices, both the *Anti-Jacobin* and the *Anti-Jacobin Review and Magazine* ran regular features critiquing journals they considered to be Jacobinical in tendency. Despite the popularity of the literary parodies—much less frequent and less inspired in the later *Anti-Jacobin Review and Magazine*—it is this corrective critical program that would have most tellingly defined the anti-Jacobin rhetorical strategy to contemporary readers. Throughout the pages of these journals, anti-Jacobin writers are vigilant critics of bias in the reformist press, pledging, in the words of Canning's "Prospectus," to resist "every attempt which may be made either by argument or (what is more in the charitable spirit of modern reformers) by force, to convert us to a different opinion" (*A-J* 1:7). For this purpose, the *Anti-Jacobin* ran a feature listing various forms of error—designated under the categories of "LIES," "MISREPRESENTATIONS," and "MISTAKES"—found in Jacobin publications. Similarly, the *Anti-Jacobin Review and Magazine* ran a regular feature entitled "The Reviewers Reviewed," aimed at correcting "the principles and conduct of modern critics"—especially in journals like the *Critical* and *Monthly Reviews*, which, in the words of a 1799 letter to the editor, plant subversion "in the false statements of splenetic contradiction, or in the more specious manoeuvres of uncandid misconstruction" (*AJR* May 1799: 64). In *The Satirist*, a feature entitled "Comparative Criticism" focused on the "*quackery* of reviewing" by juxtaposing quotations from reviews of the same work from different journals to expose liberal inconsistency and folly, what it dismisses as "the fallacy, incongruity, absurdity, and wickedness of those *intellectual nuisances*" (*S* 1 Dec. 1807: 243).

Despite the categorical tone of anti-Jacobin criticism, what is at issue in either the texts being examined or the critical analyses of these texts is the rhetorical construction (or misconstruction) of meaning. The texts in question were either book reviews or what today would be called news stories. Whether concerning estimates of books or events, however, they involved interpretation, and it is on this basis, not of logical certainty but of rhetorical probability, of opinion, that the anti-Jacobin metareviewers quiz the Jacobin press. A necessary corollary of this emphasis is a distinctly modern—the term would be "newfangled" when the shoe was on the other foot—and skeptical relativism potentially at odds with traditional Tory certainties. Despite the confidence expressed in Canning's Prospectus that various forms of falsehood collected by his journal's literary censors "will naturally divide themselves into different classes, according to their different degrees of stupidity or malignity" (A-J 1:7–8), such quasi-logical taxonomies as the *Anti-Jacobin* regularly featured actually served to shift the political debate wholly to the uncertain grounds of rhetoric. "LIES," "MISREPRESENTATIONS," and "MISTAKES" involve interpretations of interpretations, so that seemingly straightforward categories like lies and mistakes are subject to the very effects of imposture or error they are designed to expose. Even allowing them to be unproblematic, however, there is still the matter of misrepresentations, "which, taking for their ground-work facts in substance true, do so colour and distort them in description, as to take away all semblance of their real nature and character" (A-J 1:8). This category wholly occupies the equivocal realm of fallacy on the grounds of expression and interpretation alike. In it the radically rhetorical assumptions of anti-Jacobin critique are clearly evident. Canning's "Introduction" to the *Anti-Jacobin's* first number observes that misrepresentations are problematic because they are products of long-standing usage—ordinarily not a bad thing for a Burkean Tory. His discussion of this difficulty, however, seems to owe much to Thomas Paine in its reductive roots-and-branches rhetoric. Canning speaks of a "difficulty" faced by the readers of Jacobian writing:

> It is [this difficulty], that many or most of the Misrepresentations which are obtruded upon our daily notice, have their root and foundation in lies of older dates; which either from the circumstance of their never have received a decisive contradiction,

or, by dint of being impudently repeated after it, have obtained a
sort of prescriptive credit, and are referred to upon all occasions
as if established beyond dispute. It will be necessary, therefore,
in many instances, for the complete confutation of modern Falsehoods, to trace them diligently and patiently to their origin; and
not only to dam up the current, but to cut off the source. (*A-J* 20
Nov. 1797: 11–12)

Paine described Burkean arguments in similar terms, employing
the same radical critique to get at the root assumptions behind
Burke's doctrine of prescription (which Bentham would presumably have listed among "Fallacies of Authority"). The argument
that falsehood may eventually be admitted as truth if repeated
often enough, moreover—elsewhere the *Morning Post* is accused
of "Having thus affirmed the truth of its Lie, by a solemn repetition of it" (*A-J* 9 Apr. 1798: 117)[7]—bears the distinct impress of
sensationalist psychology. Truth by this means is reduced from
conviction arrived at by argument to a conditioned impression.
Canning goes so far as to assert that certain misrepresentations,
even if glaringly false, have become so familiar "that they are
constantly, and without shame, appealed to by the Jacobins, and
are even by many well-meaning persons often admitted, not only
as true in themselves, but as the test and standard whereby the
probability of other assertions is to be estimated" (*A-J* 20 Nov.
1797 :12). But this is no more than Burke argues of tradition. His
concept of "amiable error"—premised on the notion that misguided reinforcements of tradition, if well-meant, are justifiable
(*RRF* 8:87)—effectively means that repeated error may come to
seem true, which is as good as actually being true in a world of
rhetorical probability. Canning would like to accept this pragmatic doctrine when it applies to the existing order but draws
the line at further demonstrations, "which when once assumed
as established Truths may be stated and re-stated in a thousand
different shapes" (*A-J* 20 Nov. 1797: 14). Jacobin error is not only
unamiable error but positive error. Devoting themselves to exposing "the Jacobinical design of giving it authenticity by inces-
sant repetition" (*A-J* 4 Dec. 1797: 116), anti-Jacobins attempt to
have and eat their cake in many ways, subverting liberal moral
relativism with its own skeptical techniques in the service of a
king and church sanctioned by immemorial usage.

It is through this rhetorical melding of Enlightenment rationalism with Tory loyalism that reform and reaction meet in anti-
Jacobin critique. The anti-Jacobin reviewers portray Jacobin
imposture as proceeding from "a System of Exaggeration and
Falsehood" (*A-J* 26 May 1798: 37). The corollary of this is the
erection of their own critical method into a system founded in opposition to system, a kind of conservative dissent directed to the
exposure and correction of "this complicated baseness, this cool,
deliberate, systematic fabrication of Jacobinical falsehood and
malignity," as one anti-Jacobin critic puts it (*A-J* 11 June 1798:
333). Yet what is likely an irreconcilable contradiction between
the negative and positive aspects of anti-Jacobinism—critique
and loyalty, respectively—renders this system as vulnerable to
critique as, it asserts, is that of its opponents. In an essay on "The
Rise, Progress, Operations, and Effects of Jacobinism in these
Realms," the *Anti-Jacobin Review and Magazine* speculates that
many Jacobin votaries have "have been deluded and duped to
embrace opinions without examining their grounds." Once
prompted "to retrace in their recollection the series of arts employed to render them proselytes," however, they will see their
error (*AJR* July 1798: 109–10). This imputes an irrationalist
basis to Jacobin doctrine, or, more precisely, imputes to it methods of inculcating assumptions, in Canning's words, "either by argument or (what is more in the charitable spirit of modern
reformers) by force, to convert us to a different opinion" (*A-J* 1:7).
Against such coercive methods anti-Jacobins claim to employ
truth and logic. An installment of "The Reviewers Reviewed"
thus confidently asserts that "Reason and argument are the
proper weapons to be employed in repelling all attacks of a literary nature; and, as the *means* of employing them with effect are
now supplied, we trust no other will ever be had recourse to"
(*AJR* Sept. 1798: 351). These are brave words, but they are
hardly credible when elsewhere radical publishers prosecuted by
the government are compared to "receivers of stolen goods." The
article in which this ominous analogy occurs, a "Reviewers Reviewed" piece on a *Critical Review* analysis of "Kingsbury's *Reply
to the Bishop of Landaff's Address*," concludes its argument by
inviting the attorney general to investigate the *Critical Review*
(*AJR* July 1798: 79). Less heavy-handed, perhaps, but no less
provocative in its insidious rhetoric is Canning's *Anti-Jacobin*

"Prospectus" with its pledge to confute Jacobin falsehoods, "which may be found in the Papers devoted to the cause of SEDITION and IRRELIGION, to the pay or principles of FRANCE" (*A-J* 1:7). A glance at the words in uppercase print is sufficient to make argument unnecessary.

The stakes in these critical engagements might involve nothing less than treason, however ill-founded the charges. Noting the outcry among radicals against government prosecution of a pamphlet entitled *Wakefield's Reply to the Bishop of Landaff's Address,* an *Anti-Jacobin* reviewer charges that reform writers, "by a kind of *rhetorical perversion*, to which they have frequent recourse, have represented *persecution* and *prosecution* as synonymous terms." Yet even this *"rhetorical perversion"* had an object beyond the obvious one of defending the publisher of Wakefield's tract, a Mr. Cuthell. Also charged with the selling of this tract was none other than the publisher of the *Analytical Review*, Joseph Johnson, whose plight the *Anti-Jacobin* reviewer suggests is more dear to his hireling writers than that of Mr. Cuthell: "It is by his *orders* to men who he *pays* for scribbling in his miserable Review, that every writer who exposes the *defects*, as they are *delicately* termed, of Mr. Wakefield's pamphlet, is abused in the most scurrilous and indiscriminate manner." Charging that their "affectation of liberality" is therefore a sham, the *Anti-Jacobin* reviewer urges Johnson's editorial staff "to throw off a mask which will no longer conceal their object, and boldly, *if they dare*, pronounce an eulogy on the *loyalty* of this favourite publisher and friend of the PRIESTLEYS, the DARWINS, the GODWINS, and other *unprejudiced* authors, who have kindly taken upon themselves, for the last twenty years, the important task of *enlightening* the public mind" (*AJR* July 1798: 79, 84–85) The unfortunate Cuthell notwithstanding, the reviewer here is concerned solely with impressing on his readers the *Analytical Review*'s association with a notorious bookseller and his stable of radical authors. In this inflammatory context, it is enough merely to allude to *"enlightening* the public mind" to provoke loyal readers. The same strategy is at work elsewhere in "Detection of the Monthly Magazine," which in fact goes no further than where the name of Johnson ("the *enlightened* friend of the Priestleys, the Darwins, and the Godwins") appears on the *Monthly's* title page along with that of—a

Frenchman: "We now have adduced a sufficient body of *presumptive* evidence, to induce a grant jury of honest, upright, well-affected men, to find a bill against the *Monthly Magazine*; and we shall, hereafter, bring forward such positive and direct testimony, as will—even should the grand advocate of sedition himself be employed in its defence—ensure its final conviction, by a jury composed of a similar description of persons" (*AJR* Aug. 1798: 198, 201).

It was just such threats passing as critical comment that prompted Hazlitt to call William Gifford "the invisible link, that connects literature with the police" (*CWH* 9:13). Gifford was by this time editor of the *Quarterly Review*, but Hazlitt might also be thinking here of Gifford's former editorship of the original *Anti-Jacobin, or Weekly Examiner*, where under the categories of "LIES," "MISREPRESENTATIONS," and "MISTAKES" reform rhetoric was vigilantly monitored. Certainly, there is no mistaking the underlying threat of the following notice, under the heading of "MISREPRESENTATIONS," of a paragraph in the *Morning Chronicle* critical of the Chancellor of the Exchequer. "It would be difficult to assert more audaciously what is wholly untrue," it asserts, "—to distort more perversely an evident meaning—or to insinuate more mischievously, opinions which, in the present spirit of the Country, it might not be *prudent* distinctly to avow" (*A-J* 20 Nov. 1797: 20). Passages like this manage to subject rhetorical fallacy to the scrutiny of rational analysis—in effect, seeking to enlighten via reason—while at the same time resorting to insinuated threats carrying the brutally regressive force of reaction, a contradiction anti-Jacobin critique often detects in the shows of "liberality" and "candor" affected by literary Jacobins. In the latter connection, an article on "Finance" in the *Anti-Jacobin* criticizes the hypocrisy of reform press attacks on an English war tax, particularly in attempts to link such taxes with harsh monetary measures effected by France's revolutionary government. Having, or so the *Anti-Jacobin* writer asserts, no substantial criticisms to make of the English measure, radical writers must resort to rhetorical misconstruction: "Accordingly, the Jacobin Press now echoes the opprobrious epithets of '*Jacobin,*' '*French,*' and '*Revolutionary.*' The measure is to be spoken of only by the term '*Requisition*'; and if they can fix this word upon it, they hope the bare mention of it will excite all the horror which (*in spite of all their efforts to the contrary*) deservedly attended it, in the way in which it was applied in *France.*" This is a remarkable instance of having it both ways by accusing one's opponent of having it both ways. The *Anti-Jacobin* reviewer nicely exposes a cunning sophism whereby Jacobinism is promoted "under the pretence of censuring and attacking it," and does so, moreover, under the banner of rational critique: "But can they really flatter themselves that the bare sound of the word will be sufficient for the purpose, without any examination of the thing to which it was intended to be applied?" (*A-J* 30 Nov. 1797: 89–91). Yet the critical act of detecting a Jacobin strategy behind a loyalist veil is directed to reappropriating this strategy in order to elicit from loyal readers just such a visceral response to the sound of a word. When the *Anti-Jacobin* wryly observed that "Jacobinism shines by its own light," it was merely participating in the game of rhetorical appropriation and counterappropriation Hazlitt traced to Burke's critical subversions of revolution. If light there was, surely no one could reliably trace it to either side of the question, so refracted was it by the dense medium of rhetorical fallacy.

A notable feature of anti-Jacobin reviewing is its knowing attention to details of critical method—often to the point of unintended irony. The following passage, taken from a "Reviewers Reviewed" item in the *Anti-Jacobin Review and Magazine*, is exemplary in this respect:

> According to the specimen here given, they select a passage which is the most susceptible of misinterpretation—they quote that part of it which is most capable of being misunderstood—they then with confidence put a false construction upon the mutilated extract, and, the better to gain credit for that construction, they accompany it with some truism, which nobody can possibly dispute, and bestow some unimportant praise, to assume an appearance of candour. Upon the strength of this triumph, so surreptitiously obtained, they pronounce a general sentence of condemnation, and they succeed but too often in exciting so strong a prejudice in the mind of the reader, as to prevent him from examining the work itself, in order to form his own judgment upon it. (*AJR* July 1798: 71)

William Gerard Hamilton himself could not have more nicely expounded the fallacies of omission and misconstruction than they are inferred here. Viewed in isolation, indeed, this explanation of reviewing practice seems as knowingly pragmatic as any counsel offered in *Parliamentary Logic*. The techniques exposed here are calculated to bypass genuine critical analysis by creating the mere impression of critical analysis. Far from acting as a provisional check on rhetoric, criticism appears to have appropriated rhetoric's traditionally acclamatory role. To quote Campbell once again: "It is not ultimately the justness either of the thought or of the expression, which is the aim of the orator; but it is a certain effect to be produced in the hearers." Such reviewing methods, the *Anti-Jacobin* critic implies, exploit associations in readers' minds concerning critical analysis by rigorously analyzing passages selected for their susceptibility to misconstruction. The result is a closed system in which fallacy may confirm itself independent of genuine critical scrutiny. Readers are conditioned by this means to reject the whole on the basis of a fallacious reading of a part of the whole. The same readers, however, must also either accept or reject this reading of a reading on the basis of assertion and "the specimen here given." Thus questions raised by the reviewer may also raise doubts about his own review, premised as it is on what an *Anti-Jacobin* correspondent terms "Polemical Criticism, however just and acute" (*A-J* 16 Apr. 1798: 158). Under the heading of "MISREPRESENTATIONS," indeed, *The Anti-Jacobin* makes this candid reply to charges by the *Morning Post* that it edited a paragraph quoted from that journal: "We confess we dropt this sentence. It is so dull and wicked, so base and cowardly, so total a dereliction of every feeling that should animate an Englishman, and evinces so complete a devotement to the overbearing insolence of France, that we secretly applauded ourselves for having spared our Readers the disgusting perusal" (*A-J* 9 Apr. 1798: 125).

The very admission seems to imply that probity is beside the point, and in any case the point concerns not critical proofs but the continually repeated assertion of Jacobin imposture. A polemical strategy applying critique rhetorically depends for its success not on reflexive examination of its own practice but on reiterated charges brought against that of an opposing position. In the *Anti-Jacobin*'s final issue, then, calculating the number of

Jacobin falsehoods they have exposed, the editors boast that "the conviction on which We so confidently rely, is not the effect of a *solitary* impression on our Readers' minds, but of one four hundred and twenty times repeated (this being the fair amount of the number of Lies, &c. We have detected)—an agglomeration of impulse, which no prejudice could resist, and no pre-conceived partialities could weaken or remove" (*A-J* 9 July 1798: 622). Like its Jacobin foes—or those it imagines, and repeatedly refers to, as such—anti-Jacobin criticism merely repeats its arguments against selected critical abuses feature after feature, issue after issue, volume after volume. It is such a rhetorical strategy that has produced the "agglomeration of impulse" proudly pointed to in the final issue of the original *Anti-Jacobin*. This is not to dismiss the force of anti-Jacobin counterarguments, or to deny validity to their critique of reform's rhetorical impostures—only to remark a common method linking these opposed ideological positions. The truism that it takes one to know one is repeatedly illustrated by anti-Jacobin criticism as it knowingly lays bare the craft of periodical reviewing.

The role of satire in anti-Jacobin criticism is for this reason more problematic than it is in the verse parodies, though again the latter's cleverness may in fact cancel any corrective purpose it professes. This is at any rate what happens in the criticism, where critique often recedes into technique. Features like "LIES, MISREPRESENTATIONS, and MISTAKES" and "The Reviewers Reviewed" not only appropriate to satirize but satirize to appropriate. Under the veil of irony—something Bentham looked for in vain in *Parliamentary Logic*—anti-Jacobin critics expose in their Jacobin foes, but also apply against them, techniques of imposture more in keeping with rhetorical than critical practice. Assuming that criticism plays a reflexive role relative to other forms of rhetoric and that, within the contingent realm of rhetorical usage, it provisionally carries the normative authority of logic, irony can only tacitly subvert this authority. The metareviewing features regularly run in the anti-Jacobin journals constitute rhetorics in which parody and criticism effectively cancel each other out. While they uncover falsehood in Jacobin rhetoric, moreover, much as *Political Primer* and *Elements of Opposition* do with respect to Tory or Whig rhetoric, they also go some way toward formulating a system of rhetorical imposture capable of being applied on either side of a question. As in a work like *Parliamentary Logic*, the distinction between exposing and expounding rhetorical imposture becomes less and less relevant in light of simply describing its effective application. Again, Peacock's Mr. Sarcastic is the cautionary (or salutary?) instance of this blurring of theory, practice, and irony. Following his election to Parliament in *Melincourt*, any ethical purpose underlying Mr. Sarcastic's ironic displays of rhetorical imposture has receded amid his political success.

As in radical descendents like the *Black Dwarf*, critical features in anti-Jacobin journals regularly walked a fine line between critique and satire, earnest and jest. The result was often an exposure of tricks of the reviewing trade verging on the prescriptive self-parody that outraged Bentham in Hamilton. Much of *The Anti-Jacobin*'s "LIES, MISREPRESENTATIONS, and MISTAKES" feature is concerned, or at least purports to be concerned, with matters of fact—i.e., "These two paragraphs require no comment. They are 'direct falsehoods, and were known to be such by the Writer'" (*A-J* 27 Nov. 1797: 47)—or more subtle exposures of fallacy: "Very circumstantial! but a *Lie* nevertheless" (*A-J* 11 Dec. 1797: 156). At other times, critical comment takes the more equivocal, because ironic, form of advice. Under its "LIES" section in a 1799 number, for instance, *The Anti-Jacobin* ran a piece subtitled "*A new and approved Method of conveying Abuse, recommended to the Practice of all True Jacobins, by the Members of the lately affiliated Clubs at the Crown and Anchor.*" The following passage of quasi-counsel could have appeared in works like *The Political Primer* or even, in more concise form, *Parliamentary Logic*:

> Take any Gentleman (the more respectable the better) and charge him with what you and all the world know to be false; then revile him for it, as if it were true:—this done, retract your Lie as soon as possible; but instead of shewing any shame for it, or any sorrow for the insult you have heaped on an innocent person, be particularly careful to glory in the one, and add to the other, by sneeringly observing that you are pleased to see he is not quite as bad as you thought him. Thus, without any provocation, without any apparent cause, you may ingeniously gratify your spleen against every Friend of his King and Country, who

happens at the same time to be distinguished for talents, integrity, and virtue. (*A-J* 19 Feb. 1798: 502)

The reviewer then quotes a passage appearing in both the *Morning Post* and *Morning Chronicle* in which Lord Grenville has been abused in this manner. First the theory, then a practical demonstration: as Hamilton advises at the beginning of his book, "settle method first." Elsewhere, once again under "LIES," another trick (or method) is described wherein "When any one of them publishes a Lie more attrocious [*sic*] than usual, the next in course copies it, and boldly asserts it to be taken from a 'Ministerial Paper'" (*A-J* 25 Dec. 1797: 218). Yet another technique is inferred from certain habitual usages in Jacobin rhetoric: "Whenever the Jacobins have a falsehood in contemplation more atrocious than common, they generally preface it with the words—"*It is a fact.*"—We do not despair of seeing them soon exhibit their fabrications in the form of an *Affidavit*" (*A-J* 5 Feb. 1798: 435). A later article remarking this phrase even claims to have found it literally translated in French papers (*A-J* 12 Feb. 1798: 470). Thereafter, its every occurrence is noted until the very word "*fact*" in a Jacobin context becomes a byword for lie. A piece actually attacking the *Morning Post* for retracting a misstatement, indeed, advises that "A melancholy *Lie*, beginning "*It is a fact,*" is worth a thousand such sneaking recantations as these" (*A-J* 12 Feb. 1798: 470).

In *The Satirist; or, Monthly Meteor*, this strain of quasi-critical parody is developed in full-length features. "Hints to Newspaper-Editors," by the aptly named Crop the Conjuror, offers this rhetorical analysis of a press article: "first we have the cool paragraph—then the paragraph insinuant—next the paragraph declaratory—after this the paragraph inquisitive—then the paragraph adverse—and last of all, the *puff impartial!*" (*S* 1 Aug. 1809: 135). Another feature, "Elements of Politics," running to six parts through 1808–9, offers ironic advice much like that found in *Elements of Opposition* and *The Political Primer*, the elements in question being oratory and "LITERARY POLITICS." Some definitions given in the first installment include this one of "POPULARITY" as "that applause which is obtained by the *artful* from the mouths of the *artless*" (*S* 1 Nov. 1808: 391–92). Some of its axioms recall Hamilton, for while the putative intent is to satirize the actual advice follows practice so closely (pace Peacock's Mr. Sarcastic) that it seems plausible, if not admirable—an axiom, for instance, which advises that "Truth is not to be spoken at all times. This axiom is particularly useful, where *half* the truth will answer your purpose better than the *whole*" (*S* 1 Mar. 1809: 228). Similar advice in a later issue suggests that "The whole is greater than its part. *Ex. gr.* a mass of falsehood with a few truths scattered throughout it, will always overbalance any of the truths taken separately" (*S* 1 Mar. 1809: 353). It is in the *Satirist's* first issue, however, where it reviews *Advice to a young Reviewer, with a specimen of the Art*, that the fine line trod by this strain of irony shades into perfect indeterminacy. An extract quoted from the work under review indicates a satiric purpose wholly in keeping with the *Satirist's* own:

> Since much depends upon the rhythm and terseness of expression, both of which are sometimes destroyed by dropping a single word or transposing a phrase, I have known much advantage to arise from not quoting in the form of a literal extract, but giving a brief summary in *prose* of the contents of a *poetical* passage; and interlarding your own language with occasional phrases of the poem, marked with inverted commas. These and a thousand other little witty expedients, by which the arts of quizzing and banter flourish, practice will soon teach you. If it should be necessary to transcribe a dull passage, not very fertile in topics of humour and raillery, you may introduce it as a *favourable* specimen of the author's manner.

The reviewer praises *Advice to a young Reviewer* as an admirable parody of "the *cant trim* and trick of the critical trade," though he says he wondered whether its author might be Francis Jeffrey. While this is surely enough to damn the work, the reviewer has no need to be so heavy-handed. Even as he allows his professional appreciation to stand, despite the possible Whig connection, he points to a notice in the *Eclectic Review* claiming Jeffrey's *Edinburgh Review* to be none other than the satire's object. These circumstances, not only his attribution but a more damaging attribution by a liberal journal, make it all the easier to praise the work in question. The reviewer is even able to quote the *Eclectic* reviewer's own charges against the *Edinburgh*, to the effect that "Its peculiar qualifications are well known to consist in a complete sacrifice of feeling to wit, and of justice to malignity," without compromising his own seeming liberality as a reviewer. What finally amounts to a review of a review of an anatomy of reviewing, then, stands itself as a creditable specimen of the craft. The implications of this do not escape comment by the *Satirist* reviewer. "This is a tolerably smart *tirade,*" he says. "Reviews, we believe, have hitherto considered each other as inviolable characters; but if the system of mutual attack and abuse is introduced, who shall say to what length it may be carried?" (*S* 1 Dec. 1807: 313–14).

Who indeed? Priestley and Campbell advise that abuse, particularly ridicule, should be used with caution. Defining "ridicule" as a response to inconsistency, Priestley points out that if nothing elicited ridicule but inconsistencies with truth, then "it would bid fair to be the test of truth." The fact that ridicule is provoked by "analogies, contrasts, and comparisons" not inconsistent with truth, however, indicates that it is capable of making both truth and error appear contemptible and is thus ultimately "indeterminate" (*LOC* 214). Campbell notes that, while ridicule is better suited to refuting error than supporting truth, even then "it is not properly levelled at the false, but at the absurd in tenets." That absurdity is "a thing hardly confutable by mere argument" in Campbell's view suggests both that ridicule has its place in criticism and that it is no substitute for argument (*PR* 20–21). Like Burke, anti-Jacobin critics recognized that the subversive techniques of literary Jacobinism were treacherously double-edged, but were less cognizant of these dangers when they appropriated these instruments to their own uses. A letter to the editor of *The Satirist*, "On the Utility of Ridicule, When Applied as the Test of Truth" by one C. M. S. Cant, warns of rhetorical pitfalls in the satirico-critical methods of periodical reviewing, asserting that "no proper motive can recommend forbearance towards a literary felon." This tendency in modern letters he traces to the influence of Shaftesbury who, he claims, offered readers an "an easy and amusive criterion of Truth" less arduous than the exertions of ancient logic and philosophy. What in idle minds "will pass for incontrovertible argument," then, may in fact end up subverting the power of argument to demonstrate truth:

It is replete with folly, for it proposes to conquer difficulty without exertion: it is detestable, for that envenomed levity with which it assaults the most salutary principles. Its effects are indiscriminate, and therefore baneful; for reason suffers when a variety of subjects are tortured by being adapted to the same criterion. The scoffer takes a ready method to attain his purpose: for the most serious maxims can claim no security from ludicrous ideas. The mind is taken by surprise, the image is presented, and the smile excited, before the most attentive observer perceives the design.

The letter writer is careful to exempt Tory satirists from this category, even pronouncing it "the duty of THE BRITISH SATIRIST to assert the dignity of Literature, and protect the best interests of Society." Yet what he darkly terms "the tendency of *indiscriminate Ridicule*" must by definition inform even loyal satire. The danger posed by this tendency to society involves nothing less than regression to a natural state as "those happy effects which had reclaimed a community from savage licentiousness, are reversed by the sarcastic quibbles of men." (*S* 1 Aug. 1808: 13, 9–10, 13–14).

A pamphlet by Josiah Hard, entitled *Imposture Exposed in a Few Brief Remarks on the Irreligiousness, Profaneness, Indelicacy, Virulence, and Vulgarity of certain Persons, who style Themselves Anti-Jacobin Reviewers* (1801), goes further. Hard suggests that sharp ideological lines between Jacobin and anti-Jacobin in this reviewing war are only apparent, that techniques of critical subversion associated with the one carry the same dangers when employed by the other. Though written from an unequivocally conservative viewpoint, the pamphlet's argument deliberately takes the logic of anti-Jacobin appropriations of Jacobin critique to its necessary conclusion. It begins by underlining its own character as a critical exposure, rather in the vein of conspiracy tracts popular during the revolutionary decade such as Barruel's sensational *Memoirs* (1796–97), except that in this case the conspirators being exposed are Tories, or purport to be. "The Anti-Jacobin Reviewers, with that indiscretion which is often the fated concomitant and ban of artifice, have suffered the mask, on several occasions, to slip aside," he avers, "and thus betrayed the genuine features of their character. To point out some of these to the attention of the public, is the sole object of the present publication." These "features" are very like those of liberal writers targeted by anti-Jacobin criticism in that they include an indiscriminate irreverence, particularly in religious matters, attributable only to Jacobinical tendencies. The "real principles" of these seeming Tory loyalists, then—Hard dismisses them as "*soi-disant* Anti-Jacobin Reviewers"—emerge from the rhetorical methods they employ. While Hard himself professes an uncomplicated Church-and-King Toryism, his reading of anti-Jacobin criticism displays an acute understanding of the ways by which rhetorical imposture may circumvent rational argument even in criticism. Singling out a particular issue of the *Anti-Jacobin Review and Magazine*, he notes how "these Reviewers, under a pretense of reproving the author of a work, entitled 'Hierogamy,' for expressions *almost* indecent; introduce those expressions, in such a way, that, simply from the detached state in which they are unwarrantably placed, and the emphasis and point which are shamefully given to them by the Reviewer, they become not *almost*, but *altogether* indecent, and *grossly* so." Under the guise of moral reprobation, then, anti-Jacobin reviewers deliberately manipulate reader responses to sensational association. Elsewhere, however, Hard wonders how conscious these reviewers are of such insidious appropriations in their own rhetoric. With respect to their position on Sunday Recreations, he concludes that they have deluded themselves into believing they promote morality and religion rather than mischief. "But if it were otherwise; if they were *aware* of the mischievous tendency of the reasonings which they were labouring to establish, where shall we find words to express the *infamy* of their conduct!" he exclaims— adding, however, that "whether, in this transaction, it were ignorance or malice that influenced them, the effect is the same." It is this subversive effect, palliated by the "barren formality" of professions to the contrary, that leads Hard to accuse anti-Jacobin critics of "*declaring* that they are the *best* of Critics, and of *proving* that they are the worst."[8]

Yet this proof issues from an "effect," an impression. That this should be all that matters, finally, suggests how rhetorically charged was periodical reviewing during the revolutionary decade and the years following. If only the effect matters, and if the methods producing that effect are employed by anti-Jacobin and Jacobin alike, then what really distinguishes these positions? Hard claims that the two are effectively the same, going so far as to demand that anti-Jacobin journals "discard the term *Anti* from their title page, and from every other part of their Review, in which they have occasion to designate *themselves*."[9] Practicing what it preached against, anti-Jacobin criticism did not ultimately intensify the ideological divisions from which it emerged so much as blur them by opportunistically turning conviction to account. In 1809, noting the failure of attempts to revive the previous decade's Jacobin baiting, William Cobbett would observe of anti-Jacobin writers that "They have found anti-Jacobinism such a thriving trade, that they were loath to give it up" (*CPR* 25 March 1809: 425). When anti-Jacobins declared victory at the turn of the century, they mistook the assimilation of literary Jacobinism into the neutrality of a common method for its disappearance. They themselves had demonstrated, through their appropriation of reviewing practices they criticized, that ideology might itself be subordinated to method—thus demonstrably not, in Coleridge's words, "securing a purity in the principle without mischief from the practice." The result is the emergence of a kind of generic critical ethos in English periodical culture during the first decades of the nineteenth century in which, notwithstanding sharp party divisions, all participants are of a kind. In "Remarks on the Periodical Criticism of England," Lockhart's pseudonymous Von Lauerwinkel sketches a portrait of the general type:

> An English Reviewer is a smart, clever man of the world, or else a violent political zealot. He takes up a new book either to make a jest of it, and amuse his readers and himself at the expense of its author, or he makes use of the name of it merely as an excuse for writing what he thinks the author might have been better employed in doing, a dissertation, in *favour* of the minister, if the Review be the property of a Pittite, *against* him and all his measures, if it be the property of a Foxite bookseller.[10]

The distinction opening this passage is only apparent, for the roles of worldling and ideologue might be variously assumed by the same writer in the expedient medium of periodical reviewing. In any case, both worldling and ideologue can employ the same techniques to turn to account whatever works they criticize. The ideologue may even choose whether to manipulate his critique for or against ministry or opposition to meet the demands of exigent circumstance—much like the parliamentary Machiavel posited by Hamilton. To be sure, party lines continued to condition perceptions of particular journals and writers or groups of writers during the post-Revolutionary period. At the same time, the "barren formality" noted by Hard in anti-Jacobin reviewing argues that conviction itself might be formalized into a rhetorical stance. Where Regency periodical criticism is concerned, the method is the man.

Hazlitt's sense of what he calls "Literary Jacobinism" does not appear to develop the term beyond its provenance in Burkean critique. He applies it to a writer, Walter Savage Landor, known to hold radical political views. His definition of the term—"that despotism of the mind, which only emancipates itself from authority and prejudice, to grow impatient of every thing like an appearance of opposition, and to domineer over and dictate its sudden, crude, violent, and varying opinions, to the rest of the world"—seems faithful to Burke's analysis. Yet the coercive critical temper it describes as aptly characterizes anti-Jacobin criticism in the late 1790s and early 1800s. That Hazlitt held much the same views as Landor suggests that the issue for him was not political principle but something more pervasive, a "complexional disposition," to use Burke's phrase, characterizing the tenor and techniques of literary practice on both sides of a question. As Hazlitt elsewhere says of Robert Southey's various career as ultra-radical and ultra-Tory, "the one maintained second-hand paradoxes; the other repeats second-hand common-places" (*CWH* 7:169). Implicit in such offhand comments is the sense of an identity between Jacobin and anti-Jacobin sensibilities at odds with neo-Burkean Whig literary histories where Jacobin decadence is reversed by anti-Jacobin rigor. A *Blackwood's* article "On the Reciprocal Influence of Periodical Publications, and the Intellectual Progress of this Country" (1824) in fact argues that the salutary influence of the old reviews—it cites the example of the *Monthly Review* (a frequent target of "The Reviewers Reviewed" in the *Anti-Jacobin Review and Magazine*)—has sadly declined in the wake of modern reviewing practices. Instances given of the latter include the *Quarterly*, *Edinburgh*, and *Westminster Reviews*, all of differing political stripe but all, the writer asserts, following "nearly the same plan and object," and so exerting a uniformly harmful influence through "the talent in essay-writing which they display, and the severity in which they indulge."[11] No mention is made of the anti-Jacobin press per se, which was surely a dim memory by 1824 when this essay appeared. Yet the unsavory character of modern reviewing as it is described here, technical facility in the service of interested censure, was as much a hallmark of anti-Jacobin as it was of Jacobin periodical reviewing—indeed, anti-Jacobin critics claimed to be more adept, if more principled, practitioners of the reviewing craft than their Jacobin counterparts. The *Republican*'s tribute to Lord Castlereagh's reviewing skills seems to indicate that they were on a par on both counts.

What this suggests is that, politics aside, literary Jacobinism was about criticism appropriated to sensational rhetorical effect. *An Address to the Conductors of the Periodical Press* (1823), by one Abram Combe, indeed, argues that the chief source of religious and political controversy in the press are "the different ideas, which the various individuals attach to the same words, or terms." With its definitions and tables, Combe's pamphlet seems to be entirely in earnest, proceeding from the assumption that demonstrable truth must be "universally consistent." At the same time, his thesis that certain operative terms have a permanent general sense and a changeable local sense that may contradict the former carries a potential for irony occasionally realized in his examples. The general sense of a term like "Mental Liberty," for instance, is "The liberty of freely expressing all the thoughts, which in our conscience we believe to be true, (to those who are willing to hear them,) without any one bearing a grudge, at us upon account of them." The local sense, however, "The liberty of receiving the thoughts which are imperceptibly forced upon the mind, and of expressing those opinions, which are not in opposition to the religious or political sentiments of the community," seems unmistakably loaded. The question of Combe's intent aside, the instances of rhetorical imposture he presents emerge from the same medium of conditioned response and opportunistic calculation variously expounded and exposed in political rhetoric by Hamilton, Bentham, Hazlitt, et al. His definition of prejudice, similarly, that it conditions individuals "to listen attentively, to reiterated statements of all that ingenuity, or sophistry, can urge in favour of their preconceived ideas,"[12] lays bare the sensationalist machinery conditioning unthinking assent in periodical criticism.

Regency reviewing practice is represented in just such terms, in the period's commentary and fiction alike, as a system of calculated deception in which rhetorical effect methodically circumvents critical reception. Instances of pamphlets and essays attacking periodicals of every party disposition (but especially the Whiggish *Edinburgh Review*) for unscrupulous reviewing methods are endemic to the age and are surely the most tangible and salutary legacy of anti-Jacobin metacritique. While not exceptional in this respect, Thomas Love Peacock is a notable instance of how this critique might be put into the service of constructive, if often caustic, media commentary. In a review of "Moore's Letters and Journals of Lord Byron" appearing in the *Westminster Review*, Peacock refers to "the system which the Edinburgh Review adopted in its literary criticisms," singling out its treatment of Byron, first its harsh review of *Hours of Idleness* (1807), then its abrupt about-face in light of Byron's subsequent celebrity, charging that its critical practice—both the initial censure and, by implication, the subsequent praise—is "without principle." The latter half of Peacock's unfinished "Essay on Fashionable Literature" (1818), similarly, is devoted to an 1816 review of Coleridge's "Christabel" in the *Edinburgh*. Peacock exposes the methods employed by the *Edinburgh* reviewer, showing the article to consist of little more than variations on half a dozen standard jokes: "This ready cut and dried wit, thus stamped with eternal currency, is very convenient to a trading critic who has no wit of his own." If Peacock accuses the *Edinburgh* of reviewing without principle, moreover, he can also say here of its Tory rival, the *Quarter Review*, that it "contains more talent and less principle than it would be easy to believe coexistent."[13]

Portrayals of predatory Regency reviewing culture in Peacock's satiric fiction expose the same forms of critical expedience. *Melincourt* (1817) is Peacock's most unequivocally political novel, written from the liberal proreform perspective he shared with his friend Shelley. Yet the antecedents of its literary satire are anti-Jacobin in provenance. Isaac Disraeli's satiric novel *Vau-*

rien (1797) concerns the misadventures of Charles, a country clergyman's son who encounters in London venal literary Jacobins like Mr. Subtile and Mr. Acrid who disseminate their principles through the medium of modern letters. As Mr. Subtile points out, "Twenty years of authorship and criticship have taught me the principles of human nature and literary composition; how to interest the imagination, how to conduct the understanding, and how to variegate with the colouring gleams of a specious, a novel, a confounding ratiocination." But Charles, a young anti-Jacobin in the making, sees clearly enough for himself both the fallacy and the craft by which it is inculcated. "In this new system, the sensual and inflammatory passions are solaced and gorged," he notes; "man is flattered to be deceived; while his rational faculties are obscured by verbal misconstructions, rest on dangerous paradoxes, and wander wild in extravagant hypotheses."[14] Twenty years later, Peacock's *Melincourt* relates a set-piece story of one Desmond, a young idealistic (i.e., proreform) writer who enters the London literary world only to be disillusioned by the likes of Messrs. Vamp and Foolscape, "the paragraph-mongers of prostituted journals, the hireling compounders of party praise and censure." When he meets Mr. Vamp that gentleman is surrounded by the cut-up remains of books and pamphlets "together with a large pot of paste, and an enormous pair of scissors [*sic*]." Here is the apparatus of modern letters put to the service of special interest—this time Old Corruption, though indeed the particular end is less important than the versatility of the means. Ironically, Peacock himself takes a page from his satiric subject, the italicized passages put into Mr. Vamp's mouth—Old Corruption described as *"Persuasion in a tangible shape"* and *"notorious as the sun at noonday"*—being detachable catchphrases that serve satirist and satirized alike. As commentators have noted, Peacock's satiric texts are tissues of other texts from which selected phrases and passages have essentially been cut and pasted for satiric deployment. Chapter 39, for instance, set at the aptly named Mainchance Villa and populated by such figures as George Canning in the character of Mr. Anyside Antijack, is a virtual cento of quotations from the Tory *Quarterly Review*. In his very critique of what he elsewhere terms "a systematical cant in criticism," then, Peacock employs the same expedient techniques he detects in modern reviewing—

in the parodic service of satire, to be sure, but nevertheless exploiting the facility of the technique, if with a critical sense of its seductive facility as a technique. A few years earlier, he anatomized this attitude in a little-known verse satire entitled "Sir Proteus" where the title character first manifests himself as a how-to manual of rhetorical imposture:

> He first appeared a folio thick,
>   A glossary so stout,
> Of modern language politics,
> Where conscience was left out.[15]

Conscience (or its lack) aside, Peacock shared Hazlitt's misgivings about an age in which criticism was as ubiquitous, and promiscuous, as advertising copy. In an 1830 review of Thomas Jefferson's Memoirs in the *Westminster*, he cites Jefferson's conviction that "a complete suppression of the press could not more effectually deprive the nation of its benefits than was done by its abandoned prostitution to falsehood."[16] He himself goes further in the fragmentary "Essay on Fashionable Literature," positing something like a culture industry, to borrow an operative term from the Frankfurt School,[17] exercising in Regency letters "an influence widely diffused and mighty in its operation" (8:273). Peacock speaks here not of direct censorship but of "a degree of spurious liberty, a Whiggish moderation with which many will go hand in hand," a false consciousness insidiously limiting free enquiry.[18] It was just such "Whiggish moderation," a frequent epithet in anti-Whig polemics, that made the *Edinburgh Review* so dominant a presence in Regency reviewing culture. Along with the Tory *Quarterly Review*, it formed nothing less than an "oligarchy," according to Lockhart's Von Lauerwinkel who calls the editors of both journals "men of great talents" and "very bad Reviewers"[19]—by which he presumably means morally rather technically "bad." In his comments on Jeffrey's highly imitable reviewing style, indeed, he asserts that "It is a thousand pities that such a mind as his should have consented to wear an impress that can so easily be counterfeited," for so transparent is it "that the fault more frequently consists in what he omits to say, than in what he says" (678). Anti-Jacobin critics detested this insidious quality in the reformist press of the 1790s even more than rank sedition. The *Anti-Jacobin Review and Magazine* observes

of reform writers in 1799 that, "though not less desperate in their
end, they display more caution and prudence in their *means*.
Thus the difficulty of counteraction is enhanced, and the consequent necessity of increased vigilance and circumspection established" (*AJR* Mar. 1818: 672). Explaining such caution as a
consequence of the anti-Jacobin backlash, a "Reviewers Reviewed" notice of the *Monthly Review* on Godwin's *St. Leon* speculates that "Their experience has taught them the *precious*
method of damning with faint praise, those works which are calculated to oppose innovation; and it has also taught them, the no
less dexterous method of celebrating, with seeming censure, the
labours of new fangled philosophism" (*AJR* Nov. 1800:435). In
both cases, the "effect" is less a product of critique than of technique, the form of critical thought with the suggestive force of
rhetoric. Anti-Jacobin criticism exposes such methods of persuasion—methods insidiously directing themselves, as Coleridge
warns, to "the habit of receiving pleasure without any exertion of
thought"—even as it demonstrates by its own practice how they
may become pervasive habits of thought co-opting and conditioning even criticism itself. In an age of "newspapers and parliamentary speeches," criticism had become a means to wholly
rhetorical ends.

4

Systematic Opposition:
The Case of William Cobbett

> Had the world ever before produced so versatile,
> so abusive, and so self-contradictory a writer,
> Mr. Cobbett would have missed his principal
> distinction. As it is, he stands alone. The foul
> and indiscriminate cast of his virulence is not
> less decided than systematic, and may be
> imitated by the ingenious, but will never
> be rivalled by the most unprincipled.
> —Henry White,
> *Double Dealings of Cobbett* (1823)

During the revolutionary decade and the years following, opposition could take unexpected forms in English public life. The anti-Jacobin alarms of the late 1790s saw a ministerialist press opposing opposition in the subversive terms of rational reform. At the same time, it defended a war against revolutionary France, putatively on behalf of continental monarchy, in the language of English loyalty. Twenty years later, during the Caroline Affair, reformers attacked ministerialists, putatively on behalf of their queen, using this same language, the very language employed against them by ministerialist foes during the wars. Hazlitt's characterization of such appropriations—"There was the cant of loyalty, the cant of gallantry, and the cant of freedom mixed together in delightful and inextricable confusion"—imputes to these respective rhetorics, and to those who opportunistically turned them to account, a certain ethical autonomy. In each case, opposition or rather the form of opposition emerged not so much as a moral choice as a tactical option, its easy assimilation by reaction and reform alike suggesting a rhetorical capitulation of principle to contingency. A participant in these and other controversies, William Cobbett remarked in his *Weekly Political Register* that "Amongst all the symptoms of mortality, which corruption has exhibited of late years, there is none more strong than the *imposture*, to which it is constantly resorting" (*CPR* 3 Aug. 1811: 144).

In 1811, when he made this observation, Cobbett was a reformer. He was by now capable even of giving the French their due, if only because he had become used to being called a Jacobin himself. By this time, he would not have accused reformers of imposture, though he did so in the *Political Register*'s early years when he wrote as an independent member of the anti-Jacobin press. While Cobbett's Toryism is commonly factored into his radicalism, it is all too easy now to overlook his early, if never wholly comfortable, career as a ministerialist writer. The fact remains that while *Cobbett's Weekly Political Register* became known for its loud campaign against Old Corruption, it was founded in 1802, if not wholly as a ministerialist organ, then certainly as a loyalist one. Some time in the mid 1810s, however—commentators point to 1804 when he first became aware of the extent and depth of agricultural distresses in England[1]—Cobbett began to question what he would come to identify as "the System," though the radicalization of his thinking was more gradual. Virulent attacks on him in ministerialist quarters, then, and in the radical press even when he was a confirmed proponent of reform—notably by Carlile's *Republican*—stem from this alleged political apostasy. Cobbett often made the case for his seemingly abrupt conversion by claiming that it was not he but those around him who had changed. At other times, he portrayed it as the result of having had his eyes opened to the true nature of erstwhile ministerialist allies, Pitt chief among them. In either case, it would be fair to say that circumstances played a role. A reputation as a staunch British loyalist preceded Cobbett on his return to England from America in 1800 where he had enjoyed fame (and infamy) writing under the pseudonym of Peter Porcupine, his Toryism exacerbated by the Gallic republicanism of Jefferson's America. Back in England, his antirepublicanism seemed to translate easily into the prevailing anti-Jacobin mood. He is thought to have dined with Canning, Frere, and even Pitt, so high was his stock in government circles during this period. He was soon offered the editorship of a government paper, the *True Briton*, which he refused—partly out of a genuine native independence, but also because he knew that the impression of independence would lend him more credibility.[2] To the latter end, he began publishing *The Porcupine* in 1800, but that paper's virulently anti-Jacobin, pro-war sentiments attracted so few readers in war-weary Britain that he soon sold it.[3] Before long his loyalism began to acidify. While temperamentally a Tory, he was no ministerialist. With the Peace of Amiens in 1801, the year before he established the *Political Register*, he found himself among a small number of Tory anti-Jacobins opposing peace with France. As the organ of this "New Opposition," as it was called, effectively composed of proponents of Pitt's old war policy (no longer supported even by Pitt himself), the *Register* helped to represent Tory opposition to a Tory administration (now headed by Addington) even as it simultaneously conducted an anti-Jacobin campaign against the friends of Reform. Thereafter, Cobbett alternately drifted away from and abruptly broke with ministerialist connections in the face of successive circumstances.

Cobbett no doubt possessed a reactive and even somewhat antagonistic character. In his essay on "The Character of Cobbett," William Hazlitt asserts that "His principle is repulsion, his nature contradiction: he is made up of mere antipathies" (*CWH* 8:55). Hazlitt's portraits are often overdrawn but never caricatured. The oppositionist temper he isolates in Cobbett, moreover, is shared by others profiled in *The Spirit of the Age* (1825), where this essay was reprinted. Lord Byron, for instance, appeals to his admirers through his apparent disdain for them in Hazlitt's analysis; he "exists not by sympathy, but by antipathy" (*CWH* 11:74, 69). The Reverend Edward Irving, who enjoyed a brief celebrity in the 1820s as a fashionable London preacher, makes a similar appeal to the public by condemning its "favourite idols," its politicians, its writers, its actors, and its philosophers. He has, Hazlitt concludes, "found out the secret of attracting by repelling" (*CWH* 11:41). Thus it is that Cobbett, famously described here as a "*fourth estate*" in his own right (*CWH* 11:50), should display a temperament "at ease in systematic opposition":

> When he is in England, he does nothing but abuse the Borough-mongers, and laugh at the whole system: when he is in America, he grows impatient of freedom and a republic. If he had staid there a little longer, he would have become a loyal and a loving subject of his Majesty King George IV. He lampooned the French Revolution when it was hailed as the dawn of liberty by millions: by the time it was brought into almost universal ill-odour by some means or other (partly no doubt by himself) he had turned, with one or two or three others, staunch Buonapartist. He is always of the militant, not of the triumphant party: so far he bears a gallant shew of magnanimity; but his gallantry is hardly of the right stamp. (*CWH* 8:54–55)

"Character of Cobbett" was originally published in *Table-Talk* (1821) hard on the heels of the queen's trial, in which Cobbett figured prominently. Hazlitt's characterization of him as "gallant" likely refers to his Burkean defense of Caroline's honor throughout the controversy. That this gallantry—Hazlitt calls it "the cant of gallantry" in his remarks on the Caroline Affair—is somehow of the wrong "stamp" would seem, at least in this respect, to cast Cobbett in the same light as others of Caroline's defenders, the gallant George Canning among them. Hazlitt regarded both factions, ministerialists and radicals alike, as opportunists in this affair, Cobbett no less than the rest. His sense of what motivated Cobbett to represent himself so variously in such circumstances, however, was more complicated.

Himself a staunch Bonapartist, even after Waterloo, Hazlitt likely saw some of his own tendencies in Cobbett's contrarian attitude. He clearly admired the forthright, cudgeling prose in which Cobbett criticized imposture. He also acknowledged the substantial nature of his commentary, citing Lord Thurlow's claim that Cobbett was the only writer deserving the name of "a political reasoner" (*CWH* 8:52 n). It is to these abilities that he credited Cobbett's wide readership, the ability to base his polemics on "the common grounds of fact and argument to which all appeal." "The Reformers read him when he was a Tory," Hazlitt notes, "and the Tories read him now that he is a Reformer" (*CWH* 8:52). That the popularity of the original *Anti-Jacobin* crossed these same lines during its short run, however, suggests that Cobbett's appeal was at least as timely as it was timeless— and more consistently so than that of anti-Jacobin writers who, with exceptions like Canning, could not tell when a good thing became too much of a good thing. Once these erstwhile allies began to abuse him as a Jacobin, Cobbett could take satisfaction in the certain and shrewd knowledge that their polemical strategies had become dated. Cobbett's ability to keep moving forward (or backward when circumstances warrant) is for Hazlitt his weakness and his strength as a polemicist. In comparing him with Tom Paine, then, Hazlitt argues that Cobbett "is more desultory and various, and appears less to be driving at a previous conclusion than urged on by the force of present conviction" (*CWH* 8:52). The result is a highly circumstantial, topical commentary that does not scruple to employ rhetorical commonplaces—Hazlitt finds Cobbett too fond of repeating phrases like "*the Sons and Daughters of Corruption*" (*CWH* 8:51)—or to reverse itself seemingly from one moment to the next. Hazlitt attributes the latter tendency not to conscious trimming but to a habit of writing to the moment, so that "the last opinion is the only true one," pointedly contrasting this to Paine's writing from theory (*CWH* 8:56). If the latter speaks to "first principles," Cobbett is concerned almost wholly with "local circumstances," and the force of his rhetoric is never confined by preconceived ideas. This apparent absence of "fixed or leading principles" makes for less dogmatic writing according to Hazlitt who at times tends to discount Cobbett's obsessive, iterative qualities as a writer, likening each new issue of the *Political Register* to "a kind of new Prospectus" (*CWH* 8:57). It is surely such qualities that make Cobbett's polemics, especially when read over any length of time in the *Register*, highly predictable in overall tendency if not in the striking turns they take on the level of rhetorical and argumentative detail. Yet the absence of "leading principles" points to a more troubling inability to argue, with any consistency, *for* rather than *against* a question.

For all his Englishness, Hazlitt's Cobbett embodies the ungoverned critical impulse that so dismayed Burke, the destructive energies with which it threatened to lay waste to everything before it. As Hazlitt notes in his preface to *Political Essays*, rational reform is vulnerable not only to external criticism but to its own critique which, turned upon itself, splits the reform position "into a thousand fractions" (*CWH* 7:16). Hazlitt's Cobbett reflects in his critical engagements with friends and foes alike this bent for indiscriminate destruction, for "He must pull down and pull in pieces: it is not his disposition to do otherwise" (*CWH* 8:55). Reference made by Hazlitt to "the force of present conviction" in Cobbett's writings, then, is clearly a caveat, suggesting, if not expedience, then something very like it in its subjection to opportunity. "However his own reputation or the cause may suffer in consequence," Hazlitt observes, "he cares not one pin about that, so that he disables all who oppose, or who pretend to help him" (*CWH* 8:54). Cobbett's motives aside—Hazlitt never questions his sincerity—his attitude is not so different in effect from Hamilton's seeming indifference to considerations of party or principle, the tendency to look "rather to the *object* of each motion, than to the question itself." Even rhetorically inept performers may achieve similarly dubious results—a speaker like James Mackintosh, for instance, who from the best intentions sacrifices party interest to logic, employing "his knowledge indiscriminately, whether it makes for or against him, with deliberate impartiality and scrupulous exactness." What this suggests is that "the difference between the efficient and the inefficient," to use Hazlitt's formulation, is not merely talent but talent employed strategically. If Cobbett is neither inept nor mercenary, the indiscriminate nature of his opposition suggests that he "wants principle," a quality credited by Hazlitt to sheer self-will:

> I might say that Mr. Cobbett is a very honest man with a total want of principle, and I might explain the paradox thus. I mean that he is, I think, in downright earnest in what he says, in the part he takes at the time; but in taking that part, he is led entirely by headstrong obstinacy, caprice, novelty, pique or personal motive of some sort, and not by a stedfast regard to truth, or habitual anxiety for what is right uppermost in his mind. He is not a feed, time-serving, shuffling advocate (no man could write as he does who did not believe himself sincere)—but his understanding is the dupe and slave of his momentary, violent, and irritable humours. He does not adopt an opinion 'deliberately or for money;' yet his conscience is at the mercy of the first provocation he receives, of the first whim he takes in his head; he sees things through the medium of heat and passion, not with reference to any general principles, and his whole system of thinking is deranged by the first object that strikes his fancy or sours his temper. (*CWH* 8:55–56)

Honest as Cobbett may be, however, his contrarian bent makes him as treacherous in practice as the most machiavellian of politicians. Such perverse egoism seems at odds with the deliberative expedience counseled by Hamilton, but Cobbett's success must necessarily be of the limited tactical sort guaranteed by *Parliamentary Logic* with its austere discipline of contingency. For this reason, Hazlitt concludes that "It is a hollow thing" (*CWH* 8:58).

This is Hazlitt's estimate, to be sure, and it reflects his own sense of the pitfalls of the reform position generally. In some respects, his Cobbett is the Reformers' Cobbett, a volatile and uncertain ally at best, as worst a sudden enemy, though Hazlitt is more sympathetic than the *Republican*'s Carlile. At the same time, this Cobbett is remarkably similar in many respects to the Whigs' Cobbett and the Tories' Cobbett. After his initial anti-Jacobin honeymoon in the early 1800s, Cobbett was a marked man in ministerialist quarters because of his unreliability as an ally. In 1808, *The Satirist; or, Monthly Meteor* ran a series entitled "Strictures on Cobbett" in which Cobbett's reputation for John Bullish independence is explained away as a clever rhetorical construction:

> His versatility permits him to direct the popular opinion without resisting it; and to adopt such principles and select such patrons as may be most conducive to his temporary convenience, and his impudence enables him to hazard the most evident absurdities with all the assurance of conviction, to dazzle the eye and delude the understanding of the multitude by the magnitude of his professions, and the assumed independence of his character, and to support the most glaring mistatement of facts, and the best refuted errors of opinion with a confidence that is easily mistaken by his admirers for the "determined inflexibility of conscious rectitude." (*S* 1 Sept. 1808: 127)

There is a certain irony in subjecting a former ally to the same critical scrutiny he was to have applied to Jacobin imposture. The first article in the series, indeed, promises that "it will be our duty to trace him through all the mazes of political craftiness. If he pervert our meaning, we shall correct his misstatements; if he be guilty of voluntary falsehood, we shall display him *in terrorem* to his brethren of the Independent Whig and their coadjutors, as the prince of political *story-tellers*" (*S* 1 Sept. 1808: 128). Subsequent installments of the series quote the former opinions of Cobbett the Tory against his current proreform opinions. In 1809, indeed, a pamphlet entitled *Elements of Reform* was published containing antireform, proministerialist passages culled from *Peter Porcupine* and the early years of the *Register*.[4] From the Whig corner, *On the Double Dealings of Mr. Cobbett* (1823) by Henry White makes similar charges. White's Cobbett is "versatile," "abusive," and "self-contradictory." "A selfish despotism the predominant feature of his character, the subject he discusses is immaterial, in regard of the display of his own nature," charges White.[5]

Cobbett could, and did, argue for the consistency of his opinions, whatever might be said about his reliability as an ally. Yet there is also consistency in the charges brought against him by all and sundry, though attributions of motive differ. From a rhetorical perspective, actual motive is less important than apparent motive as inferred from effect, "a certain effect to be produced in the hearers" in Campbell's straitened definition of rhetoric. To concede to any proposition made by Cobbett "the force of present conviction" is to place emphasis on "force," which is to say rhetorical effect. As various, even contradictory, as Cobbett's views might be from one utterance to the next, the force of their expression remains constant. The Cobbett attacked by writers of every political stripe over his nearly forty years in public life may thus be, as Leonora Nattrass has recently argued, wholly a creature of rhetorical design. Nattrass rejects estimates of Cobbett as a talented if unsophisticated writer in order to rehabilitate him as a skilled participant in the age's polemical engagements. Cobbett's perceived weaknesses, then, the bluster, the inconsistency, the self-aggrandizement, "can be reread as transgressive and politically enabling rhetorical tools which are often the real interest and strength of his work." This rhetorical Cobbett inhabits the Bakhtinian Romantic public sphere, with its plurality of sociopolitical idioms, variously described by Jon Klancher and Olivia Smith, among others. According to Nattrass, Cobbett exploits these idioms, radical and reactionary, crude and refined, as part of a deliberate strategy directed to addressing a number of different audiences. The matter of Cobbett's "double dealings," as White terms it in his pamphlet, is thus subsumed by the exuberant subversiveness with which his writings manipulate opposing views. "Cobbett," Nattrass states, "pits one discourse against another, brings oppositions into unexpected congruities, and addresses normally polarized audiences within a single text, in order to *subvert* as well as to resist encroaching social polarization and to oppose the devaluing of the working class."[6] But how does this performative Cobbett bridge the gap between the play of rhetoric and the work of representing a particular interest? The qualities Nattrass isolates in Cobbett might also be found, in different proportions perhaps but still of a kind, in George Canning who, while he assuredly appealed to many forms of opinion—too many, in Lady Holland's estimate—might not be committed to any of them in his Machiavellian pursuit of present advantage. Recent appreciations of imposture in reform polemics naturally tend to assume (if only tacitly) some ulterior conviction redeeming the imposture, even if this assumption is implicit only in the choice of subject—after all, why Cobbett and not Canning? The end must justify the means in such cases.

Yet a means, even such discreditable means as William Gerard Hamilton describes in *Parliamentary Logic*, may become a salutary end in itself. Notwithstanding his protestations, Bentham draws a cautionary value from Hamilton's cynical candor, enabling as it does the fully realized inference of systematic imposture that is the *Book of Fallacies*. As this chapter will show, Cobbett could adapt methods of rhetorical imposture learned and employed while writing for the ministerialist press to the purposes of Reform. More important, he could instruct his readers in the arts of imposture at the same time, not with the object of teaching them to employ imposture themselves but of teaching them to see it for what it is when it opposes their interests. Even Hamilton advises his Machiavellian acolytes to employ fallacies with eyes open and to recognize its use by others. Much of what Cobbett's contemporaries said about him was probably true to some degree, just as the rhetorical virtuosity with which he is credited by Nattrass and others seems very plausible. This chapter will suggest that the real accomplishment of Cobbett's role in the public life of his time, however, lay in his ability to turn a seeming capitulation to the rhetorical spirit of the age—sophistical and suspect—into a systematic critique of that spirit. His positive convictions were in this respect less important than his critical exposure of the methods by which special interests—with whom he in fact had these methods in common—attacked these convictions. As Hazlitt knew, means and ends ultimately resolve themselves in character. It is surely possible to credit Cobbett's virtue and *virtù* alike, while examining how "the force of present conviction" in his rhetorical practice reflects both a cultural ethos and an examined disposition. The case of Cobbett demonstrates that principle cannot be isolated from the mischief of practice if it is to have any relevance at all in the perennially contingent circumstances of public life.

The purpose of the anti-Jacobin press, of which *Cobbett's Weekly Political Register* was to have been an essential part, was to fight a war of opinion. Principles codified in the constitution of Revolutionary France had been quickly transformed into slogans which, in Hazlitt's words, were "rife in the year 1793, were noised abroad then, were spoken on the house-tops, were whispered in secret, were published in quarto and duodecimo, in political treatises, in plays, poems, songs, and romances" (*CWH* 7:99). In the *Reflections*, Burke warned of the international nature of the revolutionary propaganda machine, saying of the French Jacobins that "They have societies to cabal and correspond at home and abroad for the propagation of their tenets" (*RRF* 202–3). Later that decade, in *Letters on a Regicide Peace*, he warned of an anarchic philosophy spread beyond the borders of France by "a kind of electrick communication every where" (*RP* 9:291–92). The English government's marshalling of public opinion in the war against Revolutionary France was therefore as much directed at revolutionary principles at home as at revolutionary incursions from abroad. In 1793 the English government sent a memorandum to its armies' commanders charging France with threatening "the fundamental principles by which mankind is united in the bond of civil society." Accused in Parliament of using force not merely to resist French conquest but to drive France back to her old opinions, Pitt replied: "We are not at war against the opinions of the closet, nor the speculations of the school. We are at war with armed opinion; we are at war with those opinions which the thought of audacious, unprincipled and impious innovations seeks to propagate amidst the ruins of empires, the demolition of altars of all religion, the destruction of every venerable, and good, and liberal institution, under whatever forms of policy they have been raised."[7]

No one understood the stakes involved in the rhetorical war against France better than William Cobbett, whether as a Tory or a Reformer. In a foreword to the *Political Register*'s first number, he took the loyalist line of the anti-Jacobin press, pledging his journal "to the preserving of those ancient and holy institutions, those unsophisticated morals and natural manners, that well-tempered love of regulated liberty, and that just sense of public honour, on the preservation of which our national happiness and independence so essentially depend" (*CPR* 16 Jan. 1802: 2). Over the next few years, then, when not celebrating the executions of alleged traitors, he was vilifying the "wretched traitor and apostate" Paine or opposing peace with France (*CPR* 26 Feb. 1803: 286; 8 Jan. 1803: 3; 23 Oct. 1802: 498). Alongside the Tory polemics, however, was a critique of imposture that would serve him even when he had shifted his loyalty to the reform cause. Like Pitt's, his critical assumptions were neo-Burkean. Explaining the rationale for his short-lived *Le Mercure Anglois de Cobbett*, for instance, a French-language version of the *Register*, he draws on Burke's rhetorical analysis of the French Revolution, arguing that its projectors owe their success "to the *force of opinion* operating in favour of their views" (12 Feb. 1803: 161). In the 1803 article in which he makes this analysis, "To Foreigners," Cobbett characterizes the press in revolutionary France as an instrument ("keener than her sword, more to be dreaded than her million of soldiers") with an influence wide enough to threaten not only the property and liberty but even the souls of those whom it captures (12 Feb. 1803: 162). Like Pitt, he portrays the French menace as a dangerous argument, either reasonable or seductive or frightening in its appeal but wholly fallacious in premise:

> In the making of these destructive impressions, she is aided, first, by the fear which men entertain of her power; for whoever speaks to a trembling audience, is sure to be heard with attention. Secondly, she has at her command a language almost universal. Thirdly, from one cause or another, she has, for the *propagation of falsehood*, the press of the whole world, while at

the same time, she possesses the power of *suppressing truth* in
every part of the world, England and Anglo-America excepted.
(12 Feb. 1803: 163–64)

Pitt spoke of "armed opinion" but evoked the very tangible possibility of literal invasion, whereas Cobbett is concerned solely
with a rhetorical threat, the provoking of "destructive impressions" through fears associated with Revolutionary France. The
Mercure Anglois would effectively counter this radical Enlightenment program in the very language and arguments of Enlightenment. What Cobbett fails to acknowledge in these early
writings is the role played by anti-Jacobin alarmism in helping
to prepare a "trembling audience" in England, though he recalled
this later. In 1823, by contrast, he would survey the elaborate
system of fortifications and tunnels built into the cliffs of Dover
("this very anti-jacobin hill") and conclude that it was conceived
to "to prevent the landing, not of Frenchmen, but of French principles."[8] In 1803 he was a part of this rhetorical campaign, dedicated only to resisting Jacobin imposture. The program he
proposes here, however, directed as it is to "exciting an efficient
resistance in others" (12 Feb. 1803: 164), sounds more sensation-
alistic than otherwise.

Even when Cobbett writes as a reformer, his polemics reflect
the mix of rhetorical persuasion and critical analysis characterizing anti-Jacobin reviewing. This is one regard at least in which
his brief (and skittish) ministerialist stint left its imprint on him.
The metacritical dimension of his commentaries on press techniques is also a legacy of his anti-Jacobin past. Just as Tory upstarts like Canning employed radical critical techniques to
subvert the reform press, so Cobbett would put techniques developed as an anti-Jacobin into the service of the antiministerialist
press. In 1804 he denied that he was engaged in "systematic opposition" to the ministry,[9] but there is no doubt that when he
turned against Pitt he turned against him utterly. The following
year, in an open letter "To the Public," he speaks of the *Register's*
"steady opposition to the present ministry of Mr. Pitt," though to
former Pittite allies Cobbett might not have seemed at all steady
where party was concerned. Even a sympathetic, if wary, observer like Hazlitt saw him as a gifted polemicist driven by contingency. Hazlitt would have been bemused but not surprised

that Cobbett's defense of his apparent reversal should turn on rhetoric. Responding in 1804 to an assertion of Pitt's that he, Cobbett, had once said that Pitt alone could save England, Cobbett denies not the words attributed to him but the construction placed on those words:

> This interpretation I deny. But allowing that this was the sense of the words used, I would observe: . . . That the same words have different forces and almost different meanings according to the purposes for which they are used; that you must not always understand language precisely as you find it explained in a dictionary, but as it is used in common life for the purpose of expressing the idea which is wished to be expressed; that though, in interpreting a statute, or a piece of argument, every word is to be taken in its strictest and literal sense, yet that greater latitude is allowed to other compositions; such, as in the familiar intercourse by letter, in conversation, &c. but most of all is latitude allowed in congratulatory or *complimentary* addresses. (*CPR* 14 July 1804: 33)

Two years later, however, Cobbett can be found querying eulogies to the recently deceased Pitt. "As to Mr. Pitt's being an excellent statesman, no man dare attempt to maintain the position by argument," he states, concluding that those would praise Pitt are able to do so only "in *assertion*" (1 Feb. 1806: 132).

If Pitt's excellence exists merely in the assertion, this is equally true of Cobbett's deprecation of the assertion. It could be argued that in eulogies to dead politicians words like "statesman" and "excellent" may be employed with some latitude. But Cobbett employs a severe critical standard here. He has either changed his mind about what is allowable in honorific address or he is exploiting an opportunity to attack not only his old bête noire but the present ministry. The grounds of his objection to honoring Pitt concern the *"great talents"* with which Pitt is being credited and what they say about those with an interest in honoring them:

> Mr. Pitt never gave *proof* of any talents, except as a debater. He was a great debater; a person of wonderful readiness and dexterity in conducting a contest of words; a most accomplished, a truly incomparable *advocate*. But, that was *all*; and that, from the use

he made of it, was pernicious to the country. His eloquence was frothy; it was always unsubstantial; it very rarely produced conviction; but, its object was answered by the plausibility of it, which furnished the means of a justification, or rather which protected against an unbearable sense of shame, those who, from motives of self-interest, gave him their support. (1 Feb. 1806: 133)

This estimate of Pitt is remarkably like Hazlitt's, though in the latter case Pitt is only one among many who have made the age "an age of talkers" (*CWH* 11:28). The talented speakers of this age speak to both sides of a question and would undoubtedly include Cobbett himself. Yet while the eloquence of Hazlitt's Cobbett, unlike that of Cobbett's Pitt, produces conviction, it is a conviction produced by circumstance rather than fixed principle. In this respect, Pitt and Cobbett occupy a common ground. Whether it speaks to the one's "plausibility" or the other's "force of present conviction," rhetoric in each case reflects a keen sense of contingency. Nevertheless, this attack on Pitt's eulogists probably worked with those with whom Cobbett hoped it would work, namely, Pitt's enemies. Faithful readers of the *Register*—and there were many, from every class and political persuasion— were already schooled in the means by which words might be employed with different "forces." The fact of Cobbett's own inconsistency in this respect would likely be less notable for these readers than the connection made between what Cobbett identifies as Pitt's only talent, an ability to make the unjustifiable plausible, and the dubious fluency with which those who most benefited by this talent have contrived to honor Pitt in death. Cobbett is concerned here with more than insincere eulogizing. He knew that the very sophistry of Pittite governance making it possible to venerate its late author would continue to make possible much graver abuses of reason and feeling through what he soon began to call the "Pitt System."[10]

This system—or "Thing" as Cobbett also called it—is nothing less than the totality of governance, legislative and monetary, as shaped by the Pitt administration during the Napoleonic wars. Like many reformers, Cobbett had come to regard the English war effort as fraudulent, merely the pretext for economic and social measures of dubious intent. Driving these measures was a system of imposture conceived to disseminate falsehood and fallacy on a scale virtually hegemonic. It is not surprising that Cobbett should emphasize the rhetorical nature of this system given the fact that he and others estimated Pitt himself almost solely in terms of verbal fluency. This quality takes on almost existential dimensions in Hazlitt's portrait of Pitt who "seemed not to have believed that the truth of his statements depended on the reality of the facts, but that the things depended on the order in which he arranged them in words" (*CWH* 7:323–24). Pittite England for Cobbett was thus a kind of monolithic rhetorical system, so that his offense in the eyes of former allies lay largely in the violation of rhetorical decorum. "The Treasury writers," he explained in 1804, "have accused me of 'deserting Mr. Pitt, whom I had so highly extolled, and of going over to Mr. Fox, whom I had so severely censured'" (*CPR* 29 Sept. 1804: 456–57). That the same writers had formerly extolled Cobbett indicates how interchangeable were these rhetorical categories in the public life of neo-Pittite England. To be sure, Cobbett had extolled them too, just as he was now attacking their imposture. To say that it takes one to know one seems a harsh estimate, but if Cobbett knew what he was doing, he was surely wise to what others were doing. Attacks against him necessarily issued from a like knowingness. Yet the credibility of his charges against the Pittites, and of theirs against him, must necessarily make tacit appeal to inside knowledge and only honorifically to principle.

The vituperative exchange of charge and countercharge, however, did prompt Cobbett to examine critically the system he now found himself opposing. His reflections on the gulf between rhetoric and conviction in honorific address—whether he was justifying such latitude in his own practice or criticizing it in others—stem from a developing critique of language use in public life that turns on a binary of praise and censure, Bentham's categories of "eulogistic" and "dyslogistic" rhetoric. An 1805 *Register* article, "Conduct of Mr. Pitt," argues that, while no purpose is served by exposing the faults of private persons, criticism of public persons has been inhibited by "a sophistical mode of statement" by which the distinction between private and public character is rendered ambiguous. The result is a public sphere in which partisans may praise the virtues and vices alike of public men while "a man is liable to punishment for uttering the TRUTH in censure of men in place and power" (*CPR* May 1805: 642). Under the pretext of protecting public men from libel, this fallacy protects them from legitimate censure by confounding criticism with libel. At times, it is difficult to tell what Cobbett despises most, punishments meted out to legitimate criticism or the doling out of venal praise, one symptom of the "Whiggish moderation" Peacock feared was neutralizing critical inquiry into a mere form of itself. Cobbett likely has something like this in mind when he complains, in a running commentary on the Regency controversy, that "To bestow praises upon men, whom nobody must attack, is, therefore, at all times very suspicious, at best, and when made use of in *an argument*, excessively base" (*CPR* 30 Jan. 1811: 229). In this connection, he criticizes arguments made in a *Courier* article, which carried the pointed title of "Dethroning of the King," favoring limitations on the powers of the Regent. Cobbett objected to the inference that to support the son was to insult the father and accused the *Courier* of using its encomiums on the King as a weapon against the Prince's supporters. The *Courier*'s response was to remind readers, in an article entitled "RESTRICTIONS ON CALUMNY," of Cobbett's extravagant praise of George III at a County Meeting in Winchester two years before (*CPR* 6 Feb. 1811: 290). In his reply, Cobbett develops his earlier point about the circular, self-validating nature of the *Courier* argument into a critique of the rhetorical hegemony—elsewhere he calls it "the smothering system" (*CPR* 18 Apr. 1812: 481)—enjoyed by the ministerialist press:

> This is, in fact, their language; so that there is no escaping them. They have their net so set for you, that to escape it is absolutely impossible. You must either yield to their argument; you must admit their conclusions; or, according to them, you are, either in act or wish, *a calumniator of the King*.—As to the words imputed to me, as having been spoken at Winchester, they are by no means a correct representation of what I then said; but, what if they were? How does it shew any *inconsistency* in me? It was not to the *praise* that I objected; but to the *use* that was made of it. I objected to its being brought forward in the way of argument; to its being made a *ground* in a controversy; because, as I said before, no one who was on the other side in the controversy, would, if he could, *dare*, contradict it; and, for this reason, to

bring it forward, in such a way, was, I said, extremely base; an opinion, of the correctness of which, if there could have been any doubt, this venal man has now, by his own act completely affirmed. (*CPR* 6 Feb. 1811: 290)

Cobbett's exposure of the *Courier* writer's venality itself combines criticism and rhetoric to an appreciable degree. While he does quote directly from the *Courier*, Cobbett also presents his own inferences from the *Courier*'s argument in the form of quotation, complete with italicized words and phrases for emphasis: "We rest our conclusions upon the assertion of the virtues of the King; we say, that this or that ought to be done, or not to be done, because the King has such and such virtues; if you *contradict* us, you are calumniators of the King; and, if you *refuse to assent* to our assertions upon which our conclusions are grounded by *waving the discussion*, you prove, that you would hold the King up to *public execration* if you *dared*" (*CPR* 6 Feb. 1811: 290). To say that this is in fact "their language" is certainly factually untrue, while to imply that it is the effective truth of the inference is to beg the question of how he comes by his insight into ministerialist press tactics. Even as he skillfully argues the implications of the *Courier*'s employment of praise as argument, moreover, he rests *his* conclusions about the *Courier* on the reiterated assertion of its imputed venality ("This is the way, in which this venal man *answers* an argument" [*CPR* 6 Feb. 1811: 290]). Almost a decade later, Cobbett would pursue a campaign against George IV during the Caroline Affair using tactics he exposed in the former Regent's detractors during the Regency controversy, his praises of the queen similarly serving as an acclamatory challenge to the King's defenders. Perhaps this is what Hazlitt meant when he wondered if Cobbett's gallantry was of the right stamp.

At the same time, Cobbett's critical polemics, at once critiquing imposture and answering it in kind, expose the fallacies underpinning the "Pitt System." Despite honorific assertions to the contrary, Cobbett viewed the English public ambivalently, believing it still to be under the influence of Pittite deception. An 1813 *Register* piece on the English war campaign characterizes the English as the "the most completely duped of any nation that ever existed in this world," while at the same time asserting that

"There is nothing in which the people are more interested than the means that are thus made use of to deceive them" (*CPR* 18 Sept. 1813: 354). This seems potentially contradictory, but Cobbett finds justification for both claims in the ministerialist press campaign against France. As deluded as English readers might be regarding the truth about their own government, "They are constantly told of the deceptions practised upon the people of France" (*CPR* 18 Sept. 1813: 354–55). What this seems to suggest is that the ministerialist press critique of French imposture has had the unintended but necessary effect of cultivating a critical faculty in the same public the ministry would mislead where its own governance is concerned. Cobbett complains that no press at all would be better than the one England currently has, yet his exposure of their deceptions not only employs critical methods developed while he was an anti-Jacobin but depends on a public educated in part by these same methods. His analysis of some tricks of the trade in this article thus applies anti-Jacobin metareviewing techniques to ministerialist press tactics while relying on a knowing readership to follow the logic of his critique. Cobbett includes his own large readership, with its impressively varied demographics, among the 1 percent of readers he claims is capable of seeing through ministerialist imposture, though again he had helped many of them become wise to French imposture during the *Register*'s early years. The system of suppression and deception he describes is premised on a sensationalist under-standing of the public mind, its visceral leaning toward the plea-sure principle and the corollary that "falsehood, even glaring falsehood, in the shape of good news, is more pleasing than truth, in the shape of bad news" (*CPR* 18 Sept. 1813: 356). The ministe-rialist press's handling of documents conveying bad news, there-fore, minimizes the negative, first by simply holding them back for a time—the rule of thumb is not more than forty-eight hours, according to Cobbett—during which interval "they go to work with both hands, to weaken the effect of the document upon the public mind" (*CPR* 18 Sept. 1813: 358). With one hand, they sum-marize the document, breaking it down to a fraction of its "real force," while appending to this summary their own commentary. With the other hand, they introduce a separate, likely fabricated, piece of good news to appear in a second edition but not men-tioned the next day: "It passes, of course, uncontradicted, and, by a vast majority of the people, and it becomes recorded in their minds as true" (*CPR* 18 Sept. 1813: 358). Cobbett cites the recent example of a victory concocted by the English press for an allied commander, Prince Benradotte ("it being manifest, that, in the slight affair in which he was engaged, he gained no victory at all"), in order to downplay a major French victory in Dresden. After detailing the process of press-spinning described above, he draws attention to the following device:

> The typographical trick played off upon this occasion is worthy of notice.—The whole mass of intelligence had for title, these words: "VICTORY GAINED BY THE CROWN PRINCE—GREAT BATTLE NEAR DRESDEN."—Only observe this trick! It was a *Victory* gained by the Crown Prince; but, it was only a *great battle* near Dresden, though the imposter well knew, that, in half a minute from the reading of the title, every one must see, that this great battle ended in a most tremendous victory, gained by the Emperor Napoleon. But, half a minute was something! Half a minute was a great deal as to the intelligent reader; and, as to the mass of readers, they would take care (most thinking people as they are!) to carry the titles full in their minds while reading the whole of the intelligence. (*CPR* 18 Sept. 1813: 357)

The parenthetical reference, ("most thinking people as they are!") ironically alludes to a remark by the Earl of Mansfield that the English were the "*most thinking*" people in Europe (*CPR* 8 June 1811: 1410). While Cobbett and the government writers differ on the end achieved by the dubious means described here, they share common assumptions about the nature of the public mind such means speak to, a mind for which merely the sensation of good news is enough to lend the subliminal force of truth to falsehood. The grounds of both the strategy and its critical exposure are epistemological, the sensationalist logic of association. The result of such regressive conditioning, Cobbett states elsewhere, is a readership that "would even assent to other fabrications, ten times more absurd, upon the bare statement of such newspapers as the *Times* and the *Courier*, rather than give themselves the trouble of exercising their own judgment, even for a single moment" (*CPR* 22 Jan. 1814: 118).

In the *Political Register* Cobbett attempted to reverse this insidious influence by alerting his readership not only to numerous instances of imposture but to their systematic nature. "The publishing of falshoods, known falshoods [*sic*]," he asserts, "is, with prints like the Morning Post, a *system*; a settled method of proceeding; a fixed line of conduct" (*CPR* 21 Nov. 1810: 970). The article in which this charge is made forms part of a series on George III's illness, an occasion when Cobbett assumes (or claims to have assumed) that even the most venal press hirelings would suspend their usual mischief. Yet even under such circumstances he detects in *Post* and *Courier* treatments "a *settled design*, a premeditated contrivance to *deceive* and *cheat* the public with respect to this most interesting of all subjects" (*CPR* 3 Nov. 1810: 813). Thus does Cobbett school his readers in the fallacious logic of imposture, effectively taking his readers aside—"Stop here, reader, and mark, for a moment, the phraseology of this ministerial writer" (*CPR* 18 Aug. 1810: 193)—to explain the rhetorical workings of public life in Pittite England. Remarking the need for such guidance in an 1812 article on "Juries and Education," he even projects a handbook in which "the *meaning and use of words*" would be taught before going on to instruction on the rights and duties of citizenship (*CPR* 8 Feb. 1812: 168). This purpose would be served by the *Grammar* he published five years later, though the *Register* represents Cobbett's most sustained effort to educate readers through its tireless critical exposure of rhetorical abuses. The sheer quantity and variety of fallacies, errors, and falsehoods dissected in its pages surely qualify it as a rhetoric in its own right—like Bentham's more systematic *Book of Fallacies*, an unfriendly companion to imposture of the kind formalized by Hamilton and other English Machiavellians. Viewed in isolation, indeed, Cobbett's insights can carry the force of axioms. "There is always great danger of being misled by mere *names*," he notes in one of his addresses to tradesmen; "and, people have often fought for a *name*, when, if they had known what the *thing* was, they would have detested it" (*CPR* 27 Mar. 1819: 832). Elsewhere a definition of what Cobbett terms "knock-me-down arguments" recalls Bentham's Fallacies of Authority: "The appeal to the superior wisdom of persons in power, particularly the Commander in Chief, is one of those arguments, which, as Swift observes, 'like a flail, there is no defence against'" (*CPR* 8 Sept. 1804: 363).

◦ş ◦ş ◦ş

Cobbett's rhetorical critique is ultimately a critique of the press and press freedoms. What, under this system of acclamation and suppression, passes for freedom of expression ("the *sham* of liberty of the press") is for Cobbett more dangerous than direct censorship. Under the sway of "this one-sided goddess," he argues, "Thoughtless men see 'writers *on both sides*,' not perceiving, that those on one side have a sharp curb in their mouths, while those on the other side are wholly without a bridle!" (*CPR* 15 Apr. 1820 342). Presumably, he refers here to the Whig/Tory monopoly, "the *ins* and the *outs*; the *'gentlemen on this side'* and the *'gentlemen opposite*,'" who oppose one another purely as a matter of form and are ready to unite to defend a system that is their "joint concern" (*CPR* 15 Apr. 1820: 355). That leaves just reform, but Cobbett has no illusions about the place of critical dissent, even where it is not wholly suppressed, in a closed system:

> If there are a few, amongst the vast multitude of public writers that supply materials for our press, who *seem* to wield the pen with some degree of *boldness*, this, in fact, will be found, on a little attention, to be merely in *appearance*. It is only because they *stand alone* in their opposition to corruption that they attract any notice; and were they not extremely guarded in what they say, they even would not long enjoy the liberty of publishing what they write. (*CPR* 13 Aug. 1814: 193–94)

What does Cobbett mean when he says that those few who bravely write in opposition do so "merely in *appearance*"? One might argue that in a sphere where impressions are all that seem to matter, this is to say much. Yet what makes dissent effective? Cobbett seems to be saying that, few in number and cautious in what they say, reform writers have been co-opted as hapless players in the same closed system that sees Whigs and Tories periodically changing sides in the House but maintaining the same basic balance of power. While not calling into question either the intentions or the actions of reform writers—he would include himself among them—Cobbett suggests that their role has been rhetorically determined for them. Opposition, either within Westminster or outside it, does not exist in the Pitt System described by Cobbett except as one of a number of other rhetorical options all contributing to the impression of authentic debate. Cobbett believed that many in Pitt's England wished on some level to be deceived and that accepted forms of deception had usurped the place of truth, which, he charges in an open letter to the Prince Regent, "if she appear at all, it is under so thick a covering, in so crawling an attitude, and with so many apologies to power, that she always disgraces her character, and not infrequently injures her cause" (*CPR* 1 Feb. 1812: 130). A press such as Cobbett describes here actually works to suppress, while pretending to conduct, reasoned discussion; argument is reduced to a mere form of rhetoric controlled by public men eulogized by writers who reserve their censure solely for dissent. "Then is the Liberty of the Press, considered as a check upon such men, a mere mockery," Cobbett observes; "while, on the other hand, it is to them a most convenient instrument in deluding the people into an approbation of, or, at least, a quiet submission to, measures, against which, were they left to judge from their own observation and feelings, their minds could not fail to revolt" (*CPR* 4 May 1805: 642). In this way may simple panegyric threaten liberty of expression itself.

Two aspects of Cobbett's views on the press stand out. One is that he regards the press not as a check on power but as an accomplice whose role has been acclamatory rather than critical. The other, a direct corollary of the first, is that people would judge more clearly without its interference. This is unsurprising given the value Cobbett places on plain speaking and common sense, a conviction taking almost programmatic form in works like *Cobbett's English Grammar* (1817). The *Grammar* is conceived for working men, but appended to it are six lessons containing specimens of "false grammar," drawn from Castlereagh among others, which are intended as "a warning to the Statesmen of the present day."[11] Beyond the rudiments of literacy, then, this handbook is conceived to provide a critical guide through the rhetorical thickets of neo-Pittite England. Underlying its critique is the essentialist assumption that there is a truth secure from the mischief of practice. Cobbett's belief that people would judge right if left to "their own observation and feelings" displays a Rousseauistic distrust of institutional domination. An 1811 *Register* article even nostalgically harkens back to a period before the press existed in England when people "judged more from their *own observation* and from *experience*; from what they themselves *saw* and what they *felt*." Knowledge spread more slowly but was more sure, Cobbett claims, adding that England's most just laws date from this period (*CPR* 6 Mar. 1811: 550). Greece and Rome are also cited as salutary instances of golden ages free of press coverage, though Cobbett's anticlassicism prevents him from advocating a return to ancient rhetorical practice, as Thomas Sheridan does. Elsewhere, on the subject of English eloquence, he insists that "It is, upon a subject like this, of PRYNN and LILBURNE and TOOKE, and such men that we should speak, and not of *Socrates* and *Demosthenes* and *Cicero* and *Pisistratus*, which knew as little about *a press* as the people of England know about them" (*CPR* 23 Feb. 1811: 451).[12] Yet his primitivistic suspicion of modern sophism recalls the epistemological premise of Elocution that not only is perfect candor possible but that it will be recognized by the perfectly candid. Just as those schooled in Elocution detect dissembling in "the least impropriety in tone, look, or gesture," so Cobbett's ideal citizenry, being themselves perfectly candid, would require no help in judging the measures of those in power; indeed, a press dedicated to falsehood has only impaired their judgment. "Some truths, and valuable truths, get abroad through the means of the press," he allows elsewhere; "but these are infinitely out numbered by the falsehoods; and, if the people were left without any press at all, matters would be much better, because they would then judge and act from what they *saw* and what they *felt*, and not from what they *read*" (*CPR* 29 Aug. 1807: 334). This form of comprehension, unmediated and true, is grounded in direct observation—in the case of the Electors of Westminster, for instance, of whom Cobbett asserts that "their light has not been derived from the press, but from being upon the spot; from *hearing* and *seeing* and receiving conviction of, what the press disguises from other men" (*CPR* 29 Aug. 1807: 334). Throughout the pages of the *Register*, then, when he is not knowingly exposing the rhetorical tricks of "venal writers"—possibly his most ubiquitous phrase—Cobbett points to an ideal of candor which, while not wholly notional, is restricted to isolated cases. An address "To the People of Scotland," for example, praises the honest language of speeches and petitions made in a meeting in Paisley: "The clearness of the statements contained in the speeches; the ingenuity and force of the arguments; the spirit, eloquence and impressiveness of the language; all these give to those proceedings the stamp of superiority, and do great honour to Scotland" (*CPR* 9 Nov. 1816: 577). An 1817 number of the *Register* even allows occasional instances of this candor in arguments against reform, in this case made by Earl Grosvenor whose mild language and honest sentiments "call upon us to listen to you with the greatest respect, and, if we still retain our opinions, to show by fair statement and reasoning that the grounds of those opinions are such as to warrant us in differing, as to those opinions, from those which your Lordship has so explicitly and fairly expressed" (*CPR* 22 Feb. 1817: 226).

What connects Grosvenor's rhetorical practice with that of the Electors of Westminster and the Paisley petitioners is a common (which is to say British) idiom of candor and common sense. In his criticism of the *Courier's* position in favor of limiting the Regent's power, for instance, Cobbett draws on Burke's sentimental metaphysic of national sentiment, in this case directed not against Jacobins but the ministerialist press:

> What a disgrace it is to the English nation, that its character should be such as to embolden any one to put forth such hypocritical cant! What a shame it is for us, that any one, living amongst us, and pretty well able to ascertain the nature of the public mind, should think it his interest (for that is his guide) to publish a passage like this! What a disgrace to our national understanding, what a proof of gross national gullibility, and, indeed, what a symptom of degeneracy and baseness of spirit, that any man, after long experience at the press, should not only think it sage, but should deem it in his interest, to address the public in this manner; to put forward in their teeth sentiments and assertions like these! It is true, that all men of sense will see them in their proper light; but, the publisher of them knows well, that there are enough who will not; and, upon the supposition that there are only *one thousand* persons out of *fifteen millions*, capable of being thus imposed upon, the fact is highly disgraceful to the country. (*CPR* 30 Jan. 1811: 228)

Cobbett knew better than to overestimate John Bull. His critique tacitly extends itself to nothing less than the state of English public opinion even while attacking these same assumptions as cynical when put forward by the *Courier*. Calculations concerning "*one thousand* persons out of *fifteen millions*" allow him to have it both ways, then, acknowledging "all men of sense" in the country, including his own readers, while expressing reservations about the "public mind" nonetheless. Elsewhere, he is more categorical in his criticism. Mansfield's remark about the English as a "*most thinking*" people becomes an ironic motif in Cobbett's rhetoric in numerous connections, even forming the title of a series of *Register* articles addressed "To The Thinking People of England." There Cobbett squarely asserts to his countrymen that "you have so long been deceived; you have so long listened, and loved to listen, to falsehood; you have so long been the almost willing dupes of designing knaves; that there is scarcely a passage left by which truth can find its way to your minds" (*CPR* 30 Jan. 1813: 129). This is hardly a sanguine view. Yet, by positing a historical decline from an eloquence still occasionally glimpsed, Cobbett's critique of neo-Pittite England could at least work from a seemingly established norm even if it could not convincingly argue the conditions necessary for its national recovery.

Defining such a norm, as opposed to evoking it, was extremely problematic. Cobbett's strength, as Hazlitt noted, lay in criticism, his fearsome ability to "pull down and pull in pieces." It is one thing to employ rhetoric to this destructive purpose and another to define, much less exemplify, a language of national affirmation—though, as enemies pointed out, Cobbett had often enough praised those he had gone on to censure. Expedient tactical shifts do not a national ethos make, however, at least one whose recovery will supplant a system of imposture that Cobbett credited to Pitt and that others traced back as far as Walpole. Reconciling his rhetorical critique, its expediently deployed modes of praise and censure, with the notional England evoked in even his most corrosive writings was a problem Cobbett shared with other polemicists. Canning was only one of the more egregious examples. It is doubtful that he saw any problem with his use of loyalist rhetoric to hypnotize Tory boroughmongers, but others did, including Cobbett who once made this observation of an amendment read by Canning in Parliament: "There is in it, nothing dignified, nothing solid, nothing impressive, nothing either eloquent or elegant. It breathes neither earnestness nor sincerity, neither loyalty nor patriotism. Its panegyrics may well be mistaken for irony; and its censure consists of a wearisome series of slack-twisted and pointless sarcasm, discovering at once both impotence and malice" (*CPR* 3 Jan. 1807: 7). Cobbett would no doubt find Canning's neo-Whiggish Tory rhetoric unworthy of Burke, who invented it. Yet even Burke—"We preserve the whole of our feelings still native and entire, unsophisticated by pedantry and infidelity"—had necessarily to defend an inarticulate, because unwritten, constitution by at times employing the same "pert loquacity" from which he would defend it (*RRF* 137–38). The same deliberation required knowingly to conceive a traditional England, much less articulate it while attacking its obverse in the wiles of French sophistry, carried the danger of disingenuousness. (Hazlitt detects similar mannerism in revolutionary France's cult of simplicity, which he calls "a singularly affected and outrageous simplicity" [*CWH* 5:161–62].) Perhaps this was part of the problem that readers like Fox and Pitt had with the *Reflections*. Even when employed by a respected parliamentarian like Samuel Whitbread, the language of national ethos—rhetorically prominent as the whole concept had become since Burke, it was less an ethos than the constantly reiterated assertion of one—had a way of being compromised by the daily tactical concessions inevitable in political life. To be sure, Whitbread would pose a problem for Cobbett simply because he was a Whig, but his reputation as an Old Whig—Hazlitt praises him as "the representative of the spontaneous, unsophisticated sense of the English people"—would have made him potentially viable as a voice for the old English ethos Cobbett believed Pittite sophism had supplanted. Yet the sheer workaday force of contingency evidently had the effect of making Whitbread's rhetoric an unreliable index of national spirit, at least in any salutary sense: "There has been such a mixture of praising and of blaming in MR. WHITBREAD'S speeches; he has so often ended in *complimenting* those whom he began in *accusing*; he has so often *taken the word* of those, whom he described as totally *unworthy of all trust and confidence;* and, in short, there has been so much of backward and forward work in his proceedings, that I, as well as most others, I believe, have begun to pay much less attention to him than formerly" (*CPR* 4 May 1811: 1089). As for Cobbett himself, there were many others ready to make the same charges of him, though Hazlitt came closest to understanding the basis for this apparent double-dealing.

That so many made these charges from so many different quarters likely meant that Cobbett was doing something right. In their different ways, so too were his critics (who were also, usually for good reason, the objects of his criticism). In all cases, however, what was right lay in exposing what was wrong, not in positively embodying the rightness of the norm tacitly underlying the exposure, except at the risk of implying mannered insincerity or, in Canning's case, even irony. But candor was risky too. In his rejoinder to PUBLICOLA, mentioned above, Cobbett cites the reforming Whig M.P. Sir Francis Burdett, along with others like Tooke and Lilburne, as a model of English eloquence, though he also sees in Burdett the fate of reasoned conviction in an age when reason and conviction seem mere sports of rhetoric. In 1806, during the Middlesex election, Cobbett claimed that Burdett's words had been misrepresented by nomination rivals and that this imposture had been made worse by Whitbread who published a private letter from Burdett construable as an attack on monarchy—"and that, too," notes Cobbett, "so short a time before the day of election as to deprive Sir Francis Burdett of an opportunity of answering it, until the time should be passed for counteracting its intended effect!" (*CPR* 15 Nov. 1806: 740). The lesson in this for reformers was largely pragmatic. An address printed in the *Register* "To Sir Francis Burdett, Bart.," by the venerable reformer Major Cartwright, gives advice that could have been offered by the author of *Parliamentary Logic*, but for its good intentions:

> In times like the present, for a man to be qualified for the duties of patriotism, it is perhaps requisite that in the composition of his mind there should be a strong dash of the splenetic. Without this ingredient a parliamentary character may be deficient, and unfit for its task. 'Tis a quality that disposes to a rigorous scrutiny into misgovernment. It keeps awake and vigilant, attention to official vice. It stimulates to reprehension and satire. It displays, and it preserves, public integrity; it is a powerful supporter in the arduous labours of a reformer; and it is a far better security for the continuance of patriotism, than the professions of those who have not in the very constitution of their nature, that which renders them peculiarly hostile to the court sycophant, to

the venal senator, and the corrupt placeman. It is, in short, in political character, what discord is in music. It is essential to har-
monic energy. But neither in music nor in politics ought the
discord to be discernible to the vulgar ear. Keep therefore these
discordant tones in due subordination, that you may be the
better able to do all the good you so ardently wish. (*CPR* 1 Nov.
1806: 719)

Cartwright was by this time a revered paragon of principled dissent, but he was also a veteran of reform's polemical wars, external and internal, and he knew his audience. To affirm, one must
also oppose, balancing necessary means with estimable end. Yet
this end, which is to say its impression, must be kept in view at
all times—not unlike good news manufactured for an uncritical
wartime public. While the rhetorical system sketched here has a
salutary social purpose, then, it nevertheless counsels the artful
sublimation of criticism in honorific representations of the public
good. Only by means of such shifts is it possible to convey the impression of apparent good necessary to the persuasion to actual
good.

Cobbett no doubt saw himself walking a similarly fine line,
balancing the purity of principle against the mischief of practice.
The mischief of others was the least of it—merely an occasion for
more of his own highly destructive practice. He clearly felt that
the means to which contingency sometimes directed him were in
fact justified by the end of turning imposture against itself.
Having devoted himself to elaborating a vast system of imposture by which the English people had been duped since England
went to war under Pitt, he was even coming to believe that the
old Pitt deceptions were no longer working, venturing as early as
1806 to say that "The nation is not again to be duped in that way.
It would look with abhorrence upon the attempt" (*CPR* 1 Feb.
1806: 143). This assertion is accompanied by the caveat that another possible reaction is simple indifference, "which, of all possible feelings, is the best calculated to insure and accelerate our
destruction as an independent people" (*CPR* 1 Feb. 1806: 143).
The days when words like "*democratical*" and "*jacobinical*" were
enough to arouse a violent reaction—Cobbett remarks that "The
late minister, Pitt, of wasteful memory, drew millions out of our
pockets by the help of a few words of this sort" (*CPR* 5 Nov. 1808:

709)—were past. Yet the loyalist ethos appealed to by such words might also have had its day, due largely to its exploitation by a venal ministerialist press, but also thanks to Cobbett's own powerful critique of ministerialist rhetoric. It was, Cobbett must have discovered, impossible to debunk anti-Jacobinism without discrediting the loyalist sentiments associated with it.

Cobbett's economic writings reflect an awareness that the old loyalist line, if not wholly obsolete, was in need of refocusing. The best-known of these writings, a critique of paper money entitled *Paper Against Gold* (1815), is based on a series of articles appearing in the *Political Register* from 1810 to 1812. While the twenty-nine letters comprising this work rehearsed long-held views of Cobbett's, they were also very current. The Bullion Committee, an advisory body appointed by the government to address concerns about the solvency of paper credit, had recently recommended a return to the gold standard. Long a critic of paper money, Cobbett now found himself in the company of prominent economists like David Ricardo who argued that even paper issued by the Bank of England was steadily losing value amid rising rents and prices.[13] With his usual rigor Cobbett achieved an impressive mastery of monetary policy in order to mount a polemical assault on a system of credit and stocks that had financed Pitt's war and was continuing, he believed, to erode England's true wealth. The recommendations of the Bullion Committee had in fact been rejected by Parliament in the declared belief that Bank of England currency remained stable. Cobbett's role in the debate really began with the ministerialist defense of this position, a campaign he traced, like everything else wrong in the country, to Pittite deception. Thus, while *Paper Against Gold* presents informed economic analysis, its most telling criticisms are directed against rhetorical imposture designed to obscure the real grounds of English prosperity. It debunks the fallacy of paper credit and as such is ultimately less an economic treatise than a critique of the polemics of neo-Pittite monetary policy.

For better or worse, linguistic and monetary currency have much in common where standards of value are concerned. Scholars like Kurt Heinzelman and Marc Shell have recently investi-

gated how literary language is regulated by commercial conceptions of economy and value, arguing that fictional forms reflect
the same imperatives of economy as monetary systems.[14] Shell
introduces his study *Money, Language, and Thought* (1982) with
an account of the transition from the earliest "electrum money,"
whose exchange value derived from the precious metal from
which its coins were made, to modern "electric money," tracing a
development through the intermediate stages of stamped coins
to the even more abstract inscription of value in paper money.
Central to this monetary evolution is an ever widening "difference between inscription and thing." The authors Shell cites
range from Poe and Emerson to Hegel and Heidegger, but in each
there is a common preoccupation with constructions of value and
meaning. The equation itself is simple enough: words are to
meaning as paper is to gold, for in both value is cultural, inscribed by "the stamp of custom."[15] Cobbett was not alone among
his contemporaries in noting that value and meaning both speak
to opinion. Of his dealings as an author, Hazlitt says: "I endeav-
our to employ plain words and popular modes of construction, as
were I a chapman and dealer, I should common weights and measures," for "words are like money, not the worse for being common
... it is the stamp of custom alone that gives them circulation or
value" (*CWH* 8:244). As such assertions imply, the analogy is as
cautionary as it is descriptive. If Adam Smith, and Thomas Paine
after him, saw commerce as a great socializing influence—according to Paine, it operates "to cordialize mankind by rendering
nations, as well as individuals, useful to each other"[16]—others
were less certain about its benefits. Observers of Georgian society like Dr. Johnson and Joseph Addison noted the grandly insidious workings of advertising in general usage. Commercial
puffing had become so prevalent that it threatened to devalue
language itself—much as oversupply drives down prices. In 1761
Johnson observed:

> Advertisements are now so numerous that they are very negli-
> gently perused, and it is therefore become necessary to gain at-
> tention by magnificence of promises and by eloquence sometimes
> sublime and sometimes pathetick. Promise, large promise, is the
> soul of an advertisement. I remember a washball that had a
> quality truly wonderful—it gave *an exquisite edge to the razor!*[17]

We are so used to the attribution of aesthetic qualities to commercial products—even products as mundane as this—that we must make an effort to share Johnson's incredulity. Even so, Johnson must have suspected that advertisers were co-opting his critical vocabulary and his authority as a critic, devaluing both in the process. The same objection could be made of bad art or bad criticism generally, but they at least are recognizably bad in relation to what is recognized as good. What Johnson describes is both less distinct and more pervasive in its cultural influence. Far from providing a foil for critical and aesthetic norms, it replaces them by co-opting their very forms and employing their authority for its own ends.

For Cobbett "credit" or its absence determines the currency of either language or money. His discussion of this concept, then, in Letter XI of *Paper Against Gold*, places paper money in the same contingent sphere of 'use' occupied by rhetoric:

> *Credit* is a thing wholly dependent upon *opinion*. The word itself, indeed, has the same meaning as the word *belief*. As long as men *believe* in the riches of any individual, or any company, so long do he or they possess all the advantages of riches. But, when once *suspicion* is excited, no matter from what cause, the *credit* is shaken; and, a very little matter oversets it. So long as the *belief is implicit*, the person, towards whom it exists, goes on, not only with all the appearances, but with all the advantages, of wealth; though, at the same time, he be insolvent. But, if his wealth be not *solid*; if he have merely the *appearance* of wealth; if he be unable to pay so much as he owes, or, in other words, if he be *insolvent*, which means neither more nor less than *unable to pay*: When an individual is in this situation, he is liable, at any moment, to have his insolvency exposed. (*PG* 151)

There is nothing absolute or even logical about value because credit, the promise of value, is the mere creature of opinion, and opinion can secure only the probability of truth, not its certainty. It is enough, however, to create "the *appearance* of wealth." Cobbett argues here that insolvency is a fact, a simple inability to pay regardless of appearances to the contrary, but he has good reason to skirt the corollary of his argument about contingent value, which is that the appearance of insolvency may be as fatal as its reality, for this was in fact the basis of charges made against him by government papers, that his criticisms were undermining confidence in England's currency. Both Cobbett and his opponents, indeed, knew they were fighting on the common ground of opinion. The terms of this controversy as it played out in the press were thus largely rhetorical, speaking to the same national collectivity of belief and sentiment as the great constitutional debates initiated by Burke/Paine. The *"public credit of Old England" (PG* 98)—a sonorous phrase Cobbett repeats again and again in his arguments—was really "the collective sense of the nation" by another name.

Paper Against Gold thus correlates a nation's wisdom with its credit. Just as elsewhere Cobbett judges the public life of England on the basis of rhetoric,[18] so here he regards public credit as an index to national character. His critique of paper credit is thus a specialized subset of his rhetorical critique of Pittite governance (itself part of a broader historical critique to be examined later in this chapter). Cobbett isolates two factors in accounting for the ascendancy of paper credit in England, a venal press and a highly suggestible public, though he allows that one is largely a product of the other. The passivity and credulity making possible the continued success of Pittite deception with respect to anti-Jacobin alarms and the war with France have also, in his view, made possible paper credit with its delusive promises to pay. While tirelessly arguing against both the system and the rhetorical imposture supporting it, however, Cobbett believed that they would be defeated only by means of their own fallacious logic. Letter 11 of *Paper Against Gold* recalls a currency panic in 1797, caused not by an increase in debt, though such an increase was real enough and indeed gold and silver payments had been stopped at the Bank of England, but by fear of imminent invasion by France. Cobbett's analysis of the crisis turns on an abrupt reversal in the rhetorical strategy of the ministerialist press:

> It was now extremely curious to hear the language of the *venal newspapers*, who had, for months before, been endeavouring to excite *alarms*, and who abused Mr. Fox and his party, called them Jacobins, and, sometimes, traitors, because they said that the alarm was *false*, and was invented for bad purposes. These very news-papers now took the other side. They not only themselves

said, that the alarm was *groundless*; but they had the impudence, the unparalleled, the atrocious impudence, to *accuse the Jacobins*, as they called them, *of having excited the alarm*, for the purpose of injuring *public credit*. (*PG* 15)

The ministerialist press, which had been assiduously cultivating such fears in the public mind since 1793 as part of a campaign against English radicals, found itself attempting to calm these same fears now that they threatened England's currency. Cobbett's satisfaction in describing the resulting dilemma is evident: "In vain were all these efforts: SUSPICION, to use PAINE'S emphatical expression, was no longer ASLEEP. It was broad awake, and to stay its operations was impossible. To excite fears in the breasts of the people was a task to which the venal prints had been adequate; but to remove these fears, or to impede the progress of their effects upon the mind, was too much for any human power to accomplish" (*PG* 158). It is interesting to observe how this passage mimics the sensational emphasis, via "PAINE'S emphatical expression," of reactionary alarm. If arguments in favor of paper credit amount to honorific eulogizing, arguments against its critics employ the dyslogistic power of Bentham's "Fallacies of Danger." The sheer incongruity of this rhetorical system, constituted as it is by both neo-Whiggish cunning and loyalist bluster, gives it the regressive appeal of revolutionary and reactionary arguments alike.

In commentary on episodes like the 1797 panic, Cobbett works from an epistemological premise. In letter 12, he asserts that "our next object must naturally be to know what *impression* that event produced upon the nation, and what *measures* were adopted in consequence of it" (*PG* 162). The ensuing "history of the *stoppage*" right down to the Bullion Committee, then, merely traces a continuation of the "eulogistic" and "dyslogistic" measures employed by Pitt and his successors in defense of paper credit. Government alarms had worked by circumventing reason and eliciting the kinds of irrational reaction that made reformers despair of effecting change through logical argument. Now the shoe was on the other foot, and ministerialist writers found their arguments for calm powerless against the very conditioning they had worked so hard to inculcate during anti-Jacobin campaigns against reform. Given the antirational nature of their measures, indeed, it was axiomatic that they would be no more able "to remove these fears, or to impede the progress of their effects upon the mind" than had been their opponents in reform. It did not matter whether the present crisis was real or not—Cobbett implies that the English public correctly believed it to be real but for the wrong reasons—since the *"impression"* was that it was real. That this was due not to convincing arguments but to the reinforcement of impressions already created in the mind of the public by past measures only ensured a predictable response. Another similar case the same year concerned the ministerialist campaign against so-called country banks. These institutions issued their own bank-notes but were less secure than the Bank of England so that their frequent failures were giving paper credit a bad name. Remarking the epithets employed by the ministerialist press to describe notes issued by these banks, such as *"vile rags"* and *"dirty rags,"* Cobbett takes special notice of a writer in a London paper calling them *"destructive assignats."* The implications of this metaphor are not lost on a veteran of the old anti-Jacobin campaigns: "*Assignats* was the name given to the French revolutionary paper-money, the distresses occasioned by which are fresh in the recollection of most people; and, to give the same name to our country bank-notes was, therefore, to proclaim, as far as this writer was able to proclaim, that these notes, *being more than one half of all our circulating medium,* were as bad, if not worse, than the paper money of France, which produced so much individual misery to so many millions of people" (*PG* 41). The power of association is such that, like the "contagion among the passions" Hugh Blair describes in deployments of affective rhetoric, it may overwhelm its original purpose. What, asks Cobbett, is to prevent these destructive associations from attaching themselves to Bank of England notes in the mind of the public?—for "nothing was ever better calculated to render popular commotion violent, and to push it beyond its natural bounds" (*PG* 41). As a result of such observations, the government found itself having to deny, most emphatically, any similarity between English paper notes and revolutionary *assignats* (*PG* 359). To be sure, Cobbett's defense of the country banks is opportunistic, merely an occasion to discredit paper currency by using its defenders' own words against it, though the ministerialist campaign against the country banks was similarly expedient. Cobbett's logic is the more convincing, however. Once lost, credit is difficult to recover, involving as it does contingent qualities like belief and value. This applies to the currency of arguments and banknotes alike. The same year, noting deceptions by the ministerial-press on the subject of the king's illness, Cobbett asked: "What are we to give credit to after this?" (*CPR* 3 Nov. 1810: 815).

Cobbett's critique of arguments for paper credit are compelling. He claims that the idea behind this system, that a nation may increase its means of paying others by paying interest to itself on an increasing debt, is wrong. Paper credit represents not prosperity but debt. At the root of notions to the contrary is fallacious logic, for "this has till of late been imperceptible to the mass of the people, who were convinced of the non-depreciation by the argument built on the circumstance of the guinea and the paper being upon an equal footing" (*PG* 322). To confound paper notes with the very gold or silver they promise, while insisting on an absolute difference between English notes and French *assignats*, is to mistake words for things. "When time is taken to reflect, no rational man will attempt to maintain a proposition so shockingly absurd," Cobbett states in letter 6 (*PG* 83). This analysis turns on the distinction, elided in arguments on behalf of paper credit and in some of his own arguments against it, between rhetoric and logic. One such fallacy involves arguing from analogy— for instance, assuming an identity between private and public economy. The following passage from letter 4 notes an argument made by the Reverend John Brand comparing an individual discharging a mortgage to the nation managing its debts:

> It is a natural propensity of the mind of man, to assimilate things, which he wishes to understand, with things, which he does understand. Hence the application of the terms *mortgage, redemption,* and others, to the Debt of the Nation. But, in this work of assimilation, *or bringing things to a resemblance for the purposes of illustration,* we ought to take the greatest care, not to make use of violence, not to regard as *alike* things which are *essentially different in their properties;* for, if we do this, error must be the result, and I think, you will find, that this has been done by all those, who have reasoned like Mr. Brand; that is to say, *the whole* of those writers and speakers, who have held forth the Sinking Fund as likely to produce relief to the country. (*PG* 86)

The difference between similitude and identity is the difference between rhetorical probability and logical certainty. Cobbett here exposes paper-credit apologetics as just that, rhetorical shifts parading as arguments. In letter 26, then, he outlines what he terms a "TWO PRICES" doctrine turning on the fallacy of identifying paper and gold (*PG* 349–55). An economy in which a single commodity commands two different rates of value, depending on whether payment is in cash or coin, exhibits just the kind of systematic ambiguity associated with rhetorical imposture. "Why," Cobbett thus asks regarding accounting procedures in which cash and bullion are added in a single sum, "were things so unlike in their nature confounded together?" (*PG* 204).

Cobbett's exposures of fallacy in *Paper Against Gold* thus lay bare the campaign behind paper credit, demonstrating how mere rhetoric may undermine national prosperity. Letter 2 sets out the basic terms involved in this system, defining various types of stocks, which it characterizes as a "Babylonish collection of names, or sounds" designed to confuse rather than to clarify meaning (*PG* 36). It begins by considering the ways in which words lose their meanings through common use, "*Shrovetide*" being an case where a word originally signifying confession and absolution has come to be associated only with the unreflecting consumption of pancakes and fritters. "Monstrous, however, as is the perversion of the meaning of words, in this instance," Cobbett continues, "it is scarcely more so than in the case of the *Funds* and the *National Debt*" (*PG* 33). The putatively antirhetorical premise of this argument—that rhetoric serves to make ambiguous the true nature of things, an idea dating back to Bacon's New Science and beyond to Socratic attacks on sophists—actually demonstrates the centrality of rhetoric to both the argument and its subject. Cobbett strips away ambiguity to reveal a plain reality that is all the plainer for the rhetoric of plain speaking by which it is uncovered:

> But, it will be quite useless for us to load our subject with a multitude of words, and to ring the changes upon all the quaint terms, which, as appertaining to these matters, have, one would think, been made use of for no other purpose than that of confusing the understandings of plain men. The light wherein to view the transaction is this: The Government was (no matter how, or

from what cause) got into a war with France; and, for the alleged purpose of pushing on this war with *"vigour"* (it is odd enough that the very word was made use of, just as it is now) they borrowed a million pounds of individuals, and, at the same time, imposed taxes upon the whole nation for the purpose of paying the interest of the money so borrowed; or, in other words, the nation's taxes were *mortgaged* to the lenders of this million of pounds. (*PG* 35)

Cobbett avoids here the obsessively reiterated opinions commonly associated with his rhetoric—in this case well-aired views on the war with France—in favor of a more disinterested attitude. He pointedly distances his argument from the conventional apparatus of rhetoric, its topics and "quaint terms," seemingly in order to allow readers to see the facts in their true "light," wholly free of rhetorical mediation. Yet the force of this passage emerges less from simple exposition than from the conclusion to which the exposition leads, the qualifying "in other words" coming down to one loaded word, *"mortgaged,"* when logic must give way to rhetoric.

Even at such times, however, Cobbett largely leaves the inflammatory rhetoric to his opponents, though he still benefits from its effect. Indeed, the difficulty of distinguishing exposition from polemic in Cobbett is a defining characteristic of his writings. Letter 4, for instance, asks readers to be impartial in judging its analysis of Pitt's "GRAND SINKING FUND." This seems disingenuous given the fact that, on any number of previous occasions, Cobbett had made emphatic his unqualified contempt for Pitt and the sinking fund, and in fact his motives are far from disinterested. By urging impartiality on the reader's part and even assuming such an attitude himself, he can simply allow his past anti-Pitt rhetoric, with its lingering half-life of negatively reinforced association, to do the work for him. In this way, he is able to point out that "It is, even yet, impossible to mention the name of PITT, without exciting feelings that struggle hard against reason, and that, in some minds, overcome it" (*PG* 57), certain that these irrational variables will skew in his favor. In the ensuing analysis, he makes no effort to avoid such associations, but in fact repeats Pitt's name over and over again in relation to the sinking fund (itself always placed in italics or upper case). Though he employs a critical method, then, Cobbett puts it to distinctly rhetorical uses while pre-empting opposition to his arguments by elsewhere critiquing rhetorical tactics he might himself be accused of exploiting—and by those with whom he had developed them during his anti-Jacobin years. Having taken part in that campaign, Cobbett possessed an insider's knowledge of these tactics. In *Paper Against Gold*, he vents his loyalist leanings in defense of an old-fashioned metal currency being supplanted by newfangled paper currency, and, like former allies in the anti-Jacobin press, casts his opposition in the terms of rational critique. In letter 7, then, having reached a critical point in the argument developed in previous letters, he states that "when the design of the writer is to serve the cause of *truth*, and especially when the truths he wishes to make apparent, have been industriously enveloped in darkness; in such a case, every other quality in writing ought to yield to that of *clearness*" (*PG* 91). His putative influence here is Thomas Paine, specifically Paine's pamphlet on the *Decline and Fall of the British System of Finances* (1796), a work conceived to pierce the darkness of economic obfuscation. The fact remains, though, that Paine's warnings were not only unheeded in 1796 but utterly proscribed and Paine himself outlawed. Even during the 1797 panic, when their force in speeches by Sheridan and Fox, among others, "was so manifest, that it was impossible that the truth of it should not be *felt*," it was no match for received opinion—a mere "prejudice of the times," according to Cobbett, shared by those as hard-headed as bankers and merchants, but such as it was a convincing impression of the truth of things (*PG* 198). Whether incisive arguments against paper credit would be any more successful in 1810 was doubtful. Of a speech in Parliament on the subject of finances by Spencer Perceval, ringing the changes on old Pitt sophisms, Cobbett can only exclaim: "I would not have such workings in my mind for ten times the worth of the *reversion* of Lord Arden's sinecure. Oh! a time is coming, when all these things will be seen and felt as they ought to be" (*PG* 360).

A sound currency goes hand in hand with sound rhetoric, underwritten by a public life recognizing, in the words of Jürgen Habermas, "no authority beside that of the better argument."[19] So runs Cobbett's thesis about credit in *Paper Against Gold*, where either money or language is concerned. Given his own arguments regarding the contingent nature of value, however, Cobbett was aware, and concerned to make his readers aware, that the ethical criteria of civic virtue were of limited use in estimating rhetoric or currency, were indeed more likely to be abused, as in well-publicized meetings of bankers and merchants in 1797 organized to push paper credit—assemblies, according to Cobbett, "described by the venal writers, as being *perfectly voluntary*, and flowing from *pure public spirit*" (*PG* 177). Only critical habits of thought gained from a knowledge of how imposture works will safeguard against unreflective acclamation. "It was at the time," Cobbett observes of the Pitt years, "when the clamours, the catch-words, the misrepresentations, the falsehoods, of the fund-dealing crew had so blinded and misled the people, in every part of the kingdom, as to induce them to give the minister ample means to carry him through those measures, which led to the establishment of his political power" (*CPR* 11 Jan. 1806: 34). It is in its rhetorical critique of economic imposture that *Paper Against Gold* retains its argumentative force today when economic theories are so often acclaimed or vilified on the basis of loaded terms.

Arguments in Cobbett about parliamentary corruption or paper credit begin and end in a historical thesis: that English justice and prosperity have been in decline since the Reformation. Seemingly incidental references to the debasement of religious observances like Shrovetide, survivals of a discredited Catholic past, thus fit into a larger argument explaining the Pitt system and its hegemonic impostures in terms of national declension. For argument it is, whatever Cobbett may claim about the factual nature of history. In the preface to his *History of the Regency and Reign of King George the Fourth* (1830), a sequel to his better known *History of the Protestant Reformation in England and Ireland* (1824), Cobbett addresses charges of bias by simply stating that the business of history "is to *record facts*; and, if the facts be *true*, of what consequence are the feelings of the historian?" While allowing for bias in portrayals of character and motive, he maintains that the facts will expose undue bias in the contradiction.[20] Cobbett's *History of the Regency* is remarkably circumstantial, its almost day-to-day account of the period in question undoubtedly drawn from the *Political Register* where facts are deeply implicated with opinion. If there is any doubt, Cobbett makes clear the conclusion to which his argument is heading in his earlier Reformation history: "That change in the religion of England, which took place in the reigns of Henry VIII., Edward VI., and Elizabeth, and which is generally called the REFORMATION, has produced, in process of time, a still greater, and a most fatal, change in the nature of the English government" (*HPR* 1:3).[21] The term "fatal" betrays a bias, to be sure, but it also points to errors Cobbett detects in the magisterial argument of Reformation.

History of the Protestant Reformation in England and Ireland begins by quizzing the very designation of this event. "As to the word REFORMATION," says Cobbett in his introduction, "it means, an alteration for the better; and it would have been hard indeed if the makers of this great alteration could not have contrived to give it a good name."[22] The term is in fact an oxymoron as he reads it in Reformation apologetics, from Fox to Hume and Blackstone, merely regression in reform's clothing. With its distinctly revisionary cast, Cobbett's history is conceived to rehabilitate England's Catholic past, and associated figures like the so-called Bloody Mary, while debunking the progressivist myths of Protestant history:

> It was not a *reformation*, but a *devastation*, of England, which was, at the time when this event took place, the happiest country, perhaps, that the world had ever seen; and, it is my chief business to shew, that this devastation impoverished and degraded the main body of the people. But, in order that you may see this devastation in its true light, and that you may feel a just portion of indignation against the devastators, and against their eulogists of the present day, it is necessary, first, that you take a correct view of the things on which their devastating powers were executed. (*HPR* 1:37)

Cobbett matches eulogy for eulogy, praising what Reformation apologists censure, censuring what they praise: all the rhetorical games of periodical criticism. "Reformation" is not so much exposed as "devastation" as juxtaposed with it in nice antithesis, the place of argument supplied by repetition—no less than five times for "devastation" in this passage. Rhetoric supplements and overtakes but is never checked by critique. At the same time,

Cobbett adopts the demystifying posture of Enlightenment critique, in some respects a natural fit for the revisionary argument he is making. Like Burke's counterrevolutionary position in the *Reflections*, however, this rhetorical strategy gains much of its effect through a deployment of Enlightenment against itself. The danger of such shifts—faced cheerfully enough by rational operatives of reaction like George Canning—is that critique may employed for the overlay of rhetorical effect rather than for its exposure.

This is what Cobbett in fact argues of pro-Reformation polemics. As in the case of paper credit, much of his critique is directed to exposing rhetorical imposture, in this case enlisted in the cause of Reformation—something taking on hegemonic dimensions for him. If writers like Hume and Blackstone represent the career of Reformation in the progressivist terms of Whig history, he effectively turns this method inside out, tracing the abuses of Pittite government, as well as the rhetoric justifying them, to Reformation habits of thought and expression. The rhetorical campaign historically waged by the friends of Reformation, he argues, has insinuated itself into the grain of English sentiment through the very books read by schoolchildren—a widely used speller by Fenning, for instance, containing fables calculated to provoke anti-Catholic feeling. "How indefatigable must have been these deceivers, when they could resort to means like these!" he exclaims, "What multitudes of children, how many millions of people, have, by this book alone, had falsehood, the most base and wicked, engraven upon their minds!" (*HPR* 1:43). Even the cruelties of Bloody Mary (another calumniated queen defended by gallant Cobbett), have been "monstrously exaggerated" and Mary herself unjustly vilified since Elizabeth's reign (*HPR* 1:223). At the same time, he characterizes her victims as "thieves, felons, and traitors" rehabilitated as saints by Fox in his "lying 'Book of Martyrs'" (*HPR* 1:248, 221). Cobbett's treatment of Mary and her critics, then, reveals the same play of praise and censure that he indicts in Reformation apologetics. Oft-repeated phrases like the "fires of Smithfield" have a "horrid sound," he asserts, but is the reality any worse than the terrible punishments glossed over in the reigns of Edward VI, Elizabeth, or James I by their apologists (*HPR* 1:257)? In fighting fire with fire, Cobbett betrays the rhetorical knowingness, where skilled imposture is concerned, necessary to gain his point while undermining his own credibility to the same extent. For every point gained in this manner, a net loss is incurred. His ad hominem treatment of David Hume, whom he dismisses as "this lying historian" (*HPR* 1:116) and "malignant HUME" (*HPR* 1:134), is a study in the rhetorical law of diminishing returns, refuting every aspect of Hume on the Reformation, right down to grammar, but ultimately focusing on Hume himself. To be sure, Cobbett might be counted among early debunkers of the Enlightenment myth of the "Dark Ages," a myth still persisting in popular usage. His indictment of Hume, however, ultimately commits the same offense of criticism by invective putatively exposed in Hume and his fellow Enlightenment historians. It is as if factual authority is not enough to refute Hume the historian but he must also vilify Hume the man. "Want of room compels me to stop," Cobbett conveniently finds at one point; "but, here, in this one authority, we have ten thousand times more than enough to answer the malignant liar, HUME, and all the revilers of monastic life, which lies and revilings it was necessary to silence before proceeding" (*HPR* 1:135).

Yet along with the invective and hyperbole is a provocative critique of Reformation thinking. Underlying arguments for Reformation, according to Cobbett, is a root fallacy. "It had its very birth in division, disunion, discord," he observes in letter 7, "and its life has been worthy of its birth" (*HPR* 1:202). The result is not a religious mystery but simple injustice:

> *Two* true religions, *two* true creeds, differing from each other, contradicting each other, present us with an impossibility: what, then, are we to think of twenty or forty creeds, each differing from all the rest? If deism, or atheism, be something not only wicked in itself, but so mischievous in its effects as to call, in case of the public profession of it, for imprisonment for years and years; if this be the case, what are we to think of laws, the same laws, too, which inflict that cruel punishment, tolerating and encouraging a multiplicity of creeds, all but *one* of which must be false? A code of laws acknowledging and tolerating but one religion is consistent in punishing the deist and the atheist; but if it acknowledge or tolerate *more* than one, it acknowledges or tolerates one *false* one; and let divines say, whether a false religion is not as bad as deism or atheism? (*HPR* 1:203)

Whatever divines might say, it is surely enough for Cobbett what reason says about the illogic of such a system. More significant than the abuses for which this error is already responsible is the logical conclusion to which it tends: "The natural, the necessary effect is, that many men will believe that none of them have truth on their side; and, of course, that the thing is false altogether, and invented solely for the benefit of those who teach it, and who dispute about it" (*HPR* 1:203). Cobbett's criteria are logical, demonstrating the simple impossibility of holding more than one true faith, but he is not interested in disputing which faith is true. Rather, he is concerned with skeptical habits of thought arising from such disputes, the "complexional disposition" described by Burke in Revolutionary France through which categorical belief was being supplanted by contingent belief—or doubt.

From this logic Cobbett infers Pittite governance and its various impostures, paper credit among them. What he sees emerging from Reformation thinking is an ethos of contingency that continues to erode the permanence of property and conviction alike. Behind the demonized figures of Henry VIII and Elizabeth, then, he portrays a rising new breed of political operative, such as Thomas Cranmer, energetically pitting *virtù* against *fortuna* in the service of interest. The shift by which Cobbett's Cranmer manages to become Archbishop and swear obedience to the Pope, whose authority Henry had effectively usurped, effectively turns an oath to account as a caveat: "CRANMER, before he went to be consecrated, went into a chapel, and there made a declaration on oath, that, by the oath he was about to take, and which, for the sake of form, he was obliged to take, he did not intend to bind himself to any thing that tended to prevent him from assisting the king in making any such 'reforms' as he might think useful in the Church of England" (*HPR* 1:65). The logic of Anne Boylen's conviction for treason, as engineered by Cranmer, follows a similarly convoluted course in Cobbett's account. The problem for Cranmer was how to annul a marriage he had previously declared lawful and yet charge the wife with being unfaithful to a man to whom she had never been lawfully married. The result, as Cobbett represents it, is a narrative of events in May 1536 turning on non sequitur: "On the 15th, she is condemned as the wife of the king, on the 17th she is pronounced never to have been his wife, and, on the 19th, she is executed for having been his unfaithful wife!" (*HPR* 1:77). Letter 8 recounts the convoluted, not to say paradoxical, career that finally brought Cranmer himself to the stake:

> As Archbishop under Henry (which office he entered upon with a premeditated false oath on his lips) he sent men and women to the stake because they were not Catholics, and he sent Catholics to the stake, because they would not acknowledge the king's supremacy, and thereby perjure themselves as he had so often done. Become openly a Protestant, in Edward's reign, and openly professing those very principles, for the professing of which he had burnt others, he now burnt his fellow-Protestants, because their grounds for protesting were different from his. (*HPR* 1:251)

Having recanted his Protestant beliefs to escape execution, Cranmer "recanted his recantation" when he saw he must die regardless (*HPR* 1:251). In many respects Cranmer is the central figure in Cobbett's analysis of the effects of Reformation on politics and modern consciousness generally. Henry VIII and Elizabeth I are demonized as despots, but Cranmer represents something different—a kind of technocratic facility with paradox and fallacy that would prove versatile enough to serve the ends of interests as opposed as those of monarchy and republicanism respectively. Other such figures include Elizabeth's secretary of state, Sir William Cecil, of whom it is said that, "If success in unprincipled artifice; if fertility in cunning devices; if the obtaining of one's ends without any regard to the means; if, in this pursuit, sincerity be to be set at nought, and truth, law, justice, and mercy, be to be trampled under foot; if, so that you succeed in your end, apostacy, forgery, perjury, and the shedding of innocent blood be to be thought nothing of, this CECIL was certainly the greatest statesman that ever lived" (*HPR* 1:298). This is clearly ironic, but in 1806 Cobbett had wondered whether such traits now qualified a politician like Pitt to be designated an "excellent statesman." The implication is that, if efficiency served as criterion, then they probably did. That Cecil's successor, Francis Walsingham, is similarly portrayed as "an exceedingly prudent and cunning man, and wholly destitute of all care about means, so that he carried his end" (*HPR* 1:299), suggests that Reformation *virtù* had definitively supplanted old English virtue in public life. If Pitt's name does not figure explicitly here, perhaps this only testifies to his hegemonic influence in the decades following his death. Letter 10's catalogue of worthies leads up to the present Liverpool administration and its leader, Liverpool himself, who, Cobbett points out, once ascribed Irish starvation to a surplus of food, and whose career—under Pitt, Addington, Pitt again, Portland, and Perceval—demonstrates an uncannily durable because versatile *virtù*. "What this Bible-Saint would have done, if there had been a change of religion at every change of ministry," Cobbett concludes, "I shall not pretend to say" (*HPR* 1:300).

In fact, he does not have to. The final Letters of Cobbett's history trace the necessary effects of Reformation down to the present, making clear his post-Reformation perspective on Pittite England—paper credit and all. From the "system" established by the first Reformation, indeed, he educes four further developments: Cromwell's Commonwealth, the Glorious Revolution, and the American and French Revolutions, the latter "playing back the principles of the English Reformation-people upon themselves" (*HPR* 1:351). While logical in itself, the tendency of these developments has led to unintended consequences. In his treatment of William's war against France, Cobbett focuses on the establishment of the Bank of England to finance this war. His account of the result, including an inference of what might have been from what was, recalls Burke's deduction of the traditional English state from the chaos of revolution in France:

> Thus arose loans, funds, banks, bankers, bank-notes, and a NATIONAL DEBT; things that England had never heard or dreamed of, before this war for "preserving the Protestant religion as by law established;" things without which she had had a long and glorious career of many centuries, and had been the greatest and happiest country in the world; things which she never would, and never could, have heard of, had it not been for what is audaciously called the "REFORMATION," seeing that to lend money at interest; that is to say, for gain; that is to say, to receive money for the use of money; seeing that to do this was contrary, and still is contrary to the principles of the catholic Church; and amongst Christians, or professors of Christianity, such a thing was never heard of before that which is impudently called 'THE REFORMATION.' (*HPR* 1:403)

Passages like this, with their obsessive iteration and heavy emphasis, combine reason and passion in ways that dramatize the regressive logic they attribute to Reformation thinking. Cobbett's very rhetoric involves itself in the ethos of rationally sublimated savagery it exposes in Pitt's England for the precise reason that its opposition emerges from the same provenance. This is the seeming paradox of radical reform for Cobbett, its dialectical deduction of itself from the System it critiques. The French Revolution (or " 'Reformation' the FIFTH"), then, represents the extreme logical conclusion, even the reductio ad absurdum, of the argument of Reformation:

> Humiliation greater than the English Government had to endure, in the above event, it is difficult to conceive; but the French Revolution taught the world what "reformation" can do, when pushed to their full and natural extent. In England the "Reformation" contented itself with plundering the convents and the poor of their all, and the secular clergy in part V. But, in France, they took the whole; though we ought to mark well this difference; that, in France, they applied this whole to the use of the public; a bad use, perhaps; but, to public use they applied the whole of the plunder; while, in England, the plunder was scrambled for, and remained divided amongst, individuals! (*HPR* 1:442)

In these prescient words, Cobbett remarked a historical tendency whose logic would extend to the great revolutions of the next century. His own career, grounded in perpetual opposition, was a reflection of the same dialectical logic. As an anonymous pamphleteer rather equivocally observed in 1819 of Cobbett's "progress" from his anti-Jacobin years to radical reform (and perhaps beyond that to republicanism): "He has proceeded, step by step, as light broke in upon a vigorous intellect without early cultivation. He has stopped no where but where he thought he saw the truth. When he discovered his error, he avowed it, without regard to the fool's idol—Consistency."[23]

5

Reason in Extremis:
Narratives of Regressive Rationality

> I shall not live to behold the unravelling of the
> intricate plot, which saddens and perplexes the
> awful drama of Providence, now acting on the
> moral theatre of the world. Whether for thought
> or for action, I am at the end of my career. You
> are in the middle of yours. In what part of it's
> orbit the nation, with which we are carried
> along, moves at this instant, it is not easy to
> conjecture. It may, perhaps, be far advanced
> in its aphelion.—But when to return?
>
> —Edmund Burke,
> *First Letter on a Regicide Peace* (1796)

Disraeli's *Vaurien* (1797) asks the following questions of rational reform: "Is it possible that immoderate reason can
really become actual insanity? Can the wholesome cup of reason
overflow with all its gelid beverage, inflame with its frigidity,
and, like ice-water, taken in excessive quantities, will it heat?"
The implied answer is yes. *Vaurien* was written during the anti-
Jacobin alarms of the late 1790s, and its author, Isaac Disraeli,
father of the future Conservative prime minister, wrote as a committed foe of literary Jacobinism. The questions asked in the
above passage concern one Mr. Subtile, a radical philosopher
given to the kind of ultrarational speculation popularly associated at the time with figures like William Godwin. Disraeli's
analysis of Mr. Subtile's literary Jacobinism is Burkean in

provenance. While clearly incited by the narrowly partisan anti-Jacobin appropriation of Burke discussed in chapter 3, however, it also keeps in view more far-reaching cultural implications educed by Burke from revolutionary arguments. In his preface to the novel, Disraeli indicts not simply wild-eyed radicals of Mr. Subtile's ilk but Pittite England and its enabling of the rational hedonism on which Jacobin philosophy turns. "Our hearts," he charges, "like our fortunes, are indulged in excessive gratifications, and alike become feeble, cold, and exhausted." England, in his view, has become a "nation of jobbers" for whom the basest motives are now a matter of public honor.[1] In this, his analysis differs little from that of William Cobbett, who shared both his Country toryism and, if short-lived in Cobbett's case, connections in the anti-Jacobin press. Disraeli would not have followed Cobbett's course into radicalism, but given his distrust of "immoderate reason" such extreme reactions would not have surprised him either.

Nor would they surprise Mr. Subtile, who delights in subversive outcomes. "Every opinion has an affirmative and a negative," he instructs the novel's hero Charles, "both, to an ingenious mind, sufficiently accompanied by some probabilities; he who would distinguish himself *adopts generally the negative*, and accommodates the unknown and intangible nature of the incomprehensible with the more familiar and visible line of possibility."[2] The relation of rhetoric to probability is a commonplace of rhetorical theory. There is nothing remarkable about Mr. Subtile's comments in this respect, then, beyond their superficially outrageous cast. Perhaps, though, it is telling that a philosopher, especially one as closely identified with rational reform as Mr. Subtile, should so definitively reject any claim to logical validity in his thinking. To be sure, he is a typical representation of the so-called "New Philosophy" reviled by the anti-Jacobin press. Yet the moral relativism underlying his advice to Disraeli's young hero reflects rhetorical options available to Jacobin and anti-Jacobin alike at this time. Canning, Frere, et al. of the *Anti-Jacobin* were every bit as adept in the rational arts of incitement. For this reason, the "familiar and visible line of possibility" Mr. Subtile advises young Charles to keep an eye out for suggests nothing so much as the proverbial main chance. That the opportunities presenting themselves to the "affirmative" and "negative" of any given opinion seem to favor the "negative" suggests that for Mr. Subtile, and other Machiavellian rhetoricians on either side of a question, argument is less a matter of logical or moral judgment than rhetorical choice, a knowing and interested accommodation of reason to contingency.

The notion that certain rhetorical choices are determinative of certain lines of action, good or bad, is not surprising. It speaks to the classic rationale of rhetoric. "All the ends of speaking are reducible to four," states George Campbell; "every speech being intended to enlighten the understanding, to please the imagination, to move the passions, or to influence the will" (*PR* 1). In the various public venues examined by this study, such choices can be quite decisive, setting the courses of arguments and careers alike. This could be shown to be true even in a very equivocal case like that of Thomas Love Peacock. Peacock's reform-minded novel *Melincourt*, briefly discussed in chapter 3, is the most straightforward of his satiric novels. The difficulty posed by the multivocal dialogism of his other novels, however, tends to reflect the fact that writers (and speakers) were generally faced with difficult choices at this time. For Peacock satire, politically engaged or not, was only one of these choices. In 1810, when he published a loco-descriptive poem entitled *The Genius of the Thames*, his career seemed destined to play itself out in an exhausted tradition of minor neoclassical verse. While *Genius of the Thames* employs topographical conventions to celebrate English trade, however—"Throned in Augusta's ample port, / Imperial commerce holds her court"[3]—the step from commercial epic to cultural critique can be one of infinitesimal degree. If his radical friend Shelley questioned the assumption underlying the poem, "that commerce is prosperity,"[4] Peacock himself privately acknowledged that "the Thames is almost as good a subject for a satire as a panegyric." In a letter to his publisher Thomas Hookham, he sketches out the two scenarios, satiric and panegyrical, with telling fluency:

> A satirist might exclaim: The rapacity of Commerce, not content with the immense advantages derived from this river in a course of nearly 300 miles, erects a ponderous engine over the very place of its nativity, to suck up its unborn waters from the bosom of the earth, and pump them into a navigable canal! . . .

> A panegyrist, on the contrary, after expiating on the benefits of
> commercial navigation, and of that great effort of human ingenu-
> ity, the Thames and Severn Canal, which ascends the hills, sinks
> into the valleys, and penetrates the bosom of the earth, to unite
> the two noblest rivers of this most wealthy, prosperous, happy,
> generous, loyal, patriotic, &c, &c, &c, kingdom of England might
> say. . . .

And so on. Commentators generally stress the Satirist's emergence here, but Peacock merely lays out the options, and in fact
the Panegyrist gets the last word. More telling is the passage's
facility coupled with perhaps a tacit dismay at this facility, the
ease with which each position may be taken and abandoned in
favor of another. The bland et ceteras, the glibness of the praise
and censure alike, the casual "I must again break off for the present" ending this exercise,[5] suggest that Peacock is displaying
not two alternative positions but a technique of representation
versatile enough to accommodate any position. Its subtext of critical unease notwithstanding, this demonstration—undertaken,
however lightly, for the benefit of a bookseller—is not about
genre finally so much as about rhetorical ethos and its relation to
public life. Peacock would go on to become a satirist and an official in the East India Company, a seeming incongruity that suggests both practical necessity and perhaps further choices not
made.

The course of William Cobbett's career seems more highly determined and even determinate. The anonymous pamphleteer
cited at the end of the previous chapter, indeed, hypothetically
follows its course to the very limits of republicanism—in effect,
the exact antithesis of Cobbett's enduring loyalism:

> Indeed, the progress of Mr. Cobbett is a phenomenon that should
> excite universal admiration. He has proceeded, step by step, as
> light broke in upon a vigorous intellect without early cultivation.
> He has stopped no where but where he thought he saw the truth.
> When he discovered his error, he avowed it, without regard to the
> fool's idol—Consistency. He halted not, however, by the way, till
> he has at last arrived at *Radical Reform*. There he has now taken
> up his quarters, probably not long to abide. It is not too much to
> expect that he will take up his staff, at no distant period, and
> walk on till he shall arrive at Republicanism, at Liberty, and
> Equality.[6]

The Bunyan references notwithstanding, Cobbett's pilgrimage to *"Radical Reform"* owes less to Providence than to Reason. Each of its stages is deduced from a previous stage with Republicanism forming the logical conclusion—or reductio ad absurdum, depending on how the passage is read. If Bunyan's narrative turns on theology, this one seems to turn on argument. Perhaps it is an a priori argument, though 1819, the pamphlet's publication date, marked a pivotal point for the Reform argument. Whether or not Peterloo or even the anticipation of something like Peterloo plays a role in this line of reasoning, however, its tendency is clear. The upward arc suggested in the incremental progress from benighted to enlightened intellect follows the familiar course of Whig history. Cobbett would likely have objected to the argument that his thought was heading towards an ultimate issue in Republicanism, just as he would have quizzed the assumptions identifying this position with Liberty and Equality. He was as alert in 1819 to the regressive magic of such words as he was in 1802. One year later, he would employ hot-button arguments in defense of his queen using royalist equivalents of these words. Yet the narrative tendency encompassing these and other rhetorical options would seem as accommodating to contingency as the "line of possibility" along which Mr. Subtile expounds his subversive arguments.

Priestley attributes this narrative bias to certain inherent principles in humanity and nature alike. In one of his *Lectures*, "Of Climax, and the Order of Words in a Sentence," he asserts an identity between natural processes and rhetorical arrangement:

> In a world constituted as this is, a view of a gradual rise and improvement in things cannot fail to make an agreeable prospect. The continual observation of this furnishes us with a flock of pleasing ideas, which are constantly accumulating, and which are easily transferred, by association, upon every thing, either in composition, or in any other field of view, which presents a similar appearance. How agreeable to all persons is the idea of the days growing longer, of spring advancing, and of children growing up to men! (*LOC* 275)

The lecture goes on to assert that in rhetoric "that order of terms which constitutes the happiest climax generally coincides with the *order* of *time and nature,* in which the things they express really stand related to, or are connected with one another" (*LOC* 275–76). Priestley is concerned here with what he implies is a natural order in discourse but that he in fact ends up tracing to conventions governed by association. Chief among these conventions are those relating to "a gradual rise and improvement in things" and the "agreeable prospect" to which this process tends. What he does not add, however—namely, the fact that declension is equally intelligible to minds conditioned to perceive improvement—is surely a corollary of his argument. Conjectural histories of rhetoric cited in this study assume a pattern of progress toward or away from some salutary prospect or another, even as they also prescribe rhetorical usages themselves conditioned by such patterns of thinking. Two cases in point are Blair's *Lectures on Rhetoric and Belles Lettres* and Sheridan's *Lectures on Elocution*. Like Sheridan, Blair posits a past ideal of eloquence even as he regrets the straitened discourse of reason into which it has shrunk. Where Sheridan projects a rhetorical renaissance in which this ideal is recovered, however, Blair cautions against the interested use of primitive passion by rational opportunists like Bolingbroke, a category later to include the neo-Burkean rhetoric of clever young anti-Jacobins. Along such a path, Blair implies, lies something more regressive than primitive eloquence. In the same way, histories of political rhetoric emerging from the parliamentary anthologies of Browne and Hazlitt date the acme or nadir of English eloquence to Walpolean polity, surely the best and worst of political ascendancies judging by its nineteenth-century commentators.

Such arguments have a distinct bias toward narrative. Whig history, after all, is a narrative based on an argument about progress, for better or worse. If the *Anti-Jacobin Review and Magazine* traced "The Rise, Progress, Operations, and Effects of Jacobinism in these Realms," a lead article in the *Black Dwarf* could claim to trace the "Progress of Despotism" even as it also reported on the "Progress of Reform" (*AJR* Apr. 1817: 177–82). *The Republican* could run articles decrying the "Progress of Persecution," while running others on the "Progress of Liberal Feeling and Decay of Superstition" (*R* 8 Dec. 1820: 532). The conclusions reached by such arguments depend only partially on reason and observation in that the tendencies they project also represent rhetorical choices—the very choices entertained by

Peacock in his letter to Hookham. To be sure, what might be described as a Whig history of rhetoric is the inference of a broader historical enterprise extending to culture itself. Yet even so comprehensive a view as Adam Ferguson's, in his famous *Essay on the History of Civil Society* (1767), finally comes down to a choice of possible arguments. While accepting the progressivist assumptions of Enlightenment civil history, Ferguson nevertheless warns that "Man may mistake the objects of his pursuit; he may misapply his industry, and misplace his improvements." Action may be an effect of logical error, he suggests, for "it is certain, that many of our arguments would hurry us, for the sake of wealth and of population, into a scene where mankind being exposed to corruption, are unable to defend their possessions; and where they are, in the end, subject to oppression and ruin."[7] Ferguson refers here to arguments identifying prosperity exclusively with specific factors such as population and wealth. To argue for progress solely on this basis, effectively making these or other factors absolutely synonymous with prosperity, is to risk setting humanity on a historical course grounded in error. By the end of the century, Malthus would turn the population argument upside down by making population synonymous with misery, an idea described by William Hazlitt in his *Spirit of the Age* as "an amusing and extreme paradox." Hazlitt argues that what Malthus did was to replace one fallacy with another, for he "wished not merely to advance to the discovery of certain great and valuable truths, but at the same time to overthrow certain unfashionable paradoxes by exaggerated statements—to curry favour with existing prejudices and interests by garbled representations" (*CWH* 11:105, 112). Arguments concerning the negative effects of too little or too much population may be equally valid in themselves, but the employment of one to the exclusion of others is the sure way to fallacy—according to Hamilton's definition, "stating what is true in a qualified sense, as true in an unconditional one." Yet this is the danger Ferguson and Hazlitt see in rhetorical appropriations of cultural or, what in this context is perhaps the same thing, narrative destiny.

Hazlitt believed that Malthus had given opinion a "wrong bias" by categorically asserting a regressive relation between popula-

tion and prosperity (*CWH* 11:104). At the same time, the logic of
even skewed arguments may be consistent within the limits of a
closed system. In the *Prelude,* Wordsworth remembers Revolutionary France as such a hermetic public space, a kind of logical
interregnum where "passions had the privilege to work, / And
never hear the sound of their own names."[8] This is surely as true
of the reaction to the revolution as of the revolution itself. The
most catalytic text of the reaction, of course, was Burke's *Reflections*, at once a critique of regressive rationality and to a lesser
degree an example of it. Some of the more extreme charges made
in this work, which include allegations of cannibalism, likely
originated with sources among England's growing population of
royalist émigrés with whom Burke had frequent contact. Burke's
intense dislike of radical dissent is another factor. In November
1789, at a meeting of the Revolution Society, formed to commem-
orate the Glorious Revolution of 1688, the Reverend Richard
Price delivered a sermon that Burke took to be an incitement to
revolution in England. Out of lurid rumors from abroad and sus-
picions of treason at home Burke thus constructed, in L. G.
Mitchell's words, "a diabolid of ghosts and phantoms that men-
aced the English constitution."[9] To some, the violence of Burke's
language, not to mention what appeared to be a dramatic shift
from his earlier sympathies for the American Revolution, suggested mental imbalance. For Henry Brougham, the *Reflections*
was evidence of "the sad devastation which a disordered fancy
can make in the finest understanding." Others suggested that
Burke was "debilitated in mind as a result of the onset of old age"
or attributed his "disturbed imagination" to "political Insanity."[10]
That Burke was making much the same charges of the French
revolutionaries and their English sympathizers speaks not only
to the general disturbance of the times but to the vexed nature of
critical constructions of these times on both sides of the question.
In either case, rational critique was directed to ends more in
keeping with polemics than with principle. The passions described by Wordsworth as working so freely under names not
their own in the revolutionary interregnum were perhaps the
necessary inference of a rhetoric given absolute license by "immoderate reason."

Burke may be seen as both a critic and abettor of this inference.[11] That the irrational may be subjected to reason is a

premise of his *Philosophical Enquiry into the Origin of our Ideas of the Sublime and Beautiful* (1757), which he describes as "an attempt to range and methodize some of our most leading passions." Burke's assumption is that a rational understanding of the passions is necessary for those "who would affect them upon solid and sure principles,"[12] a cautionary note arising from a sense of the dangers posed by passion where such checks do not apply. Commentators have recently questioned the use of this text as a guide to Burke's rhetorical practice in the *Reflections*, noting that the two works are separated by more than three decades. F. P. Lock points out that by 1789 Burke himself had in fact disowned the *Enquiry*, objecting that "the train of his thoughts had gone another way, and the whole bent of his mind turned from such subjects."[13] The fact remains that contemporary readers made the connection,[14] and indeed Burke may have hoped to preempt such potentially damaging associations by distancing himself from the earlier work. Lock's reading of the *Reflections* assumes that Burke's grounding in traditional rhetoric at Trinity College served him for life,[15] even though he was propounding affective theories of the sublime at a time when rhetorical theory was moving in the same direction. The *Enquiry*'s brief associationist discussion of the emotional properties of words could in fact suggest possible affinities with New Rhetorical and Elocutionist assimilations of sensationalist psychology.[16] George Campbell at least raises the possibility of deliberately employing obscurity to rhetorical ends, thus hinting at a possible rhetorical application of sublime affect as Burke understood it. Passages from the *Enquiry* like the following, in any case, seem clearly to speak to the associationism of Campbell and Priestley: "Now, as there is a moving tone of voice, an impassioned countenance, an agitated gesture, which affect independently of the things about which they are exerted, so there are words, and certain dispositions of words, which being peculiarly devoted to passionate subjects, and always used by those who are under the influence of any passion; they touch and move us more than those which far more clearly and distinctly express the subject matter." Burke refers in this same passage to words "commonly sacred to great occasions" and thus invested with such associations even in ordinary use[17]—presumably whether or not they are used appropriately. In instances like this at least, his discussion of the sublime in language use seems to fall within the pale of New Rhetorical theory. Lock's reading of Burke within a wholly traditional rhetorical context is nevertheless corrective of recent tendencies to read a work like the *Reflections* as a piece of fiction or a dramatic performance. The *Reflections* was first and foremost conceived as an argument, intended to counter other arguments and destined in its turn to be countered by many further arguments.

This is not to say that Burke does not exploit sensational effect when reason fails him, even as he exposes such shifts in opposing arguments. Nor does he scruple to allow argument to take fabulous form when reason leads him that way. Peter Hughes goes so far as to assert that the language of the *Reflections* abolishes distinctions between reality and fiction, creating "an order of experience that changes discourse into events."[18] Yet the set pieces and gripping narratives so often evoked in critical commentary on the *Reflections* do not supplant reality so much as emerge from an argument about reality, an argument both capable of invoking the "stupendous wisdom" molding the English state (*RRF* 8:84)—Burke's reality—and of countering arguments conceived to dissemble that reality. The subversive arguments made in Price's sermon take for their starting point the Glorious Revolution and the interruption of the Royal Succession occasioned by that event, effectively maintaining that because on this occasion a monarch was called to the throne by choice, all kings therefore rule by popular sufferance. This argument, Burke charges, has so often been preached from the pulpits of dissent that it is now implicitly accepted by the faithful "as if it were a first principle admitted without dispute" (*RRF* 8:65). In this way, it has become a subliminal argument, easily made to seem harmless by "equivocations and slippery constructions" (*RRF* 8:65). To argue that such deviations prove that all sovereigns must be chosen is as extreme, in Burke's view, as to argue that inheritance is "*indefeasible* in every person, who should be found in the succession to a throne, and under every circumstance, which no civil or political right can be" (*RRF* 8:77). Price's fallacies serve only to conceal the "direct tendency" of his reform argument, which for Burke is merely treason disguised as natural right. Burke traces the error of such arguments to a willful misconstruction of the very tendencies corrected by traditionary logic in his own historical argument:

These gentlemen of the Old Jewry, in all their reasonings on the Revolution of 1688, have a revolution which happened in England about forty years before, and the late French revolution, so much before their eyes, and in their hearts, that they are constantly confounding all the three together. It is necessary that we should separate what they confound. We must recall their erring fancies to the *acts* of the Revolution which we revere, for the discovery of its true *principles*. If the *principles* of the Revolution of 1688 are any where to be found, it is in the statute called the *Declaration of Right*. In that most wise, sober, and considerate declaration, drawn up by great lawyers and great statesmen, and not by warm and inexperienced enthusiasts, not one word is said, nor one suggestion made, of a general right "to choose our *governors*; to cashier them for misconduct; and to *form* a government for *ourselves*." (*RRF* 8:66–67)

The not quite veiled allusion to religious enthusiasm implies an irrationalist inference in arguments for reform made by those who, as Burke charges elsewhere, "have nothing of politics but the passions they excite" (*RRF* 8:62). Yet these arguments also betray the more calculated workings of imposture. Price's confounding of three different revolutions as a premise for radical reform—one of them in another country and, in according to Burke, wholly without precedent in its aberrant character—recalls Cobbett's deliberate confounding of Reformation and Revolution as a rationale for neo-Pittite governance. Cobbett views all historical junctures subsequent to the English Reformation (the English Civil War, the Glorious Revolution, the American and French Revolutions) as simply so many further stages of Reformation. In both cases, certain arguments are seen as having set in motion historical tendencies that can only have led to certain conclusions, whether happy or not. Both start from preconceived conclusions and construct their historical arguments backwards from these conclusions. If Cobbett argues that Pitt is the product of Reformation, it is safe to say that Cobbett's Reformation could never have existed without Pitt, while for Price English constitutional history finds its raison d'être in the French Revolution.

These are a priori arguments of Whig history, a narrative that can claim the certainty of myth because it starts from a foregone conclusion and inexorably works itself out within this closed system. Burke discovers the principles of the Revolution of 1688 in the Declaration of Right, an act of Parliament he describes as "the cornerstone of our constitution, as reinforced, explained, improved, and in its fundamental principles for ever settled" (*RRF* 8:67). He secures his argument by pointing out that in this statute, which describes itself as "'An act for declaring the rights and liberties of the subject, and for *settling* the *succession* of the crown,'" the issues of individual right and royal succession are bound indissolubly together (*RRF* 8:67). For Burke, English constitutional history has followed an ineluctable course not only confirmed by acts like the Declaration of Right but corrected by them when necessary. The framers of this statute were as well acquainted with the arguments of abstract rights as anyone proposing them now, "But, for reasons worthy of that practical wisdom which superseded their theoretic science, they preferred this positive, recorded, *hereditary* title to all which can be dear to the man and the citizen, to that vague speculative right, which exposed their sure inheritance to be scrambled for and torn to pieces by every wild litigious spirit" (*RRF* 8:82–83). They thus employed a logic that was in part rational and in part historical, with reason subordinate to the logic of tradition but nevertheless serving to correct occasional, and inevitable, departures from that logic. Such a corrective influence, Burke argues, was exerted by the "small and a temporary deviation" made necessary by the succession of William III (*RRF* 8:68). If this sounds paradoxical, Burke not only himself imposes what seems like a rhetorical solution on the problem but implies that the framers of the Declaration of Right had effectively done so themselves. In a passage describing the comportment of Lord Somers, the Whig parliamentarian who introduced the act, Burke notes the use of "pious, legislative ejaculation" rather than the usual "dry, imperative style of an act of parliament": "It is curious to observe with what address this temporary solution of continuity is kept from the eye; whilst all that could be found in this act of necessity to countenance the idea of an hereditary succession is brought forward, and fostered and made the most of, by this great man, and by the legislature who followed him" (*RRF* 8:69). Burke's old patron, William Gerard Hamilton, himself could not have suggested a more effective or perhaps even a more expedient course.

Yet behind this strategy, what Burke calls the "politic, well-wrought veil" thrown over every circumstance that might weaken what the act sought to strengthen (*RRF* 8:69), was the stark fact that English legislators at this juncture did indeed have the option of taking the extreme course advocated by radicals a century later. Burke acknowledges as much, but the fact that this course was not taken, that every means was used to avoid "the very appearance of it," is for him the main point (*RRF* 8:69). From this view, the arguments of Price and the Revolution Society are based only on what might have been the issue of the Glorious Revolution and are for this reason purely speculative. The mere fact that their option might have been chosen does not alter the fact that another was actually acted upon. The reforms they infer as inevitable from their speculative reading of English constitutional history are thus grounded in fallacy. "These gentleman," Burke concludes, "may value themselves as much as they please on their Whig principles; but I never desire to be thought a better Whig than Lord Somers; or to understand the principles of the revolution better than those by whom it was brought about; or to read in the declaration of right any mysteries unknown to those whose penetrating style has engraved in our ordinances, and in our hearts, the words and spirit of that immortal law" (*RRF* 8:70–71).

Driving this splendid rhetoric is nevertheless a sense of what other options might have been chosen by French legislators. So astounded is Burke by the ferment caused by the revolution that he cannot rule out any developments in its career, for better or worse. Nor can he be sure that radical deviations from even such venerable statutes as the Declaration of Right are not also possible in England. "The gentlemen of the Society for Revolution see nothing in that of 1688 but the deviation from the constitution," he asserts; "and they take the deviation from the principle for the principle" (*RRF* 8:73). It is just such a regular system of fallacy that Burke sees as methodizing the anarchy in France. This seems to be one possible implication of the passage (quoted from in an earlier chapter) in which Hazlitt imagines Burke extracting the principles of social order from the chaos of Revolutionary France, "watching the passions of men gradually unfolding themselves in new situations, penetrating those hidden motives which hurried them from one extreme into another" (*CWH* 7:319–20). Unlike his Burke, however, Hazlitt arrives at this conclusion after the fact. The brilliant paradox involved in locating the provenance of the Burkean state in the ferment of revolution surely does not imply that Burke's could have been a foregone conclusion. If the traditional state magisterially propounded by Lord Somers (and Burke) lies somewhere between the extremes at play in this chaos, the revolutionary dialectic Hazlitt posits here makes any extreme equally viable as an option. The profoundly conservative thesis argued in the *Reflections* is but one possible course immanent in this dialectic, and Burke knows it. The French people followed a course prepared by the "delusive plausibilities" of revolutionary argument (*RRF* 8:89), but if the original premise was flawed, what has followed is perfectly consistent with this premise. Burke can therefore assert that "This was unnatural. The rest is in order," even as he argues that none of it was necessary, that it was an "unforced choice" (*RRF* 8:89, 91). Within the closed system of its delusively plausible logic, the career of revolution is wholly accountable.

What Burke does and does not concede of the choice that might have been taken is that it is a choice at all. Just as Price's argument confounds three different revolutions in educing the grounds for a fourth—at least this is where Burke sees the argument going—Burke confounds two systems of monarchy in his argument, subtly shifting his focus from an eloquent evocation of English mixed government to France's now imperiled ancien régime. From this rhetorical conflation, indeed, might be traced later neo-Pittite conflations of English libertarianism and continental legitimacy during the Napoleonic Wars. Burke has effected it by tacitly identifying the grounds on which both the English and French systems are putatively founded, a historical inheritance in which opposed but reciprocal interests render "deliberation a matter not of choice, but of necessity; they make all change a subject of *compromise*, which naturally begets moderation" (*RRF* 8:86). A too absolute devotion to their kings he dismisses as a recent development among the French, an "amiable error" (*RRF* 8:87). The difference between this error and Price's, one venial and the other "unnatural" and unspeakably destructive, must lie in the fact that one represents only a deviation from the rule, while the other makes deviation the rule—after which the rest naturally follows. Burkean "amiable error" is little more than the exaggeration of a just principle, an idea taken too far but still subject to correction. For Price and his confederates, the Glorious Revolution lives on in its subversive potential, not in the actual remedies prescribed to offset this potential. That this revisionary reading of the past should emerge so fortuitously as a rationale for radical action in the present suggests opportunism to Burke. Yet the terms of his own argument indicate that probability and choice—the grounds of rhetorical contingency—operate on both sides of the question.

Burke, indeed, argues ultimately from convention rather than logic. When he characterizes the premise of the French Revolution as "unnatural," he means that it represents a deviation from usage or custom, though he does not scruple to allow his own arguments to carry the categorical force of logic. He debunks the revolutionary argument, with its necessitarian underpinnings, by asserting that it in fact represents an "unforced choice" even as he asserts that the course for which he argues is "a matter not of choice, but of necessity," though this proposition is true only within the parameters of convention. The necessary issue of this course is "moderation," which is to say that tradition "naturally begets moderation" in the same way, presumably, that what has actually happened in France, as monstrous as it is, is the natural issue of an unnatural cause. But it is more than this in that it naturally points to further, even more monstrous, inferences of the logic Burke detects in revolutionary arguments, a logic whose career he describes in *Letters on a Regicide Peace* as "Going straight forward to it's [*sic*] end, unappalled by peril, unchecked by remorse, despising all common maxims and all common means" (*RP* 9:190-2). One man's "'line of possibility,'" to quote Disraeli's Mr. Subtile once again, is another's *reductio ad absurdum*. "False they are, unsound, sophistical," Burke asserts of Jacobin arguments in the *Letters*; "but they are regular in their direction. They all bear one way" (*RP* 9:226). As such, they can only lead from extreme to extreme. If the promised end of revolution is unrealistic, this does not render implausible the worst predictions about where it will actually end—at least this is the drift of Burke's argument. Burke seems to be responding here to Paine's assertion in *Rights of Man*, that "the present age will hereafter merit to be called the Age of Reason, and the present generation will appear to the future as the Adam of a new world," which is in turn a response to what Paine takes to be a "political Adam" set up by Burke in the *Reflections*,[19] a kind of original progenitor of English constitutionalism to whom all future generations are forever bound. Burke's rejoinder in the *Letters* is to follow the logic of Paine's (and the Jacobins') rational program of primitive recovery not along the progressive course of human perfectibility but straight to Hobbesian savagery:

> Endeavouring to persuade the people that they are no better than beasts, the whole body of their institution tends to make them beasts of prey, furious and savage. For this purpose the active part of them is disciplined into a ferocity which has no parallel. To this ferocity there is joined not one of the rude, unfashioned virtues, which accompany the vices, where the whole are left to grow up together in the rankness of uncultivated nature. But nothing is left to nature in their systems. (*RP* 9:246)

This seems paradoxical, but for Burke nothing is natural that is forced from nature. His terrible evocation of a regressive natural state at the end of the revolutionary vista recalls Hazlitt's observation of "singularly affected and outrageous simplicity" (*CWH* 5:262) in the culture of Jacobin France. According to Hazlitt, this doctrinaire primitivism equates revolution with "the turning the Thuilleries into a potatoe-garden [*sic*]"—but then, as he reflects, what is the use of polite arts in a shipwreck or a famine (*CWH* 13:213, 137)?

Burke believed that in the French Revolution such arts had achieved the equivalent of a natural disaster in the very midst of civil society. Chief among these were the arts of argument. When he asserts to his countrymen that "nor as yet have we subtilized ourselves into savages" (*RRF* 8:137), he refers to rationalizations that have taken the French beyond the certain limits of the known to the speculative reaches of unredeemed nature. That his arguments must pursue them there is the necessary consequence of a dialectic set in motion by his own critique. He in fact characterizes this potential danger as a strategy in "Letter to a Member of the National Assembly" (1791), a work written on the

heels of the *Reflections*, in which he argues that false principles
are most effectively debunked by following them to consequences
that can be demonstrated to subvert the results they project. "If
this kind of demonstration is not permitted," he points out, "the
process of reasoning called *reductio ad absurdum,* which even
the severity of geometry does not reject, could not be employed at
all in legislative discussions."[20] Yet logic pushed to the limit or
beyond may assume the regressive force of rhetoric. This is the
possible end (or fate?) awaiting Burke's argument as it follows
revolutionary logic to its extreme conclusion in primitive triumph. That this triumph is in fact a foregone conclusion, an "unforced choice," is clear to Burke in the *Reflections* as he describes
the terrible ease with which the revolutionaries have secured
their prize—"Their whole march was more like a triumphal pro-
cession than the progress of a war" (*RRF* 8:90)—amid the waste
of civil society. The triumph is a recurring image in the *Reflections*, describing a savage progress through accounts of everything from Cromwell's rebellion to events in France. The occasion
of Price's sermon recalls for Burke a similar occasion in the previous century, which "had, though in a different place, a triumph
as memorable as that of Dr. Price; and some of the great preachers of that period partook of it as eagerly as he has done in the
triumph of France" (*RRF* 8:116–17). The occasion was the trial of
Charles I and an eyewitness account of the king's entry into
London preceded by one Hugh Peters, a chaplain in the parliamentary army: "'I saw,' says the witness, 'his majesty in the coach
with six horses, and Peters riding before the king *triumphing*'"
(*RRF* 8:116–17). In the Reverend Peters, Burke sees a type not
merely of Price but of Enlightenment itself and the regressive
course it must necessarily take if left uncorrected. Peters, he
says, "had as much illumination, and as much zeal, and had as
effectually undermined all *the superstition and error* which
might impede the great business he was engaged in, as any who
follow and repeat after him, in this age, which would assume to
itself an exclusive title to the knowledge of the rights of men, and
all the glorious consequences of that knowledge" (*RRF* 8:116–
17). That Peters would later be executed for treason, "himself a
sacrifice to the triumph which he led as Pontiff" (*RRF* 8:116–17),
is for Burke a grim demonstration of the same logic impelling
this unfortunate divine to triumph over a lawful king in the first

place. Conor Cruise O'Brien notes that Burke himself triumphs visibly here "with this deadly *argumentum ad hominem*,"[21] but this in turn is an inevitable consequence of the course along which his own argument has taken him. The spectacle surrounding Price's sermon is part of a larger tendency leading inexorably forward to enlightenment or back to utter savagery, depending on how the argument is cast. For Burke its barbarous ferocity—which he compares to a primitive victory celebration (*RRF* 8:117–18)—is not simply at odds with the Enlightenment principles underlying it, but the necessary issue of their unchecked career. Even, however, as (in the true spirit of Enlightenment) he exposes the fallacy of these principles, his own argument necessarily becomes its irrational opposite, evoking sensational images of sacrifice and cannibalism.[22] At such times, the logical interregnum created by his fatalistic conjectures threatens to render inoperative the stabilizing counterarguments of tradition. Yet he is convinced that he has no choice but to pursue revolutionary arguments from seemingly logical premises to regressive inferences. "At home we behold similar beginnings," he warns in the *Reflections*. "We are on our guard against similar conclusions" (*RRF* 8:154).

In *Letters on a Regicide Peace*, Burke identifies a type of rhetorical *virtù* perfectly suited to debate in a discursive no-man's-land. Of the "Jacobin minority" among the larger community, he warns that "No sort of argumentative materials, suited to their purposes, have been withheld" (*RP* 9:226). Perhaps like his progeny among the emerging anti-Jacobin press, Burke understood this temper so well because his rhetoric drew its energy from that which it opposed. As early as his ironic tour de force in "A Vindication of Natural Society" (1756), where he assumes the persona of a free-thinking deist, he was accustomed to playing this Faustian game of argument by sympathetic identification. In the *Vindication*, Burke anticipates both the arguments of Jacobin philosophy and the parodic attitudinizing of anti-Jacobin reaction when he exhorts readers to abandon conventional society and religion in order to "vindicate ourselves into perfect Liberty."[23] Four decades later, *Letters on a Regicide Peace* would push the limits of argument still further for the simple reason that

England was now at war with militant opinion. The polemical shock-troops of this strange new kind of revolutionary state were remarkable for nothing so much as their refusal to respect ordinary boundaries, whether of morality or logic: "The foundation of their Republick is laid in moral paradoxes. Their patriotism is always prodigy. All those instances to be found in history, whether real or fabulous, of a doubtful publick spirit, at which morality is perplexed, reason is staggered, and from which affrighted nature recoils, are their chosen, and almost sole examples for the instruction of their youth" (*RP* 9:242–43). As Burke describes it in the *Second Letter*, this is not the result of a simple deviation from reason by passion but the systematic playing of reason into the hands of passion. Its adepts, compared by Burke to "robbers, assassins, and rebels," are the products not of debauchery but of systematic, if "inverted," indoctrination (*RP* 9:296). "Never, before this time," he claims in "Letter to a Noble Lord" (1796), "was a set of literary men, converted into a gang of robbers and assassins. Never before, did a den of bravoes and banditti, assume the garb and tone of an academy of philosophers."[24]

The outlines of this argument, a logical proposition pursued to its extreme issue in catastrophe, describe an archetypal Romantic narrative. The unproduced play William Wordsworth wrote in 1795, *The Borderers*, precedes by one year Burke's model of revolutionary society in *Letters on a Regicide Peace* as "a den of outlaws upon a doubtful frontier" (*RP* 9:247). In its setting and dramatis personae, indeed, Wordsworth's play emerges from Burke's anti-Jacobin arguments, though it finally attempts to interpose a redeeming tragic consciousness where Burke sees only unreflecting, and so unredeemed, reason working out the logic of its own destruction. Burke's "doubtful frontier" refers to the paradoxical rhetorical constructions on which the revolutionary mind has projected a society unchecked by conventional restraints. The lawless border country in which Wordsworth's play is set could therefore be viewed as a fictional referent of this rhetoric, the premise of uncovenanted Nature to which revolutionary arguments tend. Yet, situated as it is in the reign of Henry III on the borders of England and Scotland and so nominally answerable to that historical actuality, it speaks to such a premise only so far as it is recreated along these lines in the arguments of

Wordsworth's arch-rationalist villain Oswald. Outside of the closed system of logic expounded by Oswald, it is what it is. This is the case, at least, until the play's narrative is inexorably caught up in this speculative system and, to use Hazlitt's phrase, is given a "wrong bias." Oswald, described by a member of Marmaduke's virtuous band of outlaws as "One of crooked ways" (*B* 1.8),[25] is the true borderer in this play, a former seafarer and a veteran of the Crusades "where he despised alike / Mahommedan and Christian" (*B* 1.18–19). He is a Godwinian only insofar as the revolutionary inference of Godwin's philosophic anarchism might be extended to violent action, notwithstanding its quietistic emphasis. That he is meant to be a type of the French revolutionary character, however, whether sublimated in Godwinian rationalism or fully realized in the intrepid Jacobin adventurers described by Burke, must be certain. John Rieder suggests that Oswald is at once like Burke and Burke's revolutionary villains,[26] though perhaps this is actually to remark how closely the counterrevolutionary logic of Burkean critique follows its revolutionary subject. Burke and Oswald are both willing to pursue dangerous propositions to extreme conclusions, but they differ as to motive. To the extent that his argument does not take on a fatalistic life of its own, Burke's purpose is cautionary. For Oswald, by contrast, the means to his end—the moral destruction of the play's susceptible hero, Marmaduke, through systematically inculcated error—is an end in itself. The method is the main thing; everything after that is mere waste.

Oswald is a man with a past and a thesis inferred from that past. While this seems superficially Burkean, Oswald in fact finds his sanction not in past continuity, but in a past disruption of continuity. The precipitating event, a ship's mutiny in which he was persuaded by the false testimony of others to condemn an innocent man, is not an exemplary spot in time, then, but a traumatic disjunction effectively separating him from himself— much like the deviation Burke sees as having been checked during the Glorious Revolution by the Declaration of Right. It is this exception, this deviation from what is normative, that Oswald has resolved to make the principle on which he will drive Marmaduke to a similarly extreme moral position. This is as close to a motive as it is possible to discover in Oswald. Beyond that, only circumstance and opportunity remain to explain the course he takes in betraying Marmaduke's humanity. As he tells Marmaduke, when they plan to expose Herbert's alleged guilt,

> Happy are we
> Who live in these disputed tracts, that own
> No law but what each man makes for himself;
> Here justice has indeed a field of triumph
>   (*B* 2.595–98)

Indeed, his plan to dupe Marmaduke into destroying the innocent Herbert, blind and outcast father of Marmaduke's beloved Idonea, finds its perfect venue in the play's primitive border setting, with its unbounded opportunities for action. What Oswald triumphantly calls justice, however, is what Burke warns against as the intellectual *virtù* by which the revolutionary genius masters *fortuna*, the tireless aptitude for logical and ethical mischief Bentham sees in Hamilton's *Parliamentary Logic* ("it was to the opposing of whatsoever is good in honest eyes, that his powers, such as they were, were bent and pushed with peculiar energy"). In one of his notes to the play, Wordsworth speaks of a moral dialectic in human nature whereby "sin and crime are apt to start from their very opposite qualities," a process he says he observed during his stay in France amid the extremities of revolution. Its effects are moral but also intellectual, involving a "perversion of the understanding."[27] Only by means of reason corrupted by logical fallacy can the paradoxical inference of vice from virtue be borne.

The action of *The Borderers* turns on error. It is not so unusual as drama in this respect, except that its emphasis on the relation between argument and action goes beyond theme to engage the logical assumptions behind narrative plotting. The course taken by the play's action, or at least pointed to before Marmaduke achieves tragic consciousness, threatens to submerge the play in its own unreconstructed natural setting. In other words, the play's narrative is pushed to a point where, as in the arguments made by Oswald (and warned of by Burke), progression may become regression. This is no ideal return to nature, grounded as it is in fallacious arguments aimed at subtilizing thought into its irrational other in unreflective savagery. The source of these arguments is Oswald who plies a double deception where Marmaduke is concerned, portraying himself as honest and Herbert as an "Arch-Imposter" (*B* 1.85). His success, then, depends on his ability not only to appear credible himself but credibly to represent Marmaduke as deceitful. The method by which he attempts this, a systematic critique of Herbert's alleged treacheries, is based on a model of rhetorical imposture grounded in fallacy. The female vagrant, whom Oswald employs to plant doubts in Marmaduke concerning Idonea's parentage, exemplifies this fallacious logic—at least as she is employed by Oswald, who reflects thus before her entrance:

> I have prepared a most apt Instrument—
> The Vagrant must, no doubt be loitering somewhere
> About this ground; she hath a tongue well skilled,
> By mingling natural matter of her own
> With all the daring fictions I have taught her,
> To win belief, such as my plot requires.
>
> (*B* 1.365–69)

Earlier in the play, an incredulous Marmaduke nevertheless lends credence to Oswald's charges against Herbert by averring that Oswald is someone "Not used to rash conjectures" (*B* 1.291). Yet it is by means of just such plausible appearances that Oswald is able to insinuate his "daring fictions" as effectively as might the most intrepid practitioner of Machiavellian *virtù*. When, in the opening act, he and Marmaduke eavesdrop on Herbert and Idonea, Oswald concedes that Herbert's love for his daughter seems so sincere that he is tempted to believe Herbert himself sincere—at any rate, this is what he leads Marmaduke to believe. In fact, Oswald *knows* Herbert to be sincere. His strategy is to make his own falsehoods plausible by conceding not absolute truth but relative plausibility to Herbert. Marmaduke's response, provoked by what Oswald has suggested, is to charge that

> Her virtues are his instruments—A Man
> Who has so practised on the world's cold sense,
> May well deceive his Child"
>
> (*B* 1.249–51)

Oswald is in this way able to employ Marmaduke's own virtue as an instrument in a strategy grounded in the same impressionistic assumptions as those on which Elocutionary theory defines truth. When pressed for evidence that Herbert has been misled by others into rejecting Marmaduke as a suitor for his daughter, Oswald simply avers that Herbert is Marmaduke's slanderer:

> He dreads the presence of a virtuous man
> Like you; he knows your eye would search his heart,
> Your justice stamp upon his evil deeds
> The punishment they merit. All is plain
>
> (*B* 1.264–67)

Oswald appears in this speech to credit uncorrupted human nature with an innate and self-evident virtue. In this, he takes his lead from a sense of where Marmaduke's biases lie, while feeling his way to a point where he can set out Marmaduke's options for him before influencing the final choice. After a lengthy speech in which Oswald alternately praises Marmaduke's virtue and then urges him to abandon compassion, Marmaduke cuts him short and appears to choose one of these two options:

> You are wasting words; hear me then, once for all:
> You are a Man—and therefore, if compassion,
> Which to our kind is natural as life,
> Be known unto you, you will love this Woman,
> Even as I do; but I should loathe the light,
> If I could think one weak or partial feeling. . . .
>
> (*B* 2.625–30)

Marmaduke's sentiments in this speech are putatively Shaftesburian, though his caveat about "weak or partial feeling" suggests that it is a short step from an absolute measure of humanity to one that is wholly relative. In fact, he sets the terms here for capitulating to the Hobbesian rejection of compassion being urged by Oswald. The choice between a compassion based on virtue—a dubious prospect given the relative uncertainty Oswald has raised concerning Herbert's supposed vices—and a pitiless cruelty sanctioned by contingency is a choice between virtue and *virtù*. The choice Marmaduke is offered by Oswald is, therefore, not one between two logically equivalent moral qualities—good and evil, virtue and vice—but between morality and method. Marmaduke is right to accuse him of "wasting words," but only insofar as these words are empty of moral purpose as judged by Marmaduke's absolute (or sentimental) morality. To the extent that they are effective in achieving an end—any end—

these same words, to paraphrase Pocock on Court and Country
ideologies, demonstrate how one may command success without
deserving it.

If Oswald employs his words to mislead Marmaduke, he attempts to mislead the other outlaws through Marmaduke. In act
2, Wallace and Lacy enter with news of Henry III's dissolution of
the Barons' League, an intrusion of historical reality threatening
the hermetic logic of Oswald's plot. As Marmaduke innocently
works to divert his men to the fatal course on which he has been
set, it is significant that stage directions have the outlaws eyeing
Oswald, so that when Marmaduke has finished his allegations
against Hebert, Wallace immediately turns to Oswald "with an
appearance of mistrust." To his skeptical "what say you?" (B
2.1068). Oswald characteristically responds not with specific
proof but with a general argument. Rather than making a case
against Herbert per se, he instead argues that Justice should
spare neither the strong nor the weak—"Justice, / Admitting no
resistance, bends alike / The feeble and the strong" (B 2.1088–
90)—an argument valid in itself but not necessarily relevant to
Herbert's case. His point that infirmities like old age may obscure guilt by "seducing reason" and thus use weakness to deflect
justice is similarly valid but serves only to incriminate Herbert
by reason of evident infirmity rather than evident guilt. Yet the
impression made by this speech sufficiently resembles a case
that Lacy can exclaim: "By heaven, his words are reason!" (B
2.1094). Misapplied as a general proposition to a particular case,
this is rank fallacy, but Oswald knows that it is enough to condemn Herbert. In a lengthy soliloquy in the next act, he reflects
on the prospect of bringing Hebert to trial:

> Carry him to the Camp! Yes, to the Camp.
> Oh, Wisdom! a most wise resolve! and then,
> That half a word should blow it to the winds!
> This last device must end my work.—Methinks
> It were a pleasant pastime to construct
> A scale and table of belief—as thus—
> Two columns, one for passion, one for proof;
> Each rises as the other falls; and first,
> Passion a unit and "against" us—proof—
> Nay, we must travel in another path,
> Or we're stuck fast for ever;—passion, then,

Shall be a unit "for" us; proof—no passion!
We'll not insult thy majesty by time,
Person, and place—the where, the when, the how,
And all particulars that dull brains require
To constitute the spiritless shape of Fact,
They bow to, calling the idol, Demonstration.

(*B* 3.1142–58)

Oswald displays here a contempt for proof that calls into doubt its validity as a guide to truth—or action. The passions his arguments skillfully sublimate offer only visceral satisfaction under the guise of justice. Passion by any other name is not reason, much less proof, but it may employ the form of either to effect the convincing impressions, if not valid conclusions, of Demonstration. For enterprising *virtù*, passion has the advantage of responding much more quickly to contingency, the single word that may blow wisdom to the wind. Once set on its course, moreover, it may go anywhere—even to a place where the weak appear guilty because they are weak. When, following this soliloquy, Marmaduke happens upon Oswald, he asserts: "Who, on such provocation as this earth / Yields, could not chuck his babe beneath the chin, / And send it with a fillip to its grave," to which the startled (or simply wary) Oswald can only reply: "Nay, you leave me behind" (*B* 3.1242–44, 1245).

In the next scene, then, it is inevitable that Marmaduke should leave humanity itself behind when he abandons Herbert, frail and unprovided for, to a lonely death on the moors. If Marmaduke's nerve has failed him in an earlier scene, preventing him from putting Herbert to the sword, this murder by omission follows more closely than any more direct act could the logic that originally set in motion the regressive course followed by his mentor Oswald. Its premise and outcome are both grounded in error, though it is the outcome of a course as logical as it is skewed. After Marmaduke's failure to murder Herbert the first time, Oswald reflects: "Now may I perish if this turn do more / Than make me change my course" (*B* 2.991–92). He goes so far as to recant his words encouraging Herbert's murder, saying they were "rashly spoken," the result of "error" (*B* 2.992–93). Yet an advantage of the spoken word, overlooked by Sheridan but noted by Bentham, is that it may easily be disavowed. The rashest or most deliberate utterances may be almost as easily retracted as they are made, Bentham points out, for "you disavow—that is, your adherent for you disavows—the very words:—and thus everything is as it should be" (*WJB* 2:465). Bentham's solution is to subject what he terms "spoken and unminuted speeches" to the critical discipline of print.[28] In a lawless border country, no such checks exist and Oswald is able to pursue his course, under the pretext of moderating or even abandoning it, to its extreme conclusion.

To regard Oswald as motiveless, however, is only to regard him as lacking ordinary motives. Following Marmaduke's abandonment of Herbert, the other outlaws have come upon proof of the old man's innocence, but this discovery sheds no light on why Oswald should pursue his destruction. Wallace can only opine that "Natures such as his, / Spin motives out of their own bowels" and suggest naked power as a rationale (*B* 3.1427–28). None among the outlaws falls back on insanity as an explanation, however, insisting instead that this "most subtle doctor" (*B* 3.1548) has succeeded in drawing a line between even the most inhuman cruelty and mere madness. At the same time, they cannot regard him as wholly civilized either, speculating that "reasoner as he is, his pride has built / Some uncouth superstition of its own" to which he has sacrificed Marmaduke (*B* 3.1440–41)—or, in the terms of Burkean critique, subtilized him. Oswald himself says as much in the scene that follows. Here, alone with Marmaduke, he frankly reveals the at once subtle and uncouth motives for his cruelty, prompting his bemused listener to wonder,

> whither are you wandering? That a man
> So used to suit his language to the time,
> Should thus so widely differ from himself
>
> (*B* 3.1568–71)

Yet the caution Oswald has previously displayed, even his seeming deference to Marmaduke's misgivings, is of a piece with the ruthless philosophy he expounds in which the only law is that which

>   sense
> Submits to recognise; the immediate law,
> From the clear light of circumstances, flashed
> Upon an independent Intellect
>
> (*B* 3.1493–96)

Once reduced to such terms, life stretches before one, "smooth as some broad way / Cleared for a Monarch's progress" (4.1836–37) —a triumphalist perspective grounded in empirical contingency, the hedonistic reflex by which *virtù* masters *fortuna*:

> My young Friend,
> As time advances either we become
> The prey or masters of our own past deeds.
> Fellowship we "must" have, willing or no;
> And if good Angels fail, slack in their duty,
> Substitutes, turn their faces where we may,
> Are still forthcoming; some which, though they bear
> Ill names, can render no ill services,
> In recompense for what themselves required.
> So meet extremes in this mysterious world,
> And opposites thus melt into each other.
> (*B* 3.1520–30)

Yet Oswald does not actually utter these "ill names." Neither does he specify the agents for whom he would desert "good Angels" beyond making vague references to "Substitutes." Even the action to which Marmaduke has putatively been guided by the "the clear light of circumstances" is hardly an action at all, much less a decisive one. When asked by Idonea if he murdered her father, Marmaduke replies,

> No, not by stroke of arm. But learn the process:
> Proof after proof was pressed upon me; guilt
> Made evident, as seemed, by blacker guilt,
> Whose impious folds enwrapped even thee; and truth
> And innocence, embodied in his looks,
> His words and tones and gestures, did but serve
> With me to aggravate his crimes, and heaped
> Ruin upon the cause for which they pleaded.
> (*B* 5.2225–32)

"But learn the process": Marmaduke's injunction here strangely echoes Burke tracing the path from sophism to savagery in revolutionary arguments. Starting in error, even "proof after proof" leads only to further error, error made more compelling in its representations but no less false in its conclusions. When, then, Oswald makes a last attempt to win Marmaduke back with his rhetoric ("This is a paltry field for enterprise"), Marmaduke simply replies: "Ay, what shall we encounter next? This issue— / 'Twas nothing more than darkness deepening darkness" (*B* 5.2252–53).

◦§   ◦§   ◦§

At the conclusion of *The Borderers*, Oswald is put to death scorning his erstwhile disciple as "A Fool and Coward blended to my wish!" (*B* 5:2286). Herbert, meanwhile, has perished Lear-like on a barren heath, and Marmaduke condemns himself to a life of wandering "over waste and wild" in search of expiation (*B* 5.2316). While Marmaduke acknowledges both his guilt and his chance for redemption, however, Oswald dies as he has lived—at least since the unlucky incident that saw him duped into condemning an innocent man to death. Just before Marmaduke's men execute him, indeed, he wholly absolves himself, crediting his impending death to a morally neutral logic of which he is the accidental agent:

> If I pass beneath a rock
> And shout, and, with the echo of my voice,
> Bring down a heap of rubbish, and it crush me,
> I die without dishonour"
>
> (B 5.2282–85)

This is a proposition that, while possibly valid in itself, leaves out of account the fact that he knowingly lured others under a rock. Yet such simple fallacies have enabled him to achieve a remarkable devastation by the play's end. Wordsworth's note to the play mysteriously alludes to circumstances witnessed in France "while the Revolution was rapidly advancing to its extreme of wickedness." David Bromwich concludes that the precise nature of these circumstances may never be known.[29] The nature of the skewed "process" by which sin and crime may arise as necessary inferences of virtue, however, is relentlessly worked out in *The Borderers*, which demonstrates Wordsworth's premise that "there are no limits to the hardening of the heart and the perversion of the understanding to which they may carry their slaves."[30]

A measure of this proposition's validity is reflected by similar outcomes in other Romantic narratives that consider the question. Two such narratives, William Godwin's *Caleb Williams* (1794) and Mary Shelley's *Frankenstein* (1818), are more than arguments conceived as novels, but both turn on assumptions about the potentially regressive relation of argument to action noted above in Burke and Wordsworth. Both issue from political perspectives diametrically opposed to Burke's, and perhaps Wordsworth's (depending on how *The Borderers* is read), but the narrative/argumentative tendency they pursue—and which they describe their characters pursuing—cuts across political lines in its inexorable career. For Burke, "Going straight forward to it's end, unappalled by peril, unchecked by remorse, despising all common maxims and all common means," this tendency is specifically identified with the French Revolution, but its career describes a logic that carries all before it, reform and reaction alike.

Godwin's novel springs from the very crucible of debate in the revolutionary decade. Even the immediate circumstances of its composition suggest a narrative driven by radical argumentative energies. Godwin began writing the novel scant weeks after the appearance of his *Enquiry Concerning Political Justice* (1793). Indeed, he was reading proofs of the *Enquiry* in January of 1793 and began *Caleb Williams* the following month, later noting the resulting connection between the two works: "The *Enquiry Concerning Political Justice* was published in February. In this year also I wrote the principal part of the novel *Caleb Williams*, which may, perhaps, be considered as affording no inadequate image of the fervour of my spirit; it was the offspring of that temper of mind in which the composition of my *Political Justice* left me."[31] This is not to say that the novel merely fictionalizes ideas propounded in the political treatise but that, "seriously and methodically" pursued throughout 1793, it was evidently carried along by the latter's argumentative impetus. If *Caleb Williams* is not an allegory of *Political Justice*, it explores inferences not developed in that work's argument and pursues these inferences to narrative ends, though it leaves others undeveloped. Where *Political Justice* argues from the perspective of *what might be*, given humanity's wholesale commitment to reason, *Caleb Williams* concerns itself with *what is*—in the absence of any such commitment. In his Preface, then, Godwin characterizes the novel's premise not in terms of a plot, but a proposition:

The following narrative is intended to answer a purpose more general and more important than immediately appears upon the face of it. The question now afloat in the world respecting THINGS AS THEY ARE, is the most interesting that can be presented to the human mind. While one party pleads for reformation and change, the other extols in the warmest terms the existing constitution of society. It seemed as if something would be gained for the decision of this question, if that constitution were faithfully developed in its practical effects. What is now presented to the public is no refined and abstract speculation; it is a study and delineation of things passing in the moral world. (*CW* 1)

Withdrawn from the first edition of *Caleb Williams* amid anti-Jacobin alarms, Godwin's preface sets the novel squarely in the Burke/Paine debate.[32] As such, it lays out the rhetorical options available to those who would praise or censure the present state of society, its narrative serving as a means of deciding the question by demonstration. In effect, Godwin proposes to employ the story of a man persecuted for his secret knowledge of a murder to test the validity of "THINGS AS THEY ARE" as a premise, asking what would happen if "that constitution were faithfully developed in its practical effects." His caveat eschewing "refined and abstract speculation" is clearly meant to distinguish a work of fiction from a political treatise. Yet this does not so much deny an argumentative dimension to *Caleb Williams* as emphasize the subsumption of its argument by the fatal tendencies of narrative. Ironically, *Frankenstein*, inscribed by Mary Shelley to her father (*"Author of Political Justice, Caleb Williams, &c."*), would push this argument further by developing some of the more speculative narrative inferences of *Political Justice* elided in *Caleb Williams*.

Arguments appear to solve little in *Caleb Williams*, in some cases threatening potentially catastrophic results. The several debates that occur throughout the novel turn on questions speaking to the great discussions of the 1790s. The first of these takes place between the aristocratic Falkland and the John Bullish Mr. Tyrrel. The grounds of enmity between these two stems originally from the prejudice Tyrrel harbors against his fellow landholder. For his part, Falkland is motivated by a chivalric regard for personal honor that proves to be the undoing of himself and several others in the novel, including Tyrrel whom he subsequently murders. The "amicable conversation" (*CW* 27) he proposes to have with Tyrrel early in the novel must thus contend with issues not amenable to reason. Despite his own feudal prejudices, however, Falkland makes his appeal to Tyrrel on rational grounds. The peaceful arrangement he proposes is necessary to their happiness, he argues, "a proposition dictated by reason, and an equal regard to the interest of each" (*CW* 29). Tyrrel seems initially inclined to agree to such a "compact," but the exchange takes an unaccountably wrong turn when Falkland offers his hand to Tyrrel in token of their compact: "But the gesture was too significant. The wayward rustic, who seemed to have been somewhat impressed by what had preceded, taken as he was by surprise, shrunk back" (*CW* 29). Thereafter, the exchange foregrounds rhetorical gesture at the expense of rational argument. Tyrrel, who is fluent enough in his rustic way, pointedly contrasts his own plainspoken manner with Falkland's fine manners and speech, which he derides as "'Your rhymes and your rebusses, your quirks and your conundrums'" (*CW* 30). Falkland, while conducting himself creditably by his own lights, is equally provoking, for "even when he was most exemplary, there was an apparent loftiness in his manner that was calculated to irritate; and the very grandeur with which he suppressed his passions, operated indirectly as a taunt to his opponent" (*CW* 31). The commentary on Burke/Paine here, in which rhetoric itself became grounds for debate, is obvious. This exchange also initiates a logic that, founded in passion and rhetorical misconstruction, will determine the fateful direction taken by the novel's action. This is the gist of the cautionary deathbed advice given to Falkland by Mr. Clare in the next chapter. Clare warns Falkland that his virtues are endangered by his archaic prejudices: "You have an impetuosity and an impatience of imagined dishonour, that, if once set wrong, may make you as eminently mischievous, as you will otherwise be useful. Think seriously of exterminating this error!" (*CW* 34). Falkland's reaction to this expostulation is wholly characteristic. He is "deeply affected" by it, as he is by forceful expression generally, whatever its intent, good or bad. Yet the "error" he is warned of, unchecked by the "reason and justice" Clare urges in his dying breaths (*CW* 35), is only a source of further error in the novel—for "once set wrong" everything else that happens in the novel travels along this bias.

Subsequent debates in the novel are equally cautionary instances of argument gone wrong. Caleb's exchanges with Mr. Falkland, a seemingly academic debate on Alexander the Great whom Caleb censures as a murderer, for instance, serve only to provoke Falkland—much to Caleb's dismay: "'I dared not utter a word, lest I should commit a new error worse than that which I had just fallen'" (*CW* 112). In the same way, Tyrrel's innocent ward Emily makes eloquent objections against his harsh treatment of her that end up angering him further: "When the first emotion wore off, he cursed himself for being moved by her expostulations, and was ten times more exasperated against her" (*CW* 57). To be sure, Caleb's rhetorical provocations are at best disingenuous, calculated as they are to elicit a guilty reaction from Falkland. Even Emily has unwittingly conditioned Tyrrel's violent reaction through constant praise of his enemy Falkland. Nevertheless, these circumstances only show the extent to which reasonable argument can be subverted by irrationalist inferences from any quarter. As Wordsworth's Oswald demonstrates, cunning may find ways to exploit the most contingent circumstances, though neither Emily nor Caleb has mastered this black art. Emily pays with her life for her comparative innocence, while Caleb very nearly does so. When the latter is arraigned in court to face theft charges, indeed, he believes his innocence to be a sufficient defense. "'I will never believe that a man conscious of innocence, cannot make other men perceive that he has that thought,'" he tells his hostile listeners. "Do you not feel that my whole heart tells me, I am not guilty of what is imputed to me?" (*CW* 171). His former protector, Falkland's plainspoken kinsman Mr. Forester, replies that the case against him is "too strong for sophistry to overturn." The following passage from Forester's speech recalls Burke on Jacobin imposture:

> I grant you that you have shown considerable dexterity in your answers; but you will learn, young man, to your cost, that dexterity, however powerful it may be in certain cases, will avail little against the stubbornness of truth. It is fortunate for mankind that the empire of talents has its limitation, and that it is not in the power of ingenuity to subvert the distinctions of right and wrong. (*CW* 172)

This rebuke is not entirely uncalled for where Caleb is concerned. Innocent as he is of the criminal charge brought against him, his talents have figured largely in his troubles. It is his false accuser, however, whose rhetorical dexterity is such that it has managed to confound virtue with *virtù*. The end of preserving honor at any cost has reduced Falkland's chivalric ideals to mere imposture. Yet he passes for a sincere man, while his innocent victim is further stigmatized.

Mr. Forester is wrong for the right reasons, then, for while his general proposition is valid, its application is false. Yet so perilous is the career of reason in a world of rhetorical appearances that even correct reason sincerely applied may be grounded in fallacy. At the novel's opening, his name now popularly associated with imposture, Caleb must begin his narration insisting that it "will at least appear to have that consistency, which is seldom attendant but upon truth" (*CW* 3). Whether this is a consistency reflected in the story's internal logic or in the seeming integrity of the teller or in both, it is clear that the criterion of truth in *Caleb Williams* is that of rhetorical probability. As Godwin concedes in *Political Justice*, "It may perhaps be found that the human mind is not capable of arriving at absolute certainty upon any subject of inquiry; and it must be admitted that human science is attended with all degrees of certainty, from the highest moral evidence to the slightest balance of probability."[33] Caleb's sincerity is apparent and probable; his story is rendered believable by the inner consistency of its working out. Just as telling, however, is the positive error at the root of his misfortunes. Error multiplied upon itself pervades the novel's action and ultimately carries Caleb with it; having once embarked on his fatal inquiries, he has implicated himself in the treacherous politics of reputation played by Falkland and must pursue his counterargument to the latter's libels to a bitter end. Mr. Raymond, the outlaw whom Caleb encounters in the third volume, can speak movingly to such dangers. While admitting the validity of Caleb's objections to outlawry, he puts forward a case for his outlawry that indicates how far he is willing to pursue a fallacious rationale to its final issue. Having chosen a course in opposition to established law and custom, he and his men cannot turn back unless the system outlawing them is changed. "'What then can I do?'" he asks. "Am I not compelled to go on in folly, having once begun?'" (*CW* 228). Caleb is deeply affected by this argument—and so he should be, bearing as it does on his own (and Falkland's) plight. By the novel's end, at the very point of bringing his persecutor to justice, he realizes that "There must have been some dreadful mistake in the train of argument that persuaded me to be the author of this hateful scene" (*CW* 320)—this despite the evident justice of his cause and convincing arguments for his own innocence. This time the eloquence with which he defends himself in the novel's climactic episode, his "uncontrolable impetuosity," is its own proof. That even Falkland is taken by his victim's apparent sincerity, having been aware of Caleb's innocence from the beginning, testifies to the power of rhetoric that it can supercede the reality of truth with its forceful appearance. Only a William Gerard Hamilton could take satisfaction in such an outcome, however—an end that, to its beneficiary's dismay, only technically justifies its means and signals no clear winner. "I began these memoirs with the idea of vindicating my character," Caleb writes in his postscript. "I have now no character that I wish to vindicate" (*CW* 326). The public discovery of Falkland's guilt is nevertheless a necessary issue of the narrative course followed by the novel. Caleb's claim to have authored this episode goes some way toward explaining his rhetorical agency in the novel, both as this agency initiates the events of the narrative and then recounts them *as* a narrative. In the end, he has not so much vindicated himself as discovered his own role in the logic making vindication necessary in the first place. He is thus literally (and logically) the author of his own misfortunes, Falkland's actual guilt notwithstanding. When he completes his narrative, it is no longer with the intention of clearing his reputation but of confuting the relentless logic of imposture that dogs this narrative to the very end, so "the world may at least not hear and repeat a half-told and mangled tale" (*CW* 326).

If, like *The Borderers*, this novel stops short of the logical endgame to which Burke intrepidly forces Jacobin argument—Caleb ends up sadder but wiser—neither does it pursue the Godwinian obverse of that argument. Where *Caleb Williams* follows the logic of convention to its likely issue in arbitrary persecution and Pyrrhic vindication, *Political Justice* follows reason to its theoretical issue in natural justice. The difference between them is the difference between the actual and the potential, though as Godwin's son-in-law demonstrates in his great revision of the Prometheus myth, this may not be so much a difference as a logical relation in which one can be educed from the other. In the case of *Prometheus Unbound*, however, the principle of dialectical reversion is a fundamental premise, whereas *Caleb Williams* is the dialectical other of *Political Justice*, and vice versa, only by inference. As much as the narrow counterargument made by Malthus in his essay on population, they remain in themselves closed systems, each representing an option that, once chosen, may follow its own logic to a bitter end. This is a crude equation, but it reflects Godwin's reception among contemporary readers like William Hazlitt who, in his essay on Godwin in *Spirit of the Age*, notes that the author of *Caleb Williams* "dwells upon one idea or exclusive view of a subject, aggrandizes a sentiment, exaggerates a character, or pushes an argument to extremes" (*CWH* 11:25). In *Political Justice*, too, Hazlitt observes that Godwin follows reason "into its remotest consequences," thereby demonstrating reason's limits (11:23). Hazlitt's choice of analogy, the failed 1824–25 Parry expedition to find a north-west Passage, seems like back-handed praise. His assessment of *Political Justice* as an "*experimentum crucis*," however, effectively puts its argument on a level with Burkean reductio ad absurdum in the *Reflections*. Just as it may be useful to prove there is no northwest Passage, "so Mr. Godwin has rendered an essential service to moral science, by attempting (in vain) to pass the Arctic Circle and Frozen Regions, where the understanding is no longer warmed by the affections, nor fanned by the breeze of fancy! This the effect of all bold, original, and powerful thinking, that it either discovers the truth, or detects where error lies" (*CWH* 11:23). Hazlitt might thus have agreed with Sir Walter Scott's sense of where Mary Shelley had taken Godwinian argument and narrative in *Frankenstein*—for the arctic imagery of his analogy evokes that novel's pursuit of Godwin's perfectibilian premise.[34] In an 1818 review of *Frankenstein*, Scott notes Mary Shelley's debt to *Caleb Williams*, but finds that "In dark and gloomy views of nature and man, bordering too closely on impiety,—in the most outrageous improbability,—in sacrificing everything to effect,—it even goes beyond its great prototype."[35]

But where does *Frankenstein* go exactly? It starts from the premise that humanity is perfectible, a view shared by even the most pessimistic of Enlightenment thinkers, which is not to say that man is capable of perfection but that he will always strive for it. The question is whether this is good or bad. Pessimists like Malthus argue that the faculty of perfectibility produces nothing but misery in the long run. Even the optimistic Godwin qualifies his use of the term in *Political Justice* to describe not perfection but "the faculty of being made better and receiving perpetual improvement."[36] It is clear that no more than a slight recasting of this definition would be enough to produce the obverse argument. Add the premise that moral character is the product of environment, a fundamental Enlightenment assumption held by Godwin (and many others, including Burke), and it is not hard to see that unchecked progress may go anywhere depending on circumstance and inclination. The narrative of *Frankenstein* runs along this bias of perfectibilian logic, the novel's original preface, ghosted by Percy Bysshe Shelley, suggesting *Frankenstein*'s speculative use of such propositions: "I have thus endeavoured to preserve the truth of the elementary principles of human nature, while I have not scrupled to innovate upon their combinations" (*F* 3). In the poetic license claimed here may be discerned the origins of what Scott terms the novel's "outrageous improbability" by which Scott presumably means Victor Frankenstein's ability to create life from inert matter. This is a fantastic premise but once it is accepted—Walton speaks of Victor's "unparalleled eloquence" and finds that his narrative contains "internal evidence of the truth of the events of which it is composed" (*F* 15, 17)—the issue becomes Victor's ethical premise in creating life. No empirical drone, Victor hypothesizes nothing less than the perfecting of human nature in an ideal creature. "A new species would bless me as its creator and source," he reflects before beginning his task; "many happy and excellent natures would owe their being to me" (*F* 36). Thereafter, the fundamental question in *Frankenstein* concerns the validity of this premise and where it leads, so it is inevitable that debates in the novel—and there are several, the legacy of *Caleb Williams*—should turn on the responsibilities of the creator. The two major debates occur between Victor and his Creature, the first framing the Creature's narrative, the second briefly following Victor's decision not to create a mate for the Creature. The terms of these debates set them within the context of the period's great reform debates, and, like the latter, they are played out against an Enlightenment historical paradigm offering options of unlimited progress and catastrophic declension.

The Creature's narrative is literally framed in by the closed system of an argument. When confronted by the Creature near Chamonix in the second volume, Victor is no mood for rational discussion. His youngest brother cruelly murdered and the innocent Justine executed for the crime, he has just seen that a rational appearance of innocence may be no match for the irrational conviction of guilt. Upon his return to Geneva, ironically, he has formed just such a conviction of the Creature's guilt in his brother's murder. That he happens to be correct misses the point where the probity of Justine's unjust condemnation is concerned. "I could not doubt it," he says of his brief glimpse of the Creature outside Geneva. "The mere presence of the idea was an irresistible proof of the fact" (56). This, then, is Victor's frame of mind when the Creature later makes his case to him in classic constitutional terms of right, obligation, and interest. "Do your duty towards me," he tells Victor, "and I will do mine towards you and the rest of mankind" (*F* 77). The model of human nature he argues from is empirical, positing a capacity for benevolence that may nevertheless be warped by unjust treatment. In relating his tale—which, weighing "the various arguments" employed, his creator has resolved to hear out (F 79)—the Creature could be a Hume or a Ferguson tracing a speculative history of civil society that explains where man has come from on the basis of where he is, and what he is or might have been or still might be on the basis of what he was, for better or worse. The tale that follows is a classic Enlightenment narrative of progress from a solitary savage state, through various stages of social and mental development, to a point where man normally achieves the status of a civil being, with all the gains and losses attendant on that status. Through no fault of his own, the Creature has failed to attain the final stage. He possesses, however, the rational accomplishments required for civilized existence and is fully aware of what he has been denied due to his monstrous appearance. He is, in fine, an intelligent, sensible being capable of logical inferences influencing virtuous and evil actions alike. Ferguson's caveat about such inferences, "Man may mistake the objects of his pursuit; he may misapply his industry, and misplace his improvements," applies to Creature and Creator alike. Yet it is the Creature who forces the creator to pursue his speculations to their logical end. Like Whig history, the narrative related by the Creature prepares the grounds of an argument about the necessary bias of its course.

The Creature's history provides the rationale for a demand that Victor create a female mate for him. At least, this is one of two options available to Victor when the Creature completes his narrative and renews his argument. The other is mutual misery of the kind Falkland foresees in his future relations with Tyrrel in *Caleb Williams*. The Creature regards a companion for himself as a "right" that Victor cannot refuse—whether out of a sense of natural justice on Victor's part or fear for his life is not clear. When Victor initially refuses this demand, the Creature responds with further arguments employing rational promises of reward and punishment:

> "Your are in the wrong," replied the fiend; "and, instead of threatening, I am content to reason with you. I am malicious because I am miserable; am I not shunned and hated by all mankind? You, my creator, would tear me to pieces, and triumph; remember that, and tell me why I should pity man more than he pities me? You would not call it murder, if you could precipitate me onto one of those ice-rifts and destroy my frame, the work of your own hands. Shall I respect man, when he contemns me? Let him live with me in the intercourse of kindness, and, instead of injury, I would bestow every benefit upon him with tears of gratitude at his acceptance. But that cannot be; the human senses are insurmountable barriers to our union." (*F* 119)

The Creature knows that barriers of sense must perpetually doom to misconstruction his attempts to communicate. His first gesture, indeed, a hand held out to his creator on the night of his creation, has been misinterpreted as surely as Falkland's gesture of amity is by Tyrrel during their ill-fated negotiation in *Caleb Williams*. Yet as reasonable as his demands may be in themselves, they depend on other things being equal. If Tyrrel and Falkland differ in degree in certain respects, they share a common humanity. A mutual pact in this case may therefore depend on arguments likely to be valid, on rhetorical probability.

Yet the chance on which Victor's pact with the Creature depends is not even this sure, assuming as it does an identity in kind that Victor (along with the novel's readers) infers on purely sentimental grounds: "His tale, and the feelings he now expressed, proved him to be a creature of fine sensations" (*F* 120). But what is the logical basis of this premise? Is Victor's conviction of the Creature's compassionate nature even as valid as his earlier unfounded, if correct, conviction that the Creature is a murderer?

Because it is a narrative conditioned by an argument, the Creature's tale necessarily carries an a priori rhetorical force. In addition, it presupposes a common, and so reasonably predictable, humanity shared by teller and listener alike. Yet to believe that such a narrative could only have been related by a compassionate being is to accept a premise valid only within the closed system of the argument framing this narrative. That we tend to accept this premise speaks less to the argument, however, than to the sentimental nature of the narrative exploited by the argument. Where Victor is concerned, the Creature's argumentative strategy proves merely that Victor is compassionate: "He saw my change of feeling, and continued" (F 120). What *is* clear about the Creature's arguments is their facility. "He is eloquent and persuasive," Victor warns Walton (*F* 178), who nevertheless finds himself moved during a subsequent exchange with the Creature, though he still acknowledges a distinction between the tale and its teller. The Creature's rejoinder to the charge of moral monstrosity, then, that "such must be the impression conveyed to you by what appears to be the purport of my actions" (*F* 188–89), does not address the charge so much as its rhetorical grounds. Protests of potential benevolence on the Creature's part are in fact educed from indisputable proofs of actual malevolence, the premise of a good nature gone bad. While these circumstances do not rule out a truly compassionate side to the Creature, they nevertheless reveal the rhetorical grounds of his appeal to Victor, the fact that it can claim no more than plausibility, in this case without the more certain knowledge of a fundamental commonalty among those involved. Victor recognizes the fallacy of the Creature's arguments only later when he is on the verge of completing a companion for the Creature, a being "of whose dispositions I was alike ignorant" (*F* 138). While he acknowledges that this being would not be obliged to honor a contract made before her creation, an issue central to Burke/Paine, this consideration is superceded by the prior question of whether a valid pact can be made among beings as unlike as he and these creatures may be. Such an agreement must rest not on valid ethical grounds but on fallacy, applying as it does conventional precedents to circumstances wholly unprecedented. Its danger lies in its unpredictable influence on future developments. When he breaks this compact, Victor incurs the wrath of the Creature and badly misreads the drift of the Creature's ensuing threats. In choosing not to establish deviation as the rule, however, he shows he has recognized the wrong bias along which his thinking and actions alike have run.

Does Mary Shelley's novel thus confirm the contemporary view that, in Hazlitt's words, *Political Justice* represented "a new and monstrous birth in morals" (*CWH* 11:19)? Hazlitt suggests that *Political Justice* merely expounds a conventional morality radically applied. "Mr. Godwin's theory, and that of more approved reasoners, differ only in this" he states, "that what are with them the exceptions, the extreme cases, he makes the every-day rule" (*CWH* 11:19). This is the gist of *Frankenstein*'s original preface concerning the "elementary principles of human nature" on which a fabulous narrative is elaborated. Despite his appearance and actions, the Creature has a human premise. Chosen for their superior proportion and beauty, his various parts are meant to produce a superior whole, differing from humanity only in degree. His actual monstrosity is therefore the result of an idea pushed to the limit—like radical deviations of the kind pondered by Burke's seventeenth-century legislators or the Godwin of *Political Justice*. The fact that the Creature's rationale is human, however, cannot justify the extreme to which this rationale has been taken. Conceived along lines calculated to make him more than human, he has been forced beyond this into subhumanity in his consequent isolation from humanity. However whole he may be potentially, he is nevertheless the creation of an incomplete premise—as Victor realizes even as he declines to complete the Creature with a companion. This inference of rational reform, that progressive change may be effected by projecting only a portion of our being, is left undeveloped in Godwin's novel. *Caleb Williams* follows the logic of Things-As-They-Are to the verge of a savage endgame driven by Falkland's unreasonable adherence to a traditional concept of self. Yet the rational counterargument, the obverse proposition put forward in *Political Justice*, is pursued only to the early death of Mr. Clare. This character's agency in the novel, as a result, is neither exemplary nor cautionary but purely critical. As such, it is practically no different than that of Falkland's kinsman Forester with his Tory common sense. The positive inference of Mr. Clare's philosophic radicalism, however—if this is not to pursue an inference too far down a hypothetical path—is never tested against the grain of Things-As-They-Are. For Hazlitt, from whose own radical perspective Falkland's end would be a given—this is surely the implication of Paine's and Wollstonecraft's criticisms of Burke's chivalric cult in the *Reflections*—the value (and courage) of *Political Justice* lies in its unflinching pursuit of a rational reform argument back to an untenable premise. "Man was indeed screwed up, by mood and figure, into a logical machine, that was to forward the public good with the utmost punctuality and effect," he observes of Godwin's argument, "and it might go very well on smooth ground and under favourable circumstances; but would it work up-hill or *against the grain?*" (*CWH* 11:20). Confronted by the living proof of this fallacy, its very "mood and figure" evoked for us in a terrifyingly immediate glimpse of what might be, Victor Frankenstein refutes not merely an idea, but a course of logic potential in an idea. At the foregone conclusion of *Caleb Williams*, this insight exists only as the possible counterargument to an argument not made.[37]

More acculturated, perhaps, than even Gothic drama and fiction to a Reason in extremis are the verse narratives of High Romanticism. Not merely products of idiosyncratic mythopoeisis, such works incorporate the logic of the period's debates in ways that recover it in elementary (or regressive) form. Blake must figure centrally in this discussion, as his poetic mythos surely forces this logic as far back to its primordial origins as rhetoric, even poetic rhetoric, allows. Yet this critical impulse may be detected in the works of other Romantics as well, if in less extreme form. Even the obscure byways of Thomas Love Peacock's narrative poems point this way, though they stop considerably short of a destination their author preferred to avoid even as his best works continually touched on its implications for reasoned discussion. The dialectical options Peacock mused over as he wrote *The Genius of the Thames*, indeed, would emerge five years later in his unfinished Zoroastrian epic "Ahrimanes." Existing only in fragmentary form, the completed poem was to have portrayed in twelve cantos nothing less than the historical struggle of good and evil. When the poem opens, the evil principle Ahrimanes is ascendant, while Oromazes, the benign deity of a former golden age, lies dormant. There are hints of a future reversion, but in what we have of the poem this remains only a possibility. In "Ahrimanes" Peacock might have seen a chance to explore the contradictory inferences vexing him in his half-joking letter to Hookham about what turned out to be a encomiastic commercial epic on the Thames River. He left "Ahrimanes" unfinished, however, turning his dialectical talents to satiric fiction. In *Headlong Hall*, then, completed the same year this poem was abandoned, an epic scene is exchanged for a country house and the cosmic struggle of darkness and light is replaced by dilettanti arguing the pros and cons of progress. It is not so much that the Satirist in Peacock triumphed over the Panegyrist as that both were transferred to a fictional form favoring their perpetual struggle. One of Peacock's early critics, James Spedding, said in 1839 that the author of *Headlong Hall* "dwells more habitually among doubts and negations than we believe good for any man."[38]

For reformers in the years immediately after Waterloo, as for some conservatives in the revolutionary decade, all roads seemed to lead to negation. Peacock never pursued his doubts much further than the point where they checked certainty. His friend Shelley would have agreed with Spedding, however, judging by his preference for the more rhetorically confident *Melincourt*. Appearing in 1817, this most politically engaged of Peacock's novels pitted reformers against reactionaries, deciding in favor of reform at a time when reality seemed to favor a different outcome. Yet nothing else Peacock wrote would take such a unequivocal line, and he was content to let Shelley use materials from "Ahrimanes" in the ambitious *Revolt of Islam* (1817). Written in the wake of Waterloo and the ebbing of reform fortunes, this poem is described in Shelley's preface as "an experiment on the temper of the public,"[39] the vagaries of which form its emotional subtext. While Shelley eschews "methodical and systematic argument" here—Peacock had effectively chosen the opposite course when he left off "Ahrimanes" to write *Headlong Hall*—his description of the poem as "narrative, not didactic" sets up a false binary. Like others of his generation, Shelley wrote his major poems against the grain of the times and these poems' narratives reflect this circumstance in what could only be described as an argumentative tendency. His two most ambitious and difficult works, *The Revolt of Islam* and *Prometheus Unbound* (1820), turn on a reform-reaction dialectic theoretically issuing in any number of possible outcomes. Their conclusions—Demogorgon must necessarily have the last word in *Prometheus Unbound*— represent reversions in a logic that, in Burke's phrase, "will snap short, unfaithful to the hand that employs it" (*RRF* 8:272). What so often appears to be a mere leap of logic in the endings of Shelley's poems, then, is in fact an inference whose logic makes inevitable its obverse. With reform comes the certainty that re- action cannot be far behind. The problem lies with those of Shelley's reform poems directed to a popular audience, what he termed his "exoteric" poetry. A work like "The Mask of Anarchy" (1819), written hard on the heels of Peterloo, thus walks a not very fine line between progressive enlightenment—the recon- structed social vision celebrated in *Prometheus Unbound* in "man / Equal, unclassed, tribeless, and nationless"—and a more parochial, even reactionary, constitutional radicalism grounded in "The old laws of England—they / Whose reverend heads with age are gray, / Children of a wiser day."[40] At this poem's conclu- sion, Godwinian quietism is argued in the sanguinary terms of revolutionary violence. Ministerialist aggression is condemned at the same time that it is answered, at least rhetorically, in kind.

The Blakean mythos turns on just such a dilemma, its pro- gressivist logic poised to snap short at conception. "Mental fight"[41] in Blake involves something like the sanguine/sanguin- ary rhetorical shifts of Shelley's verse narratives, though it is more robustly reflexive and, as a result, more aware of its own role in a regressive logic it may extend by the very act of resisting that logic. Blakean error is a product of the closed system from which it takes its original bias as historical fallacy—original, that is, from the relative (if absolute seeming) perspective of the system. In the *Book of Urizen*, engraved in 1794, William Blake reduces the debates of the revolutionary decade to their most elemental terms. The world envisioned by his arch-rationalist deity, Urizen, is intended to be a closed system, "a solid without fluctuation" (WB 4.11). Urizen's speech in chapter 2 of *The Book of Urizen* thus constitutes less a moral code than a set of standards, logical criteria on which this world depends for its inner consistency:

> One command, one joy, one desire,
> One curse, one weight, one measure
> One King, one God, one Law.
>
> (WB 4.38–40)

Urizen's authority derives from originary primacy, an auspicious sense of which attends his every utterance. If authority here flows from priority, however, priority posits itself rhetorically and so exists only in assertion. The Los cycle, of which *Book of Urizen* is a part, at once elaborates a mythic system and examines the fallacious logic by which mythic elaboration enables power to legitimize itself. Blake could have found a source for such mythopoeic imposture in the false etymologies and adventitious conflations of eighteenth-century euhemerist scholarship to whom deities like Urizen owe not only their syncretic natures but their very rationale as deities. In *A New System, or, an Analysis of Ancient Mythology* (1776), which Blake engraved for his old master Basire,[42] Jacob Bryant posits an original antediluvian culture subsequently disseminated by Noah's descendents and corrupted in various appropriations. Hazard Adams dismisses Bryant's theories as fabulous, basing his contrast between Blake and the euhemerists respectively on a distinction between history as trope and history as phenomenon. Adams marvels at "their capacity to order large amounts of so-called knowledge into elegant wholes based on entirely false premises," but in the end dismisses the euhemerists for the misguided positivism of their attempts to establish "external historical fact."[43] Euhemerist mythology, however, like more respectable lines of cultural investigation gathered under the broad rubric of eighteenth-century moral philosophy, is necessarily speculative in nature, particularly in postulating beginnings. Even the familiar outlines of Enlightenment civil history, the rises and falls of which still condition modern historical consciousness, depend on certain assumptions about cultural development ultimately traceable to common origins. The phrase "in the infancy of society" so often opening Enlightenment histories initiates a pattern as formal as those traced out in the euhemerists' diluvian confabulations, its conventional associations of pristine rudeness signaling the commencement of a narrative working toward foregone conclusions about material opulence and/or moral declension. Whether figured as the Natural State or a diluvian ur-mythology, the common origin is a kind of master trope governing the narrative patterns of eighteenth-century civil history and euhemerist mythology alike.

It is also a logical premise. Despite its obsessive detail, Bryant's *New System* merely represents itself as empirical, for its conclusions are wholly a priori. Bryant does not so much discover a key to mythology as impose a premise. His preconceived conclusions are conditioned by an Enlightenment concept of unity based on rhetorical probability rather than logical synthesis: many myths become one myth but only at the expense of eliding many particular qualities and privileging the single quality of equivalence. The error of euhemerist logic notwithstanding, however, the common origin's status depends not so much on historical as hypothetical validity, its usefulness as a provisional starting point. Priority is problematic for Blake because it is such a contingent category. A double (and double-edged) deception is thus involved in the unifying fiat delivered in the opening stanzas of *The Book of Urizen*. Urizen's a priori validity claims are clearly false, a fact made evident in the subsequent *Book of Ahania* when would-be usurper Fuzon prematurely claims victory over Urizen: "I am God, said he, eldest of things!" (*WB* 3.38). Urizen has similarly sanctioned himself in the preceding *Book of Urizen*, his authenticity as first cause questioned from the start (so to speak) in the Preludium's reference to "the primeval Priest's assum'd power" with its strong air of presupposition. Primeval in his conjectured origins but also a priest and by definition secondary, Urizen is the creator of Fuzon—as well as the other elements, in fact the whole of the created universe as Fuzon knows it—but also his narrative source. Urizen's story not only precedes Fuzon's but provides the rhetorical pattern Fuzon attempts to duplicate before his defeat. Urizenic genesis, moreover, is coeval with its scriptural representation; its author's "original" act of creation is never *not* in narrative form, for *The Book of Urizen* is effectively synonymous with the book Urizen composes in its narrative. There is no book of Albion, because Eternity has no narrative or, what is the same thing, no history— presumably what Blake means when he says in *Milton* that knowledge remains abstract "till periods of Space & Time / Reveal the secrets of Eternity" (*WB* 21.8–10). Its conjectural unity notwithstanding, then, Blake's Eternity is only as whole as its representation in Urizenic history. In this respect, it fits the classic definition of fallacy in that it is a portion mistaken for the whole. In relation to Urizen's pseudotheodicy it serves as a kind of ur-prehistory, a beginning before the beginning. Hans Kellner suggests that the historical period helps to offset "the nightmare of infinite regress" associated with a narrative property he calls the "pre-echoing initiating event," citing as an example the sentence opening George Lefebvre's *The Coming of the French Revolution*: "The ultimate cause of the French Revolution of 1789 goes deep into the history of France and of the western world." Such a cause can only be gestured to, because it has no factual validity and is thus a rhetorical convention, at most a logical premise. But, as Kellner points out, "practically, there is a point of pre-echoic entropy, beyond which the pre-echoes are not related recognizably to the initiating event of the selected story."[44] Hence the danger of "infinite regress," surely one possibility occurring to the fallen Los in *The Book of Urizen* when he looks back at Eternity, "but the space undivided by existence / Struck horror into his soul" (*WB* 13.46–47). The certainty he craves, however, is available only in the rhetorical contingency on which Urizen's world turns.

The mythos elaborated from Lambeth onwards in Blake's prophetic works flows from such rhetorically deployed logic. What appears absolute from inside their closed rational systems is in fact wholly relative. It is not redemption that metaphysical conciliators like Los effect in their fallen contexts, then, so much as acculturation, for even they are trapped in their own or others' arguments. Urizen's emergence in chapter 1 is thus announced in such a way as to implicate all in the triumphant entry of instrumental rationality onto the scene. "It is Urizen," Blake punningly announces (*WB* 3.6)—"your reason," as countless commentators note—because every reasoning being is involved in this emergent perspective. The question is, where is Urizen's perspective situated? An answer is offered in Blake's image of Urizen constructing not only Creation but himself as Creator, and all from the solid vantage ground of—where?

> Inwards, into a deep world within:
> A void immense, wild dark & deep,
> Where nothing was. Natures wide womb
> And self balanc'd stretch'd o'er the void
>   I alone, even I!
>
>   (*WB* 4.15–19)

The untenable, or provisionally tenable, nature of Urizen's position, "self balanc'd" like this over a chaos of his own creating, becomes fully evident only in the final poem of the cycle, *The Book of Los*, which brilliantly engages the problem of creating perspective—and thus ascertaining certainty from mere probability—in a universe formerly apprehended through "all flexible senses" (*WB* 3.38). Here Los must provide himself with not only a body but a context as well as a perspective mediating both. Thus, as he plunges through the boundless void of error, he begins to establish a position, however contingent, as "wrath subsided / And contemplative thoughts first arose / Then aloft his head rear'd in the Abyss / And his downward-borne fall chang'd oblique" (*WB* 4.39–42). In Blake's mythos, then, the relative is created by the fall of eternity into disunity—by Urizen's initial separation from Eternity (or Albion) and Los's subsequent construction of a contingent point of view. Urizen's rebellious act must therefore be regarded under two aspects. As an act of separation, it is subversive, necessarily calling into question the dominant unity against which it has negatively positioned itself. As such, it is inherently critical. As an act of self-construction, however, it is acclamatory. The moment Urizen privileges his portion as the whole, he turns regressive. And so the cycle continues, as the revolutionary Fuzon attempts in his turn to demystify Urizenic power ("Shall we worship this Demon of smoke / . . . this abstract non-entity, / This cloudy God seated on the waters, / Now seen, now obscur'd, King of Sorrow?" [*Ahania, WB* 2.10–11]) and, victory within his grasp, declares himself "eldest of things." Whatever its original motive, moreover, Urizen's separation from the other zoas—body (Tharmas), emotions (Luvah), and imagination (Urthona)—signals the emergence of autonomous reason. No longer part of the absolute totality that was Albion, Urizen henceforth operates relative to circumstances, like Franken-stein's Creature directing his very being to mastering these cir-cumstances:

> 6. And Urizen craving with hunger
> Stung with the odours of Nature
> Explor'd his dens around
> 7. He form'd a line & a plummet
> To divide the Abyss beneath.
> He form'd a dividing rule:
> 8. He formed scales to weigh;
> He formed massy weights;
> He formed a brazen quadrant;
> He formed golden compasses
> And began to explore the Abyss
> And he planted a garden of fruits
>
> (*Urizen, WB* 20.30–41)

From state of nature to mastery over nature, instrumental reason critically distinguishes difference only to triumphantly suppress it once separation, initially a deviation from primordial wholeness, becomes "self-balanc'd" in its relative (or rhetorical) validity. Yet, like Los's desperate incarnation of Urizen, which is calculated to expose error by giving it a form, this provisional hedging against chaos is necessary to set limits to the potential of error for endless regression.

It is in the context of this mythic narrative of reason run amok that Blake treats the debates of his age. His unfinished manu-script poem, *The French Revolution* (1791), the most topically de-limited of his verse narratives, features a debate on the nature of authority clearly drawn from Burke/Paine. For Burke the "night-mare" of infinite regress can lead only to Rousseau's Natural State. He evokes the fourteenth century in his defenses of tradi-tion,[45] therefore, in order to preempt the reversion to a much more distant past by the reform position—Paine's argument, for instance, that "the error of those who reason by precedents drawn from antiquity, respecting the rights of man, is, that they do not go far enough into antiquity. They do not go the whole way."[46] This is precisely the hypothetical prior refuted by the fictional duke of Burgundy in Blake's poem who, while he nostalgically invokes a traditional feudal past, fears a future reign of Natural Law recovered from a past so primitive as to pre-date tradition as he knows it:

> Till our purple and crimson is faded to russet, and the
>   kingdoms of earth bound in sheaves,
> And the ancient forests of chivalry hewn, and the joys of the
>   combat burnt for fuel;
> Till the power and dominion is rent from the pole, sword and
>   scepter from sun and moon,
> The law and gospel from fire and air, and eternal reason and
>   science
> From the deep and the solid, and man lay his faded head down
>   on the rock
> Of eternity. . . .
>
> (*WB* ll. 92–97)

This passage expresses the conservative's deep fear of the essential, of a nature prior to second nature. The past defended by Burgundy, what he calls "this great starry harvest of six thousand years" (*WB* l. 90), is merely part of a past. It is a portion habitually mistaken for the whole—Paine writes against Burke's traditionalism that "the fact is, that portions of antiquity, by proving everything, establish nothing"[47]—which in fact shields Burgundy from the whole that is history. This prospect, a seemingly infinite regression beyond a traditional past, prompts the archbishop of Paris to envision France reverting to a state of nature, "for a curse is heard hoarse thro' the land, from a godless race / Descending to beasts" (*WB* ll. 138–39). In *Europe*, similarly, a reactionary escape into this very past involves George III and his ministers in the same regressive nightmare threatening Burgundy's arch-feudalist vision. Going back well beyond Burke's beloved fourteenth century in their flight from reform along "the infinite shores of Thames," they find themselves in a "serpent-form'd" Druidic temple underlying both Windsor Castle and Bacon's country seat Verulam—British monarchy and empiricism alike (*WB* 10.2, 5). In a typically Blakean metamorphosis, Druidic temple suddenly becomes Natural Man—"once open to the heavens and elevated on the human neck / Now overgrown with hair and coverd with a stony roof" (*WB* 10.28–29)—as he is

overwhelmed by a "deluge" of the senses. Whether a hopeful beginning or a catastrophic ending has been reached here is a question whose answer depends on any of a number of rhetorical
options.

But how far back is too far? The great revolutionary debates of
the period—Blake's Burgundy clearly imagines a savage fate for
himself and his privileged cohort when he asks, "Shall this
marble built heaven become a clay cottage?" (*WB* 1. 89)—turn on
this question. The concluding plates of *Europe* posit a historical
course that is hardly hopeful. Protecting a historically sanctioned status quo, the reactionary Angel of Albion can think only
in terms of closure when confronted with the revolutionary Orc
and struggles to sound "the Trump of the last doom" (*WB* 13.2).
Meanwhile, English common law (in the form of Lord Chancellor
Thurlow)[48] realizes Burgundy's worst fears by fleeing into the
wilderness. This is not a return to nature, but a final regressive
stage of second nature, the distortion of essence into accident, for
Thurlow's fate ("his furr'd robes & false locks / Adhered and grew
one with his flesh" [*WB* 12.16–17]) surely parodies Burke's doctrine of second nature through which reason is naturalized into
convention. Here, however, it is subtilized into the ultimate savagery of prescriptive rule. While meant to signal an end, similarly, perhaps *the* end, Albion's apocalyptic trumpet blast has the
effect of awakening Europe (in the figure of Enitharmon) from an
eighteen-hundred-year dream, complete with the accompanying
morning imagery of enlightenment. Yet this beginning may yet
anticipate another ending in its turn—"terrible Orc, when he
beheld the morning in the east, / Shot from the heights of Enitharmon" (*WB* 14.37; 15.1)—for once set in action the logic of regression may lead anywhere. Los concludes the poem potentially
in medias res with a cry to arms "that shook all nature to the
utmost pole" (*WB* 15.10).

How far back is too far? In the *Prelude*, William Wordsworth
recalls a period at around 1793 when he sighted a new world, "a
world, too, that was fit / To be transmitted, and made visible / To
other eyes."[49] To be sure, this passage describes a discovery of
personal imaginative power, but the New World reference has
public implications as well. Whether figured as flight or quest,
the desperate trek across Salisbury Plain described in the *Prelude*, with its spectral visions of Druidic sacrifice raised from

Sarum's primitive landscape, takes place against hopes and disappointments related to reform in revolutionary France—itself inspired by reforms enacted successfully in America not two decades before (the period setting of Wordsworth's Salisbury Plain poems). Behind both historical junctures are cautionary traces of a distant savage past. If, then, a work like Peacock's *Genius of the Thames* (1810) implicitly celebrates Whig history in an encounter between a Roman legionnaire and a savage Briton, inviting modern readers to congratulate themselves on how far they have come, for Blake and Wordsworth such historical displacements are less affirming. Wordsworth's encounter with the primitive on Salisbury Plain disturbingly identifies present with past otherness—a "new world" with a vengeance, as some canceled lines from the Salisbury Plain verses suggest:

> Still, reason's ray,
> What does it more than while the tempests rise,
> With starless glooms and sounds of loud dismay,
> Reveal with still-born glimpse the terrors of our way?[50]

In *Europe*, the conflation of monuments to British imperialism/empiricism and a Druidic temple effectively situates the regressive at the very heart of the progressive. This journey beyond tradition traces not the triumphant outlines of Whig history from rude to refined but a savage otherness emerging from the Enlightenment paradigm of rational progressivism—the logical outcome of "immoderate reason" given expression in certain arguments about history.

Afterword

"Let us only suffer any person to tell us his story, morning and evening, but for one twelvemonth," writes Edmund Burke, "and he will become our master." In "Thoughts on French Affairs," where he says this, Burke compares the French Revolution with the only other *"Revolution of doctrine and theoretick dogma"* to have happened in Europe, the Reformation. He finds in each an expansive "spirit of proselytism" respecting no national or regional barriers and so setting state against state and even dividing states within themselves. Reformation ideology, he argues, dominated national and international affairs for two centuries, giving "a colour, a character, and direction to all the politicks of Europe" before being succeeded in influence by the French Revolution. The threat of the latter, as Burke sees it here anyway, is not military but rhetorical, represented by an argument convincing not so much in its logic as in its "continual repetition."[1] Knowing this when he wrote the *Reflections*, then, he put forward arguments in that work calculated to counteract what he viewed as dangerously skewed historical logic in the revisionary arguments of Richard Price and other English radicals. In 1791, when he wrote "Thoughts on French Affairs," he had not yet seen predictions made a year earlier in the *Reflections* confirmed by events in France. His argument here, however, extends the logic of the revolution beyond France, signaling a prospect no less alarming for its seemingly indeterminate nature. "What direction the French spirit of proselytism is likely to take, and in what order it is likely to prevail in the several parts of Europe, it is not easy to determine,"[2] he says, but it is clear that he fears a repeat of the two centuries following the advent of Reformation in Europe.

Here and elsewhere, Burke notes an irrationalist inference in revolutionary arguments that, notwithstanding their militant secularism, is comparable to religious zealotry. In *Second Letter on a Regicide Peace*, he argues that Jacobin polemicists are "not exceeded by Mahomet himself" in their zeal to propagate revolutionary principles. He implies further that the impulse to proselytize may be more universal than the principles at issue:

> They who have made but superficial studies in the Natural History of the human mind, have been taught to look on religious opinions as the only cause of enthusiastick zeal, and sectarian propagation. But there is no doctrine whatever, on which men can warm, that is not capable of the very same effect. The social nature of man impels him to propagate his principles, as much as physical impulses urge him to propagate his kind. The passions give zeal and vehemence. The understanding bestows design and system. The whole man moves under the discipline of his opinions. (9:278–79)

For Burke, and for the author of *The Borderers*, the most rational of arguments is capable of reverting to a barbarous issue once unmoored from property and custom. By its conclusion, indeed, the action of Wordsworth's play seems to have moved wholly under the regressive compulsion of its villain's opinions. As another character notes, the logic of even such a rational free agent as Oswald may construct "Some uncouth superstition of its own" if left unchecked. A necessary corollary of this, as Blake's Los comes to learn, is that the "design and system" of misguided, if compelling, arguments must be opposed by arguments equally compelling—at times, in effect, looking "rather to the *object* of each motion, than to the question itself." The result, for critics of Pittite governance like William Cobbett and Jeremy Bentham, was a public life in which method and probity might go hand in hand, or not. It was a public life in which one might have no choice but to fight imposture in kind, to sacrifice purity of principle to the mischief of practice. Bentham (like Coleridge from his opposing perspective) largely avoided such a fate by sacrificing practice to principle and producing writings increasingly notable for their obscurity. Cobbett, perhaps as much for temperamental as pragmatic reasons, cast his lot with practice (even, on occasion, the practice of mischief), and so paradoxically managed to stake out a measure of principle in a hard-won public role as a reform writer. While he recognized, as the elder in Coleridge's "Fable of the madning Rain" does not, that logical validity must bow to rhetorical effectiveness in practice, however, he did not entirely escape the elder's fate. At least part of his success lay in an obsessively repeated story—of paper credit, of the devastations of Reformation, of Pittite deception, of ministerial Green Bags—by which means he became master of a devoted readership. As a result, his reform arguments frequently lose themselves in the hypnotic spell of his reactionary rhetoric, compromised by their very effectiveness.

To be sure, these alternations between rebellion and reaction are not confined to reform. Burke is the presiding genius of the period's rhetorical transformations, notwithstanding his critical exposure of this very tendency in what might be termed the characteristic *virtù* of the age. In Burke, rebel and reactionary respond in kind to contingent circumstance, intransigently opposing radical change in terms subversive of new forms of tyranny that are potential in radical reform logic. It is this critical dialectic that neo-Whiggish Tories like George Canning bring to bear on reform in the anti-Jacobin press campaigns of the late 1790s and that reformers, sadder but wiser following the wars, appropriate in neo-Tory defenses of an embattled queen at the close of the Regency. The effect of these rhetorical appropriations was necessarily to subject principle to the mischief of practice in ways that, while they by no means mitigated partisan rancor, tended to methodize it. If reformers often complained that Tories and Whigs were of a kind, they had nonetheless themselves come to occupy common rhetorical ground with the "Ins" and "Outs" of the parliamentary parties. This circumstance was not lost on those in whose imaginative representations the period's debates would find more permanent form. Neither was it any less problematic for them. While in *Prometheus Unbound* Shelley could pursue reform logic along the same ideal bias as Godwin had done in *Political Justice*, in a popular work like "The Masque of Anarchy" he found it necessary address his readership in the John Bullish strain with which Godwin's Tyrrel baits Falkland in *Caleb Williams*, with the result that it effectively becomes an incitement to passive resistance. From the other side, Burke—whose parochial vision surely finds an echo in "old laws of England" invoked by Shelley's poem—applies the progressivist tendency of Whig history to his triumphant narrative of traditional English nationhood. The question, as Coleridge poses it, is how far practice may condition principle before principle becomes moot.

Blake, in whose mythos error is connate with the origin of language, must have the last word. If, in the Los cycle, Urizen rebels against what he views as Albion's hegemonic unity, he goes on to recreate a hegemony in his own image, its validity compromised by the fallacy of its claims to primordial wholeness. Inevitably, the moral universe he posits in "Words articulate" early in *The Book of Urizen* is wholly "self-balanc'd" in its own dubious rhetorical authority. Urizen's incarnation by Los thus serves only to reconcile his fall from eternity with this newly emerged contingency. The progression he follows thereafter, from natural state to natural mastery, from Lockean man stung by sensation to Newtonian man wielding compass and rule, ends with the planting of "a garden of fruits" (*WB* 22.41)—which is to say that its logic merely leads to another fall. The same logic also results in the transformation of Los (whose unfallen name of Urthona strangely associates him with the organic legitimacy celebrated by Burke in propertied interest) from eternal principle into provisional method, an alienated and upstart talent born of necessity. In "Letter to a Member of the General Assembly" (1791), Burke advises in such circumstances that, "when neither our principles nor our dispositions, nor, perhaps, our talents, enable us to encounter delusion with delusion, we must use our best reason to those that ought to be reasonable creatures, and to take our chance for the event."[3] Los, however, can only conclude, "I must Create a System, or be enslav'd by another Mans" (*Jerusalem*, 10.20–21).

Notes

Preface

1. Jon Klancher, ed. "Romanticism and its Publics," *Studies in Romanticism* 33 (winter 1994): 524.

2. See also Kevin Gilmartin, *Print Politics: The Press and Radical Opposition in Early Nineteenth-Century England,* Cambridge Studies in Romanticism (Cambridge: Cambridge University Press, 1996); Stephen Behrendt, ed., *Romanticism, Radicalism, and the Press* (Detroit: Wayne State University Press, 1997); David Worrall, *Radical Culture: Discourse, Resistance and Surveillance, 1790–1820* (London: Harvester Wheatsheaf, 1992); Olivia Smith, *The Politics of Language, 1791–1819* (Oxford: Clarendon Press, 1984); Iain McCalman, *Radical Underworld: Prophets, Revolutionaries and Pornographers in London, 1795–1840* (Cambridge: Cambridge University Press, 1987); Michael Scrivener, *Poetry and Reform: Periodical Verse from the English Democratic Press, 1792–1824* (Detroit: Wayne State University Press, 1992); and John P. Klancher, *The Making of the English Reading Audiences,* 1790–1832 (Madison, Wis.: University of Wisconsin Press, 1987).

3. Quoted in Hazlitt "Life of Thomas Holcroft," *CWH* 3:143; quoted in Walter Lippmann, *Public Opinion* (New York: Macmillan, 1961), 197.

4. Thomas Paine, *Rights of Man* (Markham, Ont.: Penguin, 1984), 161.

5. See Hazlitt, "Life of Holcroft," *CWH* 3:148–49.

6. See J. G. A. Pocock, *The Machiavellian Moment: Florentine Political Thought and the Atlantic Republican Tradition* (Princeton: Princeton University Press, 1975), 486–87.

7. Don H. Bialostosky and Lawrence Needham, eds., *Rhetorical Traditions and British Romantic Literature* (Bloomington: Indiana University Press, 1995), 1, 8.

Chapter 1: Designing Eloquence

1. Wilbur Samuel Howell, *Eighteenth-Century British Logic and Rhetoric* (Princeton, N.J.: Princeton University Press, 1971), 5–6.

2. Quoted in Howell, *Logic and Rhetoric*, 694.

3. *The Notebooks of Samuel Taylor Coleridge*, ed. Kathleen Coburn (Princeton, N.J.: Princeton University Press, 1961), 2:2626.

4. Jerome Christensen offers a different reading of this parable, but similarly sees a rhetorical emphasis: "Coleridge begins *The Friend* of 1818 as he had its earlier incarnation, by exemplifying the hazards that beset the oracular moralist in the 'Fable of the Madning Rain.' Having sounded this note of mingled caution and pathos, Coleridge proceeds to expand on the moral dangers of bluntly communicating the truth in a long introductory section wherein he contrasts an appropriately discreet communication with the irresponsible truth telling of the French Encyclopaedists, who, by indiscriminately broadcasting technically correct but circumstantially inadequate notions, stripped truth of the reserve essential to the preservation of its moral force": "The Method of *The Friend*," in *Rhetorical Traditions*, 11.

5. "A man long accustomed to silent and solitary meditation," Coleridge admits in essay 3 of the 1818 *Friend*, "in proportion as he encreases the power of thinking in long and connected trains, is apt to lose or lessen the talent of communicating his thoughts with grace and perspicuity" (*TF* 1:20).

6. In one of his theater reviews, for instance, William Hazlitt notes "single hits here and there" in Kean's *Lear*, regarding them as "interlineations of the character, rather than parts of the text" (*CWH* 18:336); Blake angrily condemns chiaroscuro in his *Public Address* where he states: "I hope my Countrymen will Excuse me if I tell them a Wholesom truth Most Englishmen when they look at a Picture immediately set about searching for Points of Light < & clap the Picture into a dark corner [*this in*] <This when done by> Grand Works is like looking for Epigrams in Homer> A point of light is a Witticism many are destructive of all Art <One is an Epigram only> & no Grand Work can have them they produce System & Monotony" (WB 579).

7. Quoted in Introduction to John Lawson, *Lectures Concerning Oratory*, ed. E. Neal Claussen and Karl R. Wallace (Edwardsville: Southern Illinois University Press, 1972), xix.

8. Howell, *Logic and Rhetoric*, 76–77.

9. See Frederick C. Beiser, *The Sovereignty of Reason: The Defence of Rationality in the Early English Enlightenment* (Princeton, N.J.: Princeton University Press, 1996).

10. *The History of the Royal-Society of London*, ed. Jackson I. Cope and Harold Whitmore Jones (St. Louis: Washington University Press, 1959), 112.

11. *An Essay Concerning Human Understanding*, ed. Peter H. Nidditch (Oxford: Clarendon Press, 1975), 476, 508

12. As Howell writes of this passage, "Thus to Locke there is a bad and a good rhetoric, and his castigation of the one must not be allowed to obliterate his acknowledgment of the other": *Logic and Rhetoric*, 491.

13. *Essays on the Intellectual Powers of Man*, ed. William Hamilton (Hildesheim: Georg Olms, 1967), 1:219–20, 227.

14. *An Inquiry into the Human Mind on the Principles of Common Sense*, ed. William Hamilton (Hildesheim: Georg Olms, 1967), 118.

15. *A Treatise Concerning the Principles of Human Knowledge*, eds. A. A. Luce and T. E. Jessup (London: Nelson, 1948–57), 2:37.

16. Howell, *Logic and Rhetoric*, 77. See Howell's discussion of John Ward's and John Holmes's retention of this definition in their Rhetorics: 105–19, 125–42.

17. According to Howell, "Systems of fixed tones and gestures became the bane of the Elocutionary movement, and, as they were often accompanied by

mysticism and quackery, they increasingly attracted the poseurs and the charlatans into the ranks of the teachers of oratorical delivery. Such teachers brought rhetoric into the deepest disrepute that it had ever known": ibid., 243.

18. H. Lewis Ulman, *Things, Thoughts, Words, and Actions: The Problem of Language in Late Eighteenth-Century British Rhetorical Theory* (Carbondale : Southern Illinois University Press, 1994), 149–50; also see Howell, *Logic and Rhetoric*, 153.

19. Paine, *Rights of Man*, 161; Wordsworth, "Preface to *Lyrical Ballads*," in *The Prose Works of William Wordsworth*, ed. W. J. B. Owen and Jane Worthington Smyser (Oxford: Clarendon Press, 1974), 1:138.

20. "The New Rhetoric and Romantic Poetics," in *Rhetorical Traditions*, 217.

21. See ibid., 217. See also John Lothian, who points out that "the result of all these diverse activities was a wide-spread cultivation of the 'critical' spirit, which was in keeping with the national interest in political and economic philosophy, in history as a branch of literature, and in the discussion of philosophical and literary principles. It ultimately produced such notable results as the *Edinburgh Review* and *Blackwood's Magazine*. Adam Smith and his successors Watson, Blair, Campbell, Greenfield and the rest, had done their work of public education well". Introduction to Adam Smith's *Lectures on Rhetoric and Belles Lettres*, ed. John Lothian (London: T. Nelson, 1963) xxxix.

22. Early nineteenth-century students of comparative grammar like Wilhelm von Humboldt and Jacob Grimm view language in exactly this way as they reject simple referentiality and posit an identity between the internal structures of language and thought itself. See Hans Aarsleff's introduction to Wilhelm von Humboldt, *On Language: The Diversity of Human Language-Structure and Its Influence on the Mental Development of Mankind*, trans. Peter Heath (Cambridge: Cambridge University Press, 1988).

23. Editors' introduction to Joseph Priestley, *A Course of Lectures on Oratory and Criticism*, ed. Vincent M. Bevilacqua and Richard Murphy (Carbondale: Southern Illinois University Press, 1965), xxxi.

24. Ibid., xxxv.

25. Ibid., xxxii–xxxiii.

26. Ibid., xxxviii.

27. Introduction to *The Philosophy of Rhetoric*, ed. Lloyd Bitzer (Carbondale: South Illinois University Press, 1963), xxv.

28. "Practical Reasoning, Rhetoric, and Wordsworth's 'Preface,'" in *Spirits of Fire: English Romantic Writers and Contemporary Historical Methods*, ed. G. A. Rosso and Daniel Watkins (Madison, N. J.: Fairleigh Dickinson University Press, 1990), 101–2.

29. Bentham writes: "Of the self-written Memoirs of Bubb Dodington, how much was said in their day!—of Gerard Hamilton's Parliamentary Logic, how little! The reason is not unobvious: Dodington was all anecdote—Hamilton was all theory. What Hamilton endeavoured to teach with Malone and Johnson for his bag-bearers, Dodington was seen to practise" (*WJB* 2:385).

30. Of Anne Elliot in *Persuasion*, Austen observes that "She had been forced into prudence in her youth, she learned romance as she grew older—the natural sequel of an unnatural beginning": *Persuasion* (Markham, Ont.: Penguin, 1965), 58.

31. Bentham offers this impersonation of Hamilton's position: "Come unto me all ye who have a point to gain, and I will show you how: bad or good, so as it be not parliamentary reform, to me it is matter of indifference" (*WJB* 2:387).

32. "It being the interest of each person so situated to give the utmost support to abuse, and the utmost currency to fallacy in every shape, it is also his interest to give the utmost efficiency to the system of education by which men are most effectually divested both of the power and will to detect and expose fallacies, and thence to suppress every system of education in proportion as it has a contrary tendency" (*WJB* 2:398).

33. According to Mill, Bentham was "the great *critical. . .* thinker of his age and country," influential not for his opinions but for his "*method*": "Bentham," in *Collected Works of John Stuart Mill*, ed. John M. Robson (Toronto: University of Toronto Press, 1929), 10:78–79.

34. Even Campbell, while he argues that the deliberate use of "obscurity" is only seemingly as effective in certain cases as "perspicuity," implicitly concedes resources open to rhetoric, discountenanced though they might be by morality (*PR* 273–78).

35. *The Halliford Edition of the Works of Thomas Love Peacock*, ed. H. F. B. Brett-Smith and C. E. Jones (New York: AMS Press, 1967), 2:229.

36. *Elements of Opposition* (London: J. Hatchard, 1803), 1, 95.

37. *The Political Primer; or, Road to Public Honours* (London: Henry Colburn, 1820), 87, iii–iv, 5, 59–60.

Chapter 2: Whiggish Energies

1. See Felix Raab, *The English Face of Machiavelli: A Changing Interpretation 1500–1700* (London: Routledge and Kegan Paul, 1964), and J. G. A. Pocock, *Machiavellian Moment*.

2. Pocock, *Machiavellian Moment*, 156, 165.

3. See ibid., 37–41.

4. *Machiavellian Rhetoric from the Counter-Reformation to Milton* (Princeton: Princeton University Press, 1994), 11, 19–20. Khan cites Pocock's cautionary remark that *virtù* "is not merely that by which men control their fortunes in a legitimized world; it may also be that by which men innovate and so delegitimize their worlds": Pocock, *Machiavellian Moment*, 166.

5. See Mary Mack's discussion of *Letters of Anti-Machiavel* in *Jeremy Bentham: An Odyssey of Ideas, 1748–1792* (Toronto: Heinemann, 1962), 398, 400–402.

6. See Beiser, *The Sovereignty of Reason*.

7. *An Essay on the History of Civil Society*, ed. Fania Oz-Salzberge (Cambridge: Cambridge University Press, 1996), 42, 207.

8. In a letter to the editor of *The Satirist* in 1811, INVESTIGATOR writes that "in this age of oratory and politics, when we have so many volumes of parliamentary debates, I am rather surprised that no dashing compiler has ever thought of collecting the various effusions of city eloquence into a couple of octavos. 'Tis not so many years since a work came out called the 'Accomplished Senator,' and I do not see why we should not also have the '*Accomplished Common Council-man*.'" (*S* 1 Mar. 1811: 234).

9. Thomas Browne, LL.D., "Advertisement," in *The British Cicero; or a Selection of the most Admired Speeches in the English Language; Arranged under Three Distinct Heads of Popular, Parliamentary, and Judicial Oratory: With Historical Illustrations: To which is Prefixed, An Introduction to the Study and Practice of Eloquence,* 3 vols. (London: Longman, Hurst, Rees, and Orme, 1808), 1:iii–iv, 1, 10, 88–89, 101, 3:8.

10. Ibid., 1:9, 3:4, 1:33, 1:75.

11. Hamilton variously advises: "Do not omit totally, but only throw into the shade the capital circumstances that make against you"; "By a collection of circumstances piece out, or if you cannot do that, drop, what is defective; but state clearly to your own mind what is so"; "In stating any thing, drop some of the circumstances that are most invidious, but retain enough not to make the fallacy obvious: add likewise others, which if they do not actually, might possibly belong to it" (PL 25, 18, 86–87).

12. *The Technological Society*, trans. John Wilkinson (New York: Knopf, 1967), 134, 53.

13. *Machiavellian Moment*, 486–87.

14. Mill, *Collected Works*, 10:10, 78–79. In his fragmentary essay "On Life," Shelley asserts the strengths and limitations of this subversive method, which he calls "the intellectual philosophy": "It destroys error, and the roots of error. It leaves, what is too often the duty of the reformer in political and ethical questions to leave, a vacancy": Percy Bysshe Shelley, *Shelley's Poetry and Prose*, ed. Donald H. Reiman and Sharon B. Powers (New York: Norton, 1977), 477.

15. Quoted in L. G. Mitchell, introduction (*RRF* 8:20).

16. Ibid., 8:31–32.

17. Frank O'Gorman, *The Rise of Party in England: The Rockingham Whigs, 1760–82* (London: George Allen & Unwin, 1975), 547 n, 175–76.

18. Pocock, "The Varieties of Whiggism from Exclusion to Reform," in *Virtue, Commerce, and History: Essays on Political Thought and History, Chiefly in the Eighteenth Century*, ed. J. G. A. Pocock (Cambridge: Cambridge University Press, 1985), 275–76.

19. Carolus Candidus, *A Short Reply to a Short Defence of the Whigs, which will shortly prove the Imputations cast upon them during the Late Election to Be Founded in Truth; being a Short Review of their Political Conduct from 1688, to the Present Time. In Short, a Complete Refutation of the Arguments of a Noble and Learned Lord* (London: John Lowndes, 1819), 2–3

20. Wemyss Jobson, *Career of the Whigs* (London: G. J. Sands and Co., 1851), 4.

21. Candidus, *Short Reply*, 5–6.

22. Candidus, *Short Reply*, 7.

23. Nicholas Phillipson, "Politeness and Politics in the Reigns of Anne and the Early Hanoverians," in *The Varieties of British Political Thought, 1500–1800*, ed. J. G. A. Pocock (Cambridge: Cambridge University Press, 1993), 214, 214–15.

24. Pocock, "Varieties of Whiggism," in *Virtue, Commerce, and History*, 240–41.

25. *A Dissertation on the Rise, Progress, Views, Strength, Interests and Characters, of the Two Parties of the Whigs and Tories* (Boston: Joseph Greenleaf, 1773), 55–58, 35.

26. In an article simply entitled "George Canning," for instance, the *Black Dwarf* characterizes Canning as "a full-grown *harlequin,*" figuring as "the pantaloon of Pitt, the clown of Castlereagh, and the merry andrew of the present *pious* and *medical minister* whom he has the *honor* to serve so much to their mutual satisfaction, and to the entertainment of the various visitors of the phantasmagoria of British liberty" (*BD* 18 Mar. 1818: 161).

27. Even Tory colleagues drew the line when in a speech Canning mocked the physical infirmity of a man imprisoned following the suspension of Habeas Corpus in 1817. The following account appears in a number of the *Black Dwarf* for that year: "Yet even in the House of Commons, even on the ministerial side, a murmur of indignation was heard as the unfeeling orator attempted to call up derision at the miseries of his persecuted slaves! There is something so abhorrent, even to the feelings of a savage, in *jesting* with anguish, that the boroughmongers recoiled from any association with the sentiments of their doughty champion; and on his lips alone appeared an unmeaning smile, when he talked of '*the eloquence of a rupture!*' in a tone of supercilious satisfaction" (*BD* 18 Mar. 1818: 164).

28. *A Letter to the Right Honourable George Canning, M.P. President of the Board of Control, &c. on his Late Speech at Liverpool* (London: R. Carlile, 1818), 3, 4, 14, 6, 5, 6, 7, 9, 7, 33–34, 4.

29. See John W. Derry, *Castlereagh* (London: Allen Lane, 1976), 111.

30. Peter Dixon, *Canning: Politician and Statesman* (London: Weidenfeld and Nicolson, 1976), 3–4.

31. Ibid., 14.

32. Ibid., 22.

33. Ibid., 22–23.

34. Ibid.

35. Ibid., 23

36. In an open letter to Canning, of which there were many in the radical press, the *Black Dwarf* states:

> There is nothing in your station, in your abilities, or in your character, which entitles you to respect. The first is generally the reward of political, and frequently of private crime. Your talents, such as they are, you have abused; and, as for your character, I know not an individual of any party, or in any class of society, who does not consider the defence of it a paradox too outrageous and untenable even for the profligate indifference of these candid, complying times. Between the shrugs and smiles of your associates, and frowns of your honest countrymen, you fall to the ground. (*BD* 15 Apr. 1818: 226–27)

37. See Roger Fulford, *The Trial of Queen Caroline* (London: B. T. Batsford, 1967); Thomas W. Laqueur, "The Queen Caroline Affair: Politics as Art in the Reign of George IV," *Journal of Modern History* 54 (Sept. 1982): 417–66; Anna Clark, "Queen Caroline and the Sexual Politics of Popular Culture in London, 1820," *Representations* 31 (summer 1990): 47–68; E. A. Smith, *A Queen on Trial: The Affair of Queen Caroline* (Dover, N.H.: Alan Sutton, 1993); ed. John Stevenson; and Marcus Wood, *Radical Satire and Print Culture, 1790–1822* (Oxford University Press, 1994). *London in the Age of Reform* (Oxford: Blackwell, 1977).

38. Clark, "Sexual Politics," 51.

39. *From the Queen's Answers to Various Addresses Presented to Her; together with Her Majesty's Extraordinary Letter to the King; and an Introduction; and Observations Illustrative of their Tendency* (London: John Hatchard and Son, 1821) 63, 1, 44–47, 64, 28, 35–36, 74, 49, 6–7 n, 6.

40. John Guy, "The Henrican Age," in *Varieties of English Political Thought,* 16.

41. Charles Phillips, *The Queen's Case Stated* (London: William Hone, 1820) 5–6.

42. Quoted in Smith, *A Queen on Trial,* 136.

43. Laquer, "Queen Caroline Affair," 461, 464.

44. Lord Hutchinson quoted in Fulford, *Trial of Queen Caroline,* 39.

45. *The King's Treatment of the Queen shortly stated to the People of England* (London: William Hone, 1820), 3.

46. "Question between the King and Queen," *The Examiner,* 11 June 1820, 369.

47. "Cant of the Queen's Accusers," *The Examiner,* 16 July 1820, 449.

48. Quoted in Fulford, *Trial of Queen Caroline,* 28.

49. "Desperation of the Corrupt," *The Examiner,* 24 December 1820, 817.

CHAPTER 3: CRITICAL STRATEGEMS

1. The famous section on the Lake School in *Lectures on the English Poets* (1818) is as loaded a piece of "political criticism" as any Hazlitt deplored in the *Courier* or *Blackwood's Magazine*:

> The change in the belles-lettres was as complete, and to many persons as startling, as the change in politics, with which it went hand in hand. There was a mighty ferment in the heads of statesmen and poets, kings and people. According to the prevailing notions, all was to be natural and new. Nothing that was established was to be tolerated. All the common-place figures of poetry, tropes, allegories, personifications, with the whole heathen mythology, were instantly discarded; a classical allusion was considered as a piece of antiquated foppery; capital letters were no more allowed in print, than letters-patent of nobility were permitted in real life; kings and queens were dethroned from their rank and station in legitimate tragedy or epic poetry, as they were decapitated elsewhere; rhyme was looked upon as a relic of the feudal system, and regular metre was abolished along with regular government. Authority and fashion, elegance or arrangement, were hooted out of countenance, as pedantry and prejudice. Every one did what was good in his own eyes. The object was to reduce all things to an absolute level; and a singularly affected and outrageous simplicity prevailed in dress and manners, in style and sentiment. (*CWH* 5:161–62)

2. Burke, "Thoughts on French Affairs," ed. L.G. Mitchell, in *Writings and Speeches*, ed. Paul Langford (Oxford: Clarendon Press, 1989), 8:347–48, 8:359.

3. Burke, "Remarks on the Policy of the Allies," ed. L.G. Mitchell, in *Writings and Speeches*, 8: 498–99.

4. Marilyn Butler, *Jane Austen and the War of Ideas* (Oxford: Clarendon, 1975), 7–8, 39, 37. See also Kenneth R. Johnston, "Romantic Anti-Jacobins or

Anti-Jacobin Romantics?" *Romanticism on the Net* 15 (August 1999): <http://users.ox.ac.uk/~scat0385/antijacobin.html>.

5. See Marilyn Butler, *Romantics, Rebels and Reactionaries: English Literature and its Background, 1760–1830* (Oxford: Oxford University Press, 1981), 113–37

6. Butler, *Jane Austen*, 34.

7. Replying to allegations about the Lord Chancellor that it claims are false, the *Anti-Jacobin* states: As we have given so early a contradiction to this Lie, we must enter our protest against its being added to those which the Jacobins claim a prescriptive right to consider as established, from the mere impudence with which they are repeated" (*A–J* 21 May 1798: 333).

8. Josiah Hard, *Imposture Exposed in a Few Brief Remarks on the Irreligiousness, Profaneness, Indelicacy, Virulence, and Vulgarity of certain Persons, who style Themselves Anti-Jacobin Reviewers* (Cambridge: J. Drighton, 1801), 3, 5–6, 10, 15–16, 18.

9. Ibid., 5–6. In *The Friend,* Coleridge observes similarly of anti-Jacobian writers that "In order to oppose Jacobinism they imitated its worst features; in personal slander, in illegal violence, and even in the thirst for blood. They justified the corruptions of the State in the same spirit of Sophistry, by the same vague arguments of general Reason, and the same disregard of ancient ordinances and established opinions, with which the State itself had been attacked by the Jacobians" (*TF* 1:216).

10. "Remarks on the Periodical Criticism of England—In a Letter to a Friend (Translated from the German of Von Lauerwinkel)" *Blackwood's Edinburgh Magazine* 2, March 1818, 671.

11. "On the Reciprocal Influence of Periodical Publications, and the Intellectual Progress of this Country," *Blackwood's Edinburgh Magazine* 16, (November 1824, 526. In *The English Metropolis*, John A. Corry writes: "That the first Reviewers were actuated by the patriotic desire to refine the public taste, and regulate the eccentricities of genius, will not be denied by the judicious reader of their periodical works; and the Monthly Review affords the most valuable and interesting History of English and Foreign literature for more than half a century": "Free Strictures on English Literature," in *The English Metropolis; or, London in the Year 1820. Containing Satirical Strictures on Public Manners, Morals, and Amusements; A Young Gentleman's Adventures; and Characteristic Anecdotes of Several Eminent Individuals who now figure in this Great Theatre of Temporary Exhibition. By the Author of a Satirical View of London.* (London: Sherwood, Neely, and Jones, 1820), 268.

12. Abram Combe, *An Address to the Conductors of the Periodical Press, Upon the Causes of Religious and Political Disputes, with remarks on the Local and General Definition of Certain Words and Terms which have often been the Subject of Controversy* (Edinburgh: Bell and Bradfute, 1823), 7, 5, 14, 33.

13. Peacock, *Works of Thomas Love Peacock*, 9:109, 108, 8:279–80, 269.

14. [Isaac Disraeli], *Vaurien: or, Sketches of the Times: exhibiting Views of the Philosophies, Religions, Politics, Literature, and Manners of the Age,* 2 vols. (London: T. Cadell, junior, and W. Davies; J. Murray and S. Highley, 1797), 1:72, 35.

15. *Works of Thomas Love Peacock*, 2:144, 134, 135, 8:270, 6:285.

16. *Works of Thomas Love Peacock*, 9:167.

17. See Max Horkheimer and Theodor W. Adorno, *Dialectic of Enlightenment*, trans. John Cumming (New York: Herder and Herder, 1969).

18. Peacock, *Works of Thomas Love Peacock*, 8:273.

19. "Remarks on the Periodical Criticism of England," *Blackwood's* 2, March 1818, 672.

CHAPTER 4: SYSTEMATIC OPPOSITION

1. See Ian Dyck, *William Cobbett and Rural Popular Culture* (Cambridge: Cambridge University Press, 1992), 225; and Ian Dyck "From 'Rabble' to 'Chopsticks': the Radicalism of William Cobbett," *Albion* (1989): 71–72. Also see Leonora Nattrass, *William Cobbett: The Politics of Style* (Cambridge: Cambridge University Press, 1995), 90–92.

2. He pointed out in a letter at this time "that for me to be able to do the government any service, I must be able to say that I am totally independent of it, in my capacity of proprietor of a newspaper": quoted in Daniel Green, *Great Cobbett: The Noblest Agitator* (London: Hodder and Stoughton, 1983), 185.

3. Ibid., 191.

4. See *Elements of Reform, or An Account of the Motives and Intentions of the Advocates for Parliamentary Reformation* (London: T. Gillet, 1809).

5. Henry White, *A Calm Appeal to the Friends of Freedom and Reform on the Double Dealings of Mr. Cobbett and the Baneful Tendency of his Writings with a Vindication of the Whigs and the Patriots of Westminster and the Borough of Southwark, against his scurrilous and malignant Aspersions* (London: H. Robertson, 1823), 5, 6.

6. Nattrass, *Politics of Style*, 4, 30. For other recent discussions of Cobbett see Gilmartin, *Print Politics*, 158–94; and John Whale, *Imagination under Pressure, 1789–1832: Aesthetics, Politics and Utility* (Cambridge: Cambridge University Press, 2000), 140–65.

7. Quoted in Hans Speier, "Public Opinion," in *The Truth in Hell and other Essays on Politics and Culture, 1935–1987* (New York: Oxford University Press, 1989), 155–56.

8. Cobbett, *Rural Rides,* ed. George Woodcock (Harmondsworth: Penguin, 1967), 200, 201.

9. Green, *Great Cobbett*, 189–90.

10. For an early occurrence see "Summary of Politics. New Ministry" (*CPR* 8 Feb. 1806: 165).

11. *A Grammar of the English Language, in a Series of Letters* (London: Henry Frowde, 1906), 1, 190.

12. Cobbett goes on in this article to criticize a *Times* correspondent named PUBLICOLA for taking his motto from the works of Virgil, which, he charges, "teach flattery, gross, fulsome, nauseous flattery of an execrable tyrant, who gained his power by deliberate perfidy and murder. . . . And, yet, it is from this author, that the writer of the Letter in question *takes his motto?* Could he not have found mottoes in Lilburne's or Tooke's speeches; or in the speeches of Lord Erskine or Sir Francis Burdett?" (*CPR* 23 Feb. 1811: 452).

13. Green, *Great Cobbett*, 358–59.

14. See Kurt Heinzelman, *The Economics of the Imagination* (Amherst: University of Massachusetts Press, 1980); and Marc Shell, *The Economy of*

Literature (Baltimore: Johns Hopkins University Press, 1978); *Money, Language, and Thought: Literary and Philosophical Economies from the Medieval to the Modern Era* (Berkeley and Los Angeles: University of California Press, 1982).

15. Shell, *Economy of Literature*, 18. In "Memorabilia of Mr. Coleridge," similarly, Hazlitt writes that Coleridge "spoke of Mackintosh as deficient in original resources: he was neither the great merchant nor manufacturer of intellectual riches; but the ready warehouseman, who had a large assortment of goods, not properly his own, and who knew where to lay his hand on whatever he wanted" (*CWH* 20:217).

16. Quoted in Joyce Appleby, "Consumption in Early Modern Social Thought," in *Consumption and the World of Goods*, ed. John Brewer and Roy Porter (London: Routledge, 1993), 168.

17. Quoted in Raymond Williams, "Advertising: The Magic System," in *Problems in Materialism and Culture: Selected Essays* (London: NLB, 1980), 172 .

18. After quoting a scurrilous passage from the *Morning Post,* for instance, he asks his reader to "say, if, as an Englishman, you do not feel shame, that such language as this, such abuse as this, such self-degrading abuse, should appear in an English print" (*CPR* 8 Sept. 1810: 800).

19. Jürgen Habermas, *The Structural Transformation of the Public Sphere: An Inquiry into a Category of Bourgeois Society* (Cambridge: MIT Press, 1991), 40–41.

20. Preface, to *History of the Regency and Reign of King George the Fourth* (London: Mills, Jowett, and Mills, 1830), par. 3.

21. "Sketch of the History of England from the Protestant Reformation to the Regency of Geo. IV." *History of the Regency,* par. 7.

22. Parenthetical references in the text to Cobbett's *History of the Protestant Reformation in England Ireland* (*HPR*) cite volume and paragraph number.

23. *A Defence of Mr. Cobbett, Against the Intrigues of Sir Francis Burdett, and his Partisans.* (London: R. Carlile, 1819), 13.

CHAPTER 5: REASON IN EXTREMIS

1. *Vaurien*, 1:62–63, xiv–xv.
2. *Vaurien*, 1:72–73.
3. *Works of Thomas Love Peacock*, 6:118
4. *The Letters of Percy Bysshe Shelley*, ed. Frederick L. Jones (Oxford: Oxford University Press, 1964), 1:325.
5. Letter to Edward Thomas Hookham, 6–8 June 1809, *The Letters of Thomas Love Peacock*, ed. Nicholas A. Joukovsky (Oxford: Clarendon, 2001), 1:35.
6. *A Defence of Mr. Cobbett*, 13.
7. Ferguson, *Civil Society*, 15, 141.
8. William Wordsworth, *The Prelude: 1799, 1805, 1850*, ed. Jonathan Wordsworth, M. H. Abrams, and Stephen Gill (New York: Norton, 1979), [1805] bk. 10, ll. 812–13.
9. Mitchell, Introduction, *Writings and Speeches of Edmund Burke*, 8:8.
10. Quoted in Mitchell, Introduction (*RRF* 8:25).

11. Of passages in the *Reflections* conflating history and prophecy, John Whale writes that "Burke's rhetoric refuses and engages with the irrational": Introduction to *Edmund Burke's Reflections on the Revolution in France*, ed. John Whale (Manchester: Manchester University Press, 2000), 9.

12. Burke, *Philosophical Enquiry into the Origin of our Ideas of the Sublime and Beautiful, Writings and Speeches of Edmund Burke*, eds. T.O. McLoughlin and James T. Boulton, vol. 1, *Writings and Speeches*, 1:227.

13. F. P. Lock, "Rhetoric and Representation in Burke's *Reflections*" in *Burke's Reflections*, 20–21. Locke quotes here from Sir James Prior, *Life of Edmund Malone* (London, 1860), 154.

14. See Whale, Introduction, to *Burke's Reflections*, 21.

15. Lock, "Rhetoric and Representation," in *Burke's Reflections*, 21, 35.

16. In this work Burke writes: "Mr. Locke has somewhere observed with his usual sagacity, that most general words, those belonging to virtue and vice, good and evil, especially, are taught before the particular modes of action to which they belong are presented to the mind; and with them, the love of the one, and the abhorrence of the other; for the minds of children are so ductile, that a nurse, or any person about a child, by seeming pleased or displeased with any thing, or even any word, may give the disposition of the child a similar turn. When afterwards, the several occurrences in life come to be applied to these words; and that which is pleasant often appears under the name of evil; and what is disagreeable to nature is called good and virtuous; a strange confusion of ideas and affections arises in the minds of many; and an appearance of no small contradiction between their notions and their actions": *Sublime and Beautiful, Writings and Speeches,* 1:310–11.

17. Burke, *Sublime and Beautiful*, 1:319–20, 310–11.

18. Peter Hughes, "Originality and Allusion in the Writings of Edmund Burke," *Centrum* 4, no. 1 (1976): 39. See also John Whale, "Burke and the Civic Imagination," in *Imagination under Pressure*, 19–41; and Frans De Bruyn, *The Literary Genres of Edmund Burke: The Political Uses of Literary Form* (Oxford: Clarendon Press, 1996).

19. *Rights of Man,* 268, 44.

20. Burke, "Letter to a Member of the National Assembly," ed. L.G. Mitchell, in *Writings and Speeches*, 8:298.

21. O'Brien, Introduction to *Reflections on the Revolution in France,* ed. Conor Cruise O'Brien (Toronto: Penguin, 1986), 384 n.

22. Burke writes: "Was this spectacle intended to make the Parisians abhor persecution, and loath the effusion of blood?—No, it was to teach them to persecute their own pastors; it was to excite them, by raising a disgust and horror of their clergy, to an alacrity in hunting down to destruction an order, which, if it ought to exist at all, ought to exist not only in safety, but in reverence. It was to stimulate their cannibal appetites (which one would think had been gorged sufficiently) by variety and seasoning; and to quicken them to an alertness in new murders and massacres, if it should suit the purpose of the Guises of the day" (*RRF* 8:190–91).

23. Burke, "Vindication of Natural Society," in *Writings and Speeches,* 1:183.

24. Burke, "Letter to a Noble Lord," ed. R.B. McDowell, in *Writings and Speeches,* 9:174.

25. Parenthetical references in the text refer to act and line numbers in the play.

26. John Rieder, *Wordsworth's Counterrevolutionary Turn: Community, Virtue, and Vision in the 1790s* (Newark: University of Delaware Press, 1997), 120.

27. [Wordsworth's 1842 Note], *The Borderers*, ed. Robert Osborn (Ithaca: Cornell University Press, 1982), 813.

28. In the *Book of Fallacies*, Bentham proposes that whenever an instance of imposture occurs in Parliament, printed reports of debates should "at the bottom of the page, by the help of the usual marks of reference, give intimation of it" (*WJB* 2:486).

29. See Bromwich's chapter on "Political Justice in *The Borderers*, in *Disowned by Memory: Wordsworth's Poetry of the 1790s* (Chicago: University of Chicago Press, 1998), 44–68.

30. [Wordsworth's 1842 Note], *The Borderers*, 813.

31. Quoted in C. Kegan Paul, *William Godwin: His Friends and Contemporaries* (London: C. Kegan Paul, 1876), 1:78.

32. See Pamela Clemit, *The Godwinian Novel: The Rational Fictions of Godwin, Brockden Brown, Mary Shelley* (Oxford: Clarendon Press, 1993), 36, 39–40.

33. Godwin, *Political Justice and its Influence on Morals and Happiness*, ed. F. E. L. Priestley (Toronto: University of Toronto Press, 1969), 1:91.

34. The breeze reference seems to pick upon the letter by Walton opening *Frankenstein*. "I feel a cold northern breeze play University Presson my cheeks," writes Walton to his sister as he prepares to leave Petersburg on the Arctic expedition which will encounter the unfortunate Victor Frankenstein: *Frankenstein: or The Modern Prometheus, The 1818 Text*, ed. Marilyn Butler (Oxford: Oxford University Press, 1998), 5.

35. Scott, review of *"Frankenstein, or the Modern Prometheus,"* *Edinburgh Magazine* 88, 1818, 334.

36. Godwin, *Political Justice*, 1:92.

37. Kirsten Leaver, on the other hand, argues that Godwin had in mind for *Caleb* Williams an ideal future reader who would recognize "the political moral of the text": "Pursuing Conversations: *Caleb Williams* and the Romantic Construction of the Reader," *Studies in Romanticism* 33 (winter 1994): 607.

38. James Spedding, "Tales by the author of *Headlong Hall*," *Edinburgh Review* 68, January 1839, 443.

39. Percy Bysshe Shelley, preface to *Revolt of Islam, The Complete Works of Percy Bysshe Shelley*, ed. R. Ingpen and W. E. Peck (New York: Gordian Press, 1965), 1:242.

40. *Prometheus Unbound, Complete Works*, III.iv.4–5; "Mask of Anarchy," *Complete Works*, stanza lxxxii, ll. 331–33.

41. See Blake's hymn to Jerusalem in the Preface to the first book of *Milton*: "I will not cease from Mental Fight, / Nor shall my Sword sleep in my hand" (Plate 1). References to Blake's illuminated poetry (WB) are cited parenthetically by plate and line numbers, his prose by page number, and his unilluminated poetry by line number.

42. Peter Ackroyd, *Blake* (London: Sinclair-Stevenson, 1995), 45.

43. Hazard Adams, "Synecdoche and Method," in *Critical Paths: Blake and the Argument of Method*, ed. Dan Miller, Mark Bracher, and Donald Ault. (Durham: Duke University Press, 1987), 58, 61.

44. Hans Kellner, *Language and Historical Representation: Getting the Story Crooked* (Madison: Wisconsin University Press, 1989), 63–64.

45. "We have not (as I conceive) lost the generosity and dignity of thinking of the fourteenth century, nor as yet have we subtilized ourselves into savages": *Reflections*, 8:137–38.

46. Paine, *Rights of Man,* 65.

47. Ibid., 65.

48. I.e., "Guardian of the secret codes" (12:15): Erdman makes the identification with Thurlow: *Prophet*, 214.

49. *Prelude*, 12:371–73.

50. "Salisbury Plain," in *The Salisbury Plain Poems of William Wordsworth*, ed. Stephen Gill (Ithaca: Cornell University Press, 1975), ll. 429–32.

Afterword

1. "Burke, "Thoughts on French Affairs," 8: 347–48, 342, 344–45, 347–48.

2. Ibid., 8:347.

3. Burke, "Letter to a Member of the General Assembly," 8:297–98.

Bibliography

Primary

Anti-Jacobin, or Weekly Examiner. In Two Volumes, The. 4th edition. London: J. Wright, 1799.

Anti-Jacobin Review and Magazine; or Monthly Political and Literary Censor.

Austen, Jane. *Persuasion.* Markham, Ont.: Penguin, 1965.

Bentham, Jeremy. *The Works of Jeremy Bentham.* 11 vols. Edited by John Bowring. New York: Russell & Russell, 1962.

Berkeley, George. *A Treatise Concerning the Principles of Human Knowledge.* Edited by A. A. Luce and T. E. Jessup. London: Nelson, 1948-57.

Black Dwarf, The.

Blackwood's Edinburgh Magazine.

Blair, Hugh. *Lectures on Rhetoric and Belles Lettres.* Edited by Harold F. Harding. Carbondale: Southern Illinois University Press, 1965.

Blake, William. *The Complete Poetry and Prose of William Blake.* Edited by David V. Erdman. Toronto: Doubleday, 1988.

Browne, Thomas, LL.D., "Advertisement." In *The British Cicero; or a Selection of the most Admired Speeches in the English Language; Arranged under Three Distinct Heads of Popular, Parliamentary, and Judicial Oratory: With Historical Illustrations: To which is Prefixed, An Introduction to the Study and Practice of Eloquence.* 3 vols. London: Longman, Hurst, Rees, and Orme, 1808.

Burke, Edmund. *Reflections on the Revolution in France.* Edited by Conor Cruise O'Brien. Toronto: Penguin, 1986.

―――. *Writings and Speeches of Edmund Burke.* 9 vols. Edited by Paul Langford. Oxford: Clarendon, 1991.

Campbell, George. *The Philosophy of Rhetoric.* Edited by Lloyd Bitzer. Carbondale: South Illinois University Press, 1963.

Carolus Candidus. *A Short Reply to a Short Defence of the Whigs, which will shortly prove the Imputations cast Upon them during the Late Election to Be Founded in Truth; being a Short Review of their Political Conduct from 1688, to the Present Time. In Short, a Complete Refutation of the Arguments of a Noble and Learned Lord.* London: John Lowndes, 1819.

Cobbett, William. *A Grammar of the English Language, in a Series of Letters.* London: Henry Frowde, 1906.

———. *A History of the Protestant Reformation in England and Ireland.* 2 vols. New York : J. Doyle, 1834.

———. *A History of the Regency and Reign of King George the Fourth.* 2 vols. London: Mills, Jowett, and Mills, 1830.

———. *Paper Against Gold; or, The History and Mystery of the Bank of England, of the Debt, of the Stocks, of the Sinking Fund, and of all the other Tricks and Contrivances, Carried on by the Means of Paper Money.* New York: John Doyle, 1834.

———. *Rural Rides.* Edited by George Woodcock. Harmondsworth: Penguin, 1967.

———. *Thirteen Sermons on Crimes of an Enormous Nature, and Crimes of Public Men.* Philadelphia: W. A. Leary, 183?.

Cobbett's Weekly Political Register.

Coleridge, Samuel Taylor. *The Collected Works of Samuel Taylor Coleridge.* 13 vols. Edited by Kathleen Coburn. Princeton, N.J.: Princeton University Press, 1969.

———. *The Notebooks of Samuel Taylor Coleridge.* 5 Vols. Edited by Kathleen Coburn. Princeton, N.J.: Princeton University Press, 1961.

Combe, Abram. *An Address to the Conductors of the Periodical Press, Upon the Causes of Religious and Political Disputes, with remarks on the Local and General Definition of Certain Words and Terms which have often been the Subject of Controversy.* Edinburgh: Bell and Bradfute, 1823.

Corry, John A. *The English Metropolis; or, London in the Year 1820. Containing Satirical Strictures on Public Manners, Morals, and Amusements; A Young Gentleman's Adventures; and Characteristic Anecdotes of Several Eminent Individuals who now figure in this Great Theatre of Temporary Exhibition. By the Author of a Satirical View of London.* London: Sherwood, Neely, and Jones, 1820.

A Defence of Mr. Cobbett, Against the Intrigues of Sir Francis Burdett, and his Partisans. London: R. Carlile, 1819.

[Disreali, Isaac] *Vaurien: or, Sketches of the Times: exhibiting Views of the Philosophies, Religions, Politics, Literature, and Manners of the Age.* 2 Vols. London: T. Cadell, junior, and W. Davies; J. Murray and S. Highley, 1797.

A Dissertation on the Rise, Progress, Views, Strength, Interests and Characters, of the Two Parties of the Whigs and Tories. Boston: Joseph Greenleaf, 1773.

Edinburgh Review.

Elements of Opposition. London: J. Hatchard, 1803.

Elements of Reform, or An Account of the Motives and Intentions of the Advocates for Parliamentary Reformation. London: T. Gillet.

Examiner, The

Ferguson, Adam. *An Essay on the History of Civil Society.* Edited by Fania Oz-Salzberge. Cambridge: Cambridge University Press, 1996.

From the Queen's Answers to Various Addresses Presented to Her; together with Her Majesty's Extraordinary Letter to the King; and an Introduction; and Observations Illustrative of their Tendency. London: John Hatchard and Son, 1821.

Godwin, William. *Caleb Williams*. Edited by David McCracken. Oxford: Oxford University Press, 1982.

———. *Political Justice and its Influence on Morals and Happiness*. Edited by F. E. L. Priestley. Toronto: University of Toronto Press, 1969.

Hamilton, William Gerard. *Parliamentary Logic: To which are subjoined Two Speeches, Delivered in the House of Commons of Ireland, and other pieces by the Right Honorable William Gerard Hamilton. With an Appendix, containing Considerations on the Corn Laws, by Samuel Johnson, LL.D. never before printed*. [Edited by Edward Malone.] London: C. and R. Baldwin, 1808.

Hard, Josiah. *Imposture Exposed in a Few Brief Remarks on the Irreligiousness, Profaneness, Indelicacy, Virulence, and Vulgarity of certain Persons, who style Themselves Anti-Jacobin Reviewers*. Cambridge: J. Drighton, 1801.

Hazlitt, William. *The Complete Works of William Hazlitt*. 21 vols. Edited by P. P. Howe. Toronto: J. M. Dent and Sons, 1930–34.

Jobson, Wemyss. *Career of the Whigs*. London: G. J. Sands and Co., 1851.

King's Treatment of the Queen shortly stated to the People of England, The. London: William Hone, 1820.

Lawson, John. *Lectures Concerning Oratory*. Edited by E. Neal Claussen and Karl R. Wallace. Edwardsville: Southern Illinois University Press, 1972.

Letter to the Right Honourable George Canning, M.P. President of the Board of Control, &c. on his Late Speech at Liverpool, A. London: R. Carlile, 1818.

Locke, John. *An Essay Concerning Human Understanding*. Edited by Peter H. Nidditch. Oxford: Clarendon Press, 1975.

Mill, John Stuart. *Collected Works of John Stuart Mill*. 33 vols. Edited by John M. Robson. Toronto: University of Toronto Press, 1929.

Paine, Thomas. *Rights of Man*. Markham, Ont.: Penguin, 1984.

Peacock, Thomas Love. *The Halliford Edition of the Works of Thomas Love Peacock*. Edited by H. F. B. Brett-Smith and C.E. Jones. New York: AMS Press, 1967.

———. *The Letters of Thomas Love Peacock*. Edited by Nicholas A. Joukovsky. Oxford: Clarendon Press, 2001.

Phillips, Charles. *The Queen's Case Stated*. London: William Hone, 1820.

Political Primer; or, Road to Public Honours, The. London: Henry Colburn, 1820.

Priestley, Joseph. *A Course of Lectures on Oratory and Criticism*. Edited by Vincent M. Bevilacqua and Richard Murphy. Carbondale: Southern Illinois University Press, 1965.

Reid, Thomas. *An Inquiry into the Human Mind on the Principles of Common Sense*. Edited by William Hamilton. Hildesheim: Georg Olms, 1967.

Reid, Thomas. *Essays on the Intellectual Powers of Man*. Edited by William Hamilton. Hildesheim: Georg Olms, 1967.

Republican, The.

Satirist; or, Monthly Meteor, The.

Shelley, Mary. *Frankenstein: or The Modern Prometheus, The 1818 Text*. Edited by Marilyn Butler. Oxford: Oxford University Press, 1998.

Shelley, Percy Bysshe. *The Complete Works of Percy Bysshe Shelley*. Edited by R. Ingpen and W. E. Peck. New York: Gordian Press, 1965.

———. *Shelley's Poetry and Prose*. Edited by Donald H. Reiman and Sharon B. Powers. New York: Norton, 1977.

———. *The Letters of Percy Bysshe Shelley*. 2 vols. Edited by Frederick L. Jones. Oxford: Oxford University Press, 1964.

Sheridan, Thomas. *A Course of Lectures on Elocution*. London: A. Millar, R. and J. Dodsley, T. Davies, C. Henderson, J. Wilkie, and E. Dilly, 1762.

Smith, Adam. *Lectures on Rhetoric and Belles Lettres*. Edited by John Lothian. London: T. Nelson, 1963.

Sprat, Thomas. *The History of the Royal Society of London for the Improving of Natural Knowledge*. Edited by Jackson I. Cope and Harold Whitmore Jones. St. Louis: Washington University Studies, 1958.

Von Humboldt, Wilhelm. *On Language: The Diversity of Human Language-Structure and Its Influence on the Mental Development of Mankind*. Translated by Peter Heath. Cambridge: Cambridge University Press, 1988.

White, Henry. *A Calm Appeal to the Friends of Freedom and Reform on the Double Dealings of Mr. Cobbett and the Baneful Tendency of his Writings with a Vindication of the Whigs and the Patriots of Westminster and the Borough of Southwark, against his scurrilous and malignant Aspersions*. London: H. Robertson, 1823.

Wordsworth, William. *The Salisbury Plain Poems of William Wordsworth*. Edited by Stephen Gill. The Cornell Wordsworth. Ithaca: Cornell University Press, 1975.

———. *The Borderers*. Edited by Robert Osborn. The Cornell Wordsworth. Ithaca: Cornell University Press, 1982.

———. *The Prelude: 1799, 1805, 1850*. Edited by Jonathan Wordsworth, M. H. Abrams, and Stephen Gill. New York: Norton, 1979.

———. *The Prose Works of William Wordsworth*. Edited by W. J. B. Owen and Jane Worthington Smyser. Oxford: Clarendon Press, 1974.

Secondary

Ackroyd, Peter. *Blake*. London: Sinclair-Stevenson, 1995.

Adams, Hazard. "Synecdoche and Method." In *Critical Paths: Blake and the Argument of Method*, edited by Dan Miller, Mark Bracher, and Donald Ault. Durham: Duke University Press, 1987.

Appleby, Joyce. "Consumption in Early Modern Social Thought." In *Consumption and the World of Goods*, edited by John Brewer and Roy Porter. London: Routledge, 1993.

Behrendt, Stephen, ed. *Romanticism, Radicalism, and the Press*. Detroit: Wayne State University Press, 1997.

Beiser, Frederick C. *The Sovereignty of Reason: The Defence of Rationality in the Early English Enlightenment*. Princeton, N.J.: Princeton University Press, 1996.

Bialostosky, Don H. and Lawrence Needham, eds. *Rhetorical Traditions and British Romantic Literature*. Bloomington: Indiana University Press, 1995.

Bromwich, David. *Disowned by Memory: Wordsworth's Poetry of the 1790s.* Chicago: University of Chicago Press, 1998.

Butler, Marilyn. *Jane Austen and the War of Ideas.* Oxford: Clarendon Press, 1975.

——. *Romantics, Rebels and Reactionaries: English Literature and its Background, 1760–1830.* Oxford: Oxford University Press, 1981.

Christensen, Jerome. "The Method of *The Friend.*" In *Rhetorical Traditions and British Romantic Literature,* edited by Don H. Bialostosky and Lawrence D. Needham. Bloomington: Indiana University Press, 1995.

Clark, Anna. "Queen Caroline and the Sexual Politics of Popular Culture in London, 1820." *Representations* 31 (summer 1990): 47–68

Clemit, Pamela. *The Godwinian Novel: The Rational Fictions of Godwin, Brockden Brown, Mary Shelley.* Oxford: Clarendon Press, 1993.

De Bruyn, Frans. *The Literary Genres of Edmund Burke: The Political Uses of Literary Form.* Oxford: Clarendon Press, 1996.

Derry, John W. *Castlereagh.* London: Allen Lane, 1976.

Dixon, Peter. *Canning: Politician and Statesman.* London: Weidenfeld and Nicolson, 1976.

Dyck, Ian. "From 'Rabble' to 'Chopsticks': the Radicalism of William Cobbett." *Albion* (1989); 71–72.

——. *William Cobbett and Rural Popular Culture,* Cambridge: Cambridge University Press, 1992.

Ellul, Jacques. *The Technological Society.* Translated by John Wilkinson. New York: Knopf, 1967.

Engell, James. "The New Rhetoric and Romantic Poetics." In *Rhetorical Traditions and British Romantic Literature,* edited by Don H. Bialostosky and Lawrence D. Needham. Bloomington: Indiana University Press, 1995.

Erdman, David V. Blake, *Prophet Against Empire: A Poet's Interpretation of the History of His Own Times.* Princeton: Princeton University Press, 1954.

Fulford, Roger. *The Trial of Queen Caroline.* London: B.T. Batsford, 1967.

Gilmartin, Kevin. *Print Politics: The Press and Radical Opposition in Early Nineteenth-Century England.* Cambridge Studies in Romanticism. Cambridge: Cambridge University Press, 1996.

Green, Daniel. *Great Cobbett: The Noblest Agitator.* London: Hodder and Stoughton, 1983.

Guy, John. "The Henrican Age." In *The Varieties of British Political Thought, 1500–1800,* edited by J. G. A. Pocock. Cambridge: Cambridge University Press, 1993.

Habermas, Jürgen. *The Structural Transformation of the Public Sphere: An Inquiry into a Category of Bourgeois Society.* Cambridge: MIT Press, 1991.

Heinzelman, Kurt. *The Economics of the Imagination* (Amherst: University of Massachusetts Press, 1980.

Horkheimer, Max, and Theodor W. Adorno. *Dialectic of Enlightenment.* Translated by John Cumming. New York: Herder and Herder, 1969.

Howell, Wilbur Samuel. *Eighteenth-Century British Logic and Rhetoric.* Princeton: Princeton University Press, 1971.

Hughes, Peter. "Originality and Allusion in the Writings of Edmund Burke." *Centrum* 4 (1976): 32–43.

Johnston, Kenneth R. "Romantic Anti-Jacobins or Anti-Jacobin Romantics?" *Romanticism on the Net* 15 (August 1999): <http://users.ox.ac.uk/~scat0385/antijacobin.html>.

Jones, Steven E. *Satire and Romanticism.* New York: St. Martin's Press/Palgrove, 2000.

Kellner, Hans. *Language and Historical Representation: Getting the Story Crooked.* Madison: Wisconsin University Press, 1989.

Khan, Victoria. *Machiavellian Rhetoric from the Counter-Reformation to Milton.* Princeton: Princeton University Press, 1994.

Klancher, Jon, ed. "Romanticism and its Publics." *Studies in Romanticism* 33 (winter 1994).

———. *The Making of the English Reading Audiences,* 1790–1832. Madison, Wis.: University of Wisconsin Press, 1987.

Laqueur, Thomas W. "The Queen Caroline Affair: Politics as Art in the Reign of George IV." *Journal of Modern History* 54 (Sept. 1982): 417–66

Leaver, Kirsten. "Pursuing Conversations: *Caleb Williams* and the Romantic Construction of the Reader." *Studies in Romanticism* 33 (winter 1994): 589–610.

Lippmann, Walter. *Public Opinion.* New York: Macmillan, 1961.

Lock, F. P. "Rhetoric and Representation in Burke's *Reflections.*" In *Edmund Burke's Reflections on the Revolution in France,* edited by John Whale. Manchester: Manchester University Press, 2000.

Mack, Mary. *Letters of Anti-Machiavel.* In *Jeremy Bentham: An Odyssey of Ideas, 1748–1792* Toronto: Heinemann, 1962.

McCalman, Iain. *Radical Underworld: Prophets, Revolutionaries and Pornographers in London, 1795–1840.* Cambridge: Cambridge University Press, 1987.

Nattrass, Leonora. *William Cobbett: The Politics of Style.* Cambridge: Cambridge University Press, 1995.

O'Brien, Conor Cruise. Introduction to *Reflections on the Revolution in France,* by Edmund Burke. Edited by Conor Cruise O'Brien. Toronto: Penguin, 1986.

O'Gorman, Frank. *The Rise of Party in England: The Rockingham Whigs, 1760–82.* London: George Allen & Unwin, 1975.

Paul, C. Kegan. *William Godwin: His Friends and Contemporaries.* London: C. Kegan Paul, 1876.

Phillipson, Nicholas. "Politeness and Politics in the Reigns of Anne and the Early Hanoverians." In *The Varieties of British Political Thought, 1500–1800,* edited by J. G. A. Pocock. Cambridge: Cambridge University Press, 1993.

Pocock, J. G. A. *The Machiavellian Moment: Florentine Political Thought and the Atlantic Republican Tradition.* Princeton: Princeton University Press: 1975.

———. "The Varieties of Whiggism from Exclusion to Reform." In *The Varieties of British Political Thought, 1500–1800,* edited by J. G. A. Pocock. Cambridge: Cambridge University Press, 1993.

Raab, Felix. *The English Face of Machiavelli: A Changing Interpretation 1500–1700*. London: Routledge and Kegan Paul, 1964.

Rieder, John. *Wordsworth's Counterrevolutionary Turn: Community, Virtue, and Vision in the 1790s*. Newark: University of Delaware Press, 1997.

Scrivener, Michael. *Poetry and Reform: Periodical Verse from the English Democratic Press, 1792–1824*. Detroit: Wayne State University Press, 1992.

Sebberson, David. "Practical Reasoning, Rhetoric, and Wordsworth's 'Preface.'" In *Spirits of Fire: English Romantic Writers and Contemporary Historical Methods*, edited by G. A. Rosso and Daniel P. Watkins. Madison, N. J.: Fairleigh Dickinson University Press, 1990.

Shell, Marc. *The Economy of Literature*. Baltimore: Johns Hopkins University Press, 1978.

———. *Money, Language, and Thought: Literary and Philosophical Economies from the Medieval to the Modern Era*. Berkeley and Los Angeles: University of California Press, 198.

Smith, E.A. *A Queen on Trial: The Affair of Queen Caroline*. Dover, N.H.: Alan Sutton, 1993.

Smith, Olivia. *The Politics of Language, 1791–1819*. Oxford: Clarendon Press, 1984.

Speier, Hans. *The Truth in Hell and other Essays on Politics and Culture, 1935–1987*. New York: Oxford University Press, 1989.

Ulman, Lewis H. *Things, Thoughts, Words, and Actions: the Problem of Language in Late Eighteenth-Century British Rhetorical Theory*. Carbondale: Southern Illinois University Press, 1994.

Whale, John. *Imagination under Pressure, 1789–1832: Aesthetics, Politics and Utility*. Cambridge: Cambridge University Press, 2000.

———, ed. *Edmund Burke's Reflections on the Revolution in France*. Manchester: Manchester University Press, 2000.

Williams, Raymond. *Problems in Materialism and Culture: Selected Essays*. London: NLB, 1980.

Wood, Marcus. *Radical Satire and Print Culture, 1790–1822*. Oxford: Oxford University Press, 1994.

Worrall, David. *Radical Culture: Discourse, Resistance and Surveillance, 1790–1820*. London: Harvester Wheatsheaf, 1992.

Index

Aarsleff, Hans, 265 n. 22
Adams, Hazard, 250
Addington, Henry, 163, 205
Addison, Joseph, 31, 71, 190
Adorno, Theodor, 45, 270 n. 17
Alexander the Great, 238
American Revolution, 205, 214, 217
Analytical Review, The, 135, 143
Anne, Queen, 95, 96
Answer to Aylsbury, 105
Answer to Chipping Sodbury, 105
Anti-Jacobinism, 161, 163, 189, 193,
    194; Anti-Jacobin critique, 131,
    135, 139, 140, 141, 144, 145–57,
    151, 152, 159, 160; Anti-Jacobin
    press, 120, 127, 133, 134–45, 148,
    156, 163, 164, 170, 171, 198, 207–8,
    212, 224, 260
*Anti-Jacobin Review and Magazine,
    The,* 18, 134, 135, 136, 137, 139,
    143, 142, 145, 146, 159–60, 160,
    212
*Anti-Jacobin, or Weekly Examiner,
    The,* 99, 101, 126, 132, 133, 134,
    136, 137, 138, 139, 140, 143, 142,
    144, 145, 146, 147, 148, 149, 164,
    269 n. 7
Arden, Lord, 198
Aristotle, 21, 85
Aukland, Lord: *Some Remarks on the
    Apparent Circumstances of the War
    in the Fourth Week of October 1795,*
    129–30, 138
Austen, Jane, 51, 265 n. 30

Bacon, Francis, 29, 28, 38, 196, 255
Bakhtin, Mikhail 17, 168
Barruel, Abbé Augustin, 152
Bath, 1st Earl of, 79
Beattie, James: *Essays on Poetry and
    Music as They Affect the Mind,* 34
Behrendt, Stephen, 263 n. 2
Beiser, Frederick C., 264 n. 9
Benradotte, Prince, 179
Bentham, Jeremy, 46, 48, 49, 54, 58,
    60–61, 62, 64, 65, 66, 68, 69, 76,
    90, 103, 104, 129, 141, 147, 148,
    156, 193, 227, 231–32, 259,
    265 n. 29, 266 nn. 31 and 32;
    Anarchical Fallacies, 57–59; *Book
    of Fallacies,* 47, 53–57, 59, 65, 66
    105, 129, 169, 180, 274 n. 28;
    "Essay on Political Tactics," 59–60,
    65; *A Fragment on Government,*
    54; *Official Aptitude Maximized;
    Expense Minimized,* 66
Bergami, Bartolomo, 103
Berkeley, George, 29, 54, 130
Bevilacqua, Vincent M., 38
Bialostosky, Don H., 20
Bill of Pains and Penalties, 103, 105
Bingham, Peregrine, 53
Bitzer, Lloyd, 43
Black Dwarf, The, 62, 93, 94, 95, 98,
    101, 102, 108, 110, 115, 123, 125,
    148, 212, 268 nn. 26 and 36
Blackstone, William, 54, 200
Blackwood's Edinburgh Magazine,
    118, 127, 128, 135, 126, 155–56

Blair, Hugh, 37, 38, 39, 70, 71, 73, 77, 78, 96, 122, 123, 194; *Lectures on Rhetoric and Belles Lettres,* 36, 70, 35, 212

Blake, William, 25, 47, 247, 259, 264 n. 6; *Book of Ahania,* 251; *Book of Los,* 253; *Book of Urizen,* 249–54, 261; *Europe* 255–56, 256, 257; "The French Revolution," 254–55, 256; *Jerusalem* 261; Los cycle, 250, 261; *Milton,* 251, 274 n. 41

Boleyn, Anne, 106, 203

Bolingbroke, Lord, 71, 77, 96, 212

Bonaparte, Napoleon, 18, 89, 90, 127

Booth, Henry, 78

Bourbons, 90

Boyle, Robert, 28

Brand, the Reverend John, 195

Bromwich, David, 234

Brougham, Henry, 111, 115–16, 21

Browne, Thomas: *The British Cicero, A Selection of the most Admired Speeches in the English Language,* 72–74, 94, 212

Bruce (convict), 117

Bruyn, Frans, 273 n. 18

Bryant, Jacob: *A New System, or, an Analysis of Ancient Mythology,* 250, 251

Bull, John, 90, 97, 167, 184, 236, 260

Bunyan, John, 211

Burdett, Sir Francis, 187

Burke, Edmund, 19, 27, 29, 31, 66, 67, 91, 93, 94, 100, 101, 104, 107, 108, 109, 110, 126, 127, 128, 129, 131, 137, 138, 140, 141, 145, 151, 155, 164, 165, 171, 184, 186, 192, 201, 203, 205, 208, 214, 217, 218, 219, 220, 224, 225, 227, 233, 235, 240, 242, 246, 249, 254, 255, 256, 260, 273 nn. 11, 16, and 22, 275 n. 45; on logic of Glorious Revolution in Reflections on the Revolution on France, 214–24; "A Vindication of Natural Society," 224; *A Philosophical Enquiry into the Origin of our Ideas of the Sublime and Beautiful,* 215; *Letters on a Regicide Peace,* 18, 67, 129–30, 170, 207, 221, 224, 225; "Letter to a Member of the General Assembly," 261; "Letter to a Member of the National Assembly," 222–23; "Letter to a Noble Lord," 225; *Reflections on the Revolution in France,* 18, 27, 91, 92, 102, 126, 127, 129, 130, 131, 134, 135, 136, 170, 186, 201, 241, 247, 258, 259; "Remarks of the Policy of the Allies," 129; "Thoughts on French Affairs," 128, 258

Burke-Paine Debate, 192, 236, 237, 246, 254

Butler, Marilyn, 133, 134, 135

Byron, Lord, 157, 163

Camden, Earl of, 79, 84, 12

Campbell, George, 35, 37, 39, 40, 42, 43, 48, 70, 72, 73, 121, 123, 124, 146, 151, 168, 209, 215, 266 n. 34; *The Philosophy of Rhetoric,* 34, 36, 37, 44, 84

Campbell, John, 78

Camden, Earl of, 219

Candidus, Carolus, *A Short Reply to a Short Defence of the Whigs,* 93, 94

Canning, George, 18, 63, 82, 91, 98–103, 109, 112, 122–23, 125, 126, 132, 133, 134, 136, 138, 139, 140, 141, 142, 158, 163, 164, 165, 169, 172, 185, 186, 187, 201, 208, 260, 228 nn. 27 and 36, 268 n. 26

Carlile, Richard, 95, 118, 162, 167

Caroline of Brunswick, 103, 104, 106, 107, 108, 109, 110, 113, 114; trial, 18, 103–17, 120, 123, 161, 164, 177, 211

Cartwright, John (Major), 187–88

Cassels (alleged spy), 97

Castlereagh, Lord, 81, 97, 98, 99, 109, 118, 119, 120, 121, 125, 132, 133, 146, 182

Catholic Emancipation, 101

Cavendish, House of, 62

Cecil, Sir William, 204

Charles I, 223

Chatham, Lord, 122, 123

Christensen, Jerome, 264 n. 4

Cicero, 27, 30, 49, 53, 69, 183
Clark, Anna, 103, 268 n. 37
Cobbett, William, 20, 62, 90, 92, 99, 101, 110, 111, 115, 121, 132, 139, 154, 210, 217, 259, 271 n. 12, 272 n. 18; apparent inconsistency, 162–70; and "Pitt System," 162, 174–75, 177, 181–82, 199; as Peter Porcupine, 162; compared to Paine, 165; difficulty expressing national ethos, 185–89; educating readers in forms of ministerialist imposture, 179–80; on candid language and national spirit, 182–86; on English readers duped by ministerialist press techniques, 177–79; on credit and rhetoric, 192–99; on Green Bags, 112–14, 260; on Pitt's eulogists, 173–74; on praise and censure of public personages, 175–77; on press, 181–85; on use of anti-Jacobin rhetorical techniques, 172–73; *Cobbett's English Grammar*, 180, 182; *Cobbett's Weekly Political Register*, 92, 95, 98, 107, 109–1,10, 111–12, 120, 162, 163, 165, 168, 170, 171, 174, 177, 178, 179, 162, 163, 165, 168, 170, 171, 172, 174, 175, 176, 177, 178, 179, 180, 183–84, 185, 189, 199; *A History of the Protestant Reformation in England and Ireland*, 199–206; *A History of the Regency and Reign of King George the Fourth*, 199; *Le Mercure Anglois de Cobbett*, 171, 172; *Paper Against Gold; or, The History and Mystery of the Bank of England, of the Debt, of the Stocks, of the Sinking Fund, and of all the other Tricks and Contrivances, Carried on by the Means of Paper Money*, 189–99; *Peter Porcupine*, 168; *The Porcupine*, 163
Coleridge, Samuel Taylor, 27, 29, 44–45, 63, 110, 116, 154, 160, 259, 261; "Christabel," 157; "Fable of the Madning Rain," 23, 24, 26, 87; *The Friend*, 22, 23, 24–25, 26, 85–87, 269 n. 9; *On the Constitution of*

Church and State, 27; *The Watchman*, 24.
Combe, Abraham, *An Address to the Conductors of the Periodical Press*, 156–57
Copley, Sir John, 116
Corry, John A., *The English Metropolis*, 270 n. 11
Country Ideology, 88–91, 93, 97, 101, 111, 208, 230
Courier, The, 109, 119, 120, 176, 177, 179, 180, 184, 185
Court ideology, 88–91, 93, 230
Cowper, William, 75
Cranmer, Thomas, 203–4
Critical Review, The, 139, 142
Criticism (and rhetoric), 121–22, 124, 123–26, 130, 147, 160
Cromwell's Commonwealth, 205

Darwin, Erasmus, 143
De Man, Paul, 20
Declaration of Right, 217, 218, 219, 226
Declaration of Rights by French National Assembly (1791), 58, 59
Demosthenes, 49, 69, 183
Devonshire, Duke of, 92
Dionysius of Halicarnassus, 53
Disraeli, Isaac, *Vaurien*, 157–58, 207–9, 221
Dissertation on the Rise, Progress, Views, Strength, Interests and Characters, of the Two Parties of the Whigs and Tories, A, 96
Dixon, Peter, 102
Duke of Brunswick, 116
Dumont, Étienne, 53, 57
Dyck, Ian, 271 n. 1
Dyslogistic rhetoric, 54–55, 59, 105, 175, 193

Eclectic Review, The, 150
Edinburgh Review, The, 95, 119, 126, 131, 150, 155, 157, 159
Edward VI, 200, 201
Elements of Opposition, 62, 147, 149
Elements of Reform, or An Account of the Motives and Intentions of the

Advocates for Parliamentary Refor-mation, 168, 271 n. 4

Elizabeth I, 200, 201, 203, 204

Ellul, Jacques, 87

Elocution, 29–34, 34, 35, 43, 45, 52, 58, 61, 68, 69, 70, 92, 128, 183, 215, 228

Emerson, Ralph Waldo, 190

Empirical (or Sensationalist) Psychology, 20, 26, 31, 37, 41, 43, 45, 48, 50, 51, 55, 56, 57, 58, 63, 69, 73, 128, 179

Encyclopedia, the, 127

Engell, James, 34

English Civil War, 217

Enlightenment, the, 17, 18, 19, 24, 25, 34, 35, 45, 70, 71, 135, 136, 137, 142 201, 202, 223, 224, 242, 243, 250, 251, 257

Erdman, David, 275 n. 48

Erskine, Lord 9

Euhemerist mythology, 250–51

Eulogistic rhetoric, 54–55, 59, 175, 193

Examiner, the, 88, 109, 114

Fenning, Daniel, 201

Ferguson, Adam, 71, 73; *An Essay on the History of Civil Society*, 69, 213

Fortuna, 66, 67, 102, 203, 227, 233

Fox, Charles, 91, 92, 94, 108, 175, 186, 192, 198

Fox, George, 200

Frankfurt School, 159

French Revolution, 19, 57, 91, 92, 102, 106, 205, 206, 217, 221, 222, 235, 258

Frere, John Hookham, 18, 126, 132–33, 134, 163, 208

Friends of the People, The (society), 92

From the Queen's Answers to Various Addresses Presented to Her, 104–6

Fulford, Roger, 268 n. 37

George III, 103, 116, 117, 180, 255

George IV (Prince Regent), 103, 106, 107, 176, 177, 182, 184

Gerard, Alexander, 38

Gibbons, Thomas, 34

Gifford, Robert, 116

Gifford, William, 144; *The Baviad,* 135–36

Gilmartin, Kevin, 263 n. 2

Glorious Revolution, the, 94, 205, 214, 216, 217, 218, 219, 221, 226

Godwin, William, 143, 207, 226; *Caleb Williams*, 235–41, 244, 246, 260; *An Enquiry Concerning Political Justice*, 235, 236, 239, 240, 241, 242, 246, 247, 260; *St. Leon*, 160

Good Council, doctrine of, 106, 114

Grenville, Lord, 64, 149

Grey, Lord, 64

Grimm, Jacob, 265 n. 22

Grosvenor, Earl of, 184

Guy, John, 106

Habermas, Jurgen, 17, 198

Hamilton, William Gerard, 56, 57, 61–62, 65, 66, 67, 76, 79, 81, 84, 92, 93, 104, 127, 129, 148, 149, 155, 156, 166, 180, 213, 218, 240, 267 n. 11; *Parliamentary Logic*, 46–53, 55, 59,60, 61, 62, 64, 65, 66, 67, 68, 76, 88, 98, 101, 146, 147, 148, 167, 169, 227

Hanoverians, the, 95

Hard, Josiah, *Imposture Exposed in a Few Brief Remarks on the Irreligiousness, Profaneness, Indelicacy, Virulence, and Vulgarity of certain Persons, who style Themselves Anti-Jacobin Reviewers*, 152–53, 155

Hartley, David, 38

Hazlitt, William, 19, 46, 81, 88, 94, 98, 99, 100, 104, 110, 116–17, 119, 121, 122, 123, 124, 125, 129, 130, 131, 132, 133, 145, 155, 156, 159, 161, 164, 165, 166, 167, 170, 172, 174, 175, 177, 185, 186, 187, 190, 212, 219, 220, 222, 226, 246, 264 n. 6; "Character of Cobbett," 163, 164; "Character of Mr. Pitt," 87; *Eloquence of the British Senate,* 74–88, 93, 131; *Lectures on the Age of Elizabeth*, 121; *Lectures on the English Poets*, 127, 269 n. 1; "Mem-

orabilia of Mr. Coleridge," 272 n. 15;
Life of Napoleon, 132; "On Modern
Comedy," 122; "On the Present
State of Parliamentary Eloquence,"
80, 81–82, 98; "On the Spy
System," 97; "The Opposition and
'The Courier,' " 97; "The Political
Automaton: A Modern Character,"
85; "Political Essays, with Sketches
of Public Characters," 18, 79,
89–91, 119, 129, 165; "The Spirit of
Controversy," 130; *The Spirit of the
Age*, 82–83, 95, 163, 213, 241
Hegel, Georg Wilhelm Friedrich, 190
Heidigger, Martin, 190
Heinzelman, Kurt, 189–90
Henley, Orator, 30
Henry III, 225, 230
Henry VIII, 106, 200, 203, 204
Hobbes, Thomas, 38, 57, 65, 222, 229
Holcroft, Thomas, 17, 18
Holland House, 102, 104
Holland, Lady, 101, 102, 169
Hookham, Thomas, 209, 213, 248
Horkheimer, Max, 45, 270 n. 17
House of Lords, 103, 115
Howard, House of, 62
Howell, Wilbur Samuel, 21, 22, 26,
27, 31, 264–65 n. 17
Hughes, Peter, 216
Humboldt, Wilhelm von, 265 n. 22
Hume, David, 31, 34, 37, 38, 202
Hunt, Leigh, 62, 114, 116
Hutcheson, Francis, 38

Irving, the Reverend Edward, 163

Jacobinism, 90, 110, 126, 127, 130,
131, 135, 138, 141, 145; literary
Jacobinism, 131, 134, 135, 136,
138, 140, 144, 151, 154, 155, 156,
207; rhetoric of, 142, 146, 152, 167,
238, 240, 259
Jacobins, 62, 101, 115, 184, 192
Jacobites, 96
James I, 201
Jefferson, Thomas, 159
Jeffrey, Francis, 150, 159
Johnson, Joseph, 143

Johnson, Kenneth R., 269 n. 4
Johnson, Samuel, 190

Kames, Lord, 29, 31, 34, 37, 38
Kellner, Hans, 252
Khan, Victoria, 68
*King's Treatment of the Queen shortly
stated to the People of England,
The*, 108
Klancher, Jon P., 17, 168, 263 n. 1
Knight, Sir John, 78

Lagueur, Thomas W., 268 n. 37
Landor, Walter Savage, 131, 155
Laqueur, Thomas, 107
Leaver, Kirsten, 274 n. 37
Lefebvre, George, 252
Leiven, Princess, 107
*Letter to the Right Honourable
George Canning, M.P. President of
the Board of Control, &c. on his
Late Speech at Liverpool*, 99–101
Levellers, 62
Lilburne, John, 183, 187
Liverpool administration, 93, 98, 102,
103, 205, 115
Liverpool, Lord, 205
Lock, F. P., 215, 216
Locke, John, 28, 29, 31, 37, 38, 50, 54,
72, 95, 261, 273 n. 16
Lockhart, John Gibson, 154, 15
Longinus, 29, 73
Lothian, John, 265 n. 21
Louis IV, 135
Louis XIV, 127
Lowth, Robert, 34

Machiavelli, 66, 68, 96; *The Prince (Il
Principe)*, 67
Machiavellianism, 62, 66, 68, 80, 102,
103, 129, 155, 167, 169, 180, 209
Mack, Mary, 266 n. 5
Mackintosh, Sir James, 82, 83, 84,
123, 125, 134, 166
Malone, Edmond, 46, 47, 65
Malthus, Thomas, 213, 242; *An Essay
on the Principle of Population*, 241
Mandeville, Bernard, 24, 54, 66, 98
Mansfield, Earl of, 179, 185

Marie Antoinette, 107
Mary I, 200, 201
Mathias, Thomas James, 136
McCalman, Iain, 263 n. 2
Methodism, 32, 34
Mill, John Stuart, 22, 36, 60, 90,
    266 n. 33
Ministerial Press, 126, 131, 132, 133,
    161, 169, 178, 184, 189, 193
Mitchell, L. G., 92, 214
Monthly Magazine, The, 143–44
Monthly Review, The, 135, 139, 155,
    160
Moore, Sir John, 132
Morning Chronicle, The, 97, 82, 144,
    149
Morning Post, The, 141, 146, 149, 180
Murphy, Richard, 38

Napoleonic Wars, 18, 89, 110, 131–33,
    161, 163, 170–72, 174, 177, 188,
    189, 192, 197, 220
Nattrass Leonora, 168–69
Needham, Lawrence, 20
New Rhetoric, the, 34–45, 36, 39, 48,
    50, 52, 58, 61, 68, 73, 74, 215, 216
New School Poetics, 127, 134
New Science, 21, 22, 27
Newcastle, Duke of, 93
Newton, Isaac, 261

O'Brien, Conor Cruise, 224
Old Times, The, 105
Oliver the Spy, 97

Paine, Thomas, 30, 134, 140–41,
    165, 171, 190, 192, 247; *Decline
    and Fall of the British System of
    Finances,* 198; *The Rights of Man,*
    17–18, 222
Parry, William Edward, 241
Peace of Amiens, 163
Peacock, Thomas Love, 176, 213, 247;
    "Ahrimanes," 248, 249; "Essay on
    Fashionable Literature," 157, 159;
    "The Genius of the Thames,"
    209–10, 248, 257; *Headlong Hall,*
    248, 249; *Melincourt,* 61, 148, 150,
    157–58, 209, 248; review of

"Moore's Letters and Journals of
    Lord Byron," 157; "Sir Proteus,"
    159
Peel, Sir Robert, 17, 19
Peninsular Campaign (1808–9), 131
Perceval, Spencer, 205, 198
Perfectibility, doctrine of 242
Peterloo, 211, 249
Peters, Hugh, 223
Petrarch, Francesco: *De Vita Soli-
    taria,* 22, 23
Phillips, Charles: *The Queen's Case
    Stated,* 106
Phillipson, Nicholas, 95, 96
Philosophic Radicalism, 247
Pisitratus, 183
Pitt, William (the Younger), 68, 81,
    82, 91, 101, 110, 116, 126, 134, 162,
    163, 170–71, 172–75, 182, 185, 186,
    188, 193, 197, 204, 205, 217
Pittite governance, 74–77, 94, 104,
    189, 192, 199, 201, 203, 217, 259,
    260; neo-Pittite governance, 87, 88,
    96–97, 98, 104, 220
Plato, 85
Plunkett, William Conyngham,
    82–83, 95
Pocock, J. G. A., 19, 66, 67, 88–89, 90,
    93, 96, 230
Poe, Edgar Allan, 190
Poetry of the Anti-Jacobin Review,
    136, 139
*Political Primer; or, Road to Public
    Honours, The,* 21, 62–63, 67, 98,
    147, 148, 149
Portland, Duke of 205; Portland
    Wigs, 91
Price, the Reverend Richard, 92,
    102, 214, 216, 219, 220–21, 223,
    224, 258
Priestley, Joseph, 18, 37, 40, 41, 42,
    44, 48, 52, 124, 134, 143, 151, 215;
    *A Course of Lectures on Oratory
    and Criticism,* 34, 36–37, 38, 83
Prior, Sir James, 273 n. 13
Prometheus, 241
Prynn, William, 183
Pulteney, William (Earl of Bath),
    79–80

Quarterly Review, The, 144, 155, 157, 158, 159
Quintilian, 53

Raab, Felix, 66
Reform and Reformers, 46, 66, 89–91, 93, 102, 104, 107, 106, 111, 112, 114, 115, 116, 119, 164, 167, 171, 181, 188, 211, 260
Reformation, the, 27, 199, 200, 201, 205, 206, 217, 259, 260
Regency, the, 103, 260
Regency reviewing, 157–60
Reid, Thomas, 30–31; *Essays on the Intellectual Powers of Man*, 28; *Inquiry into the Human Mind on the Principles of Common Sense*, 29
Reider, John, 226
Republican, The, 94, 95, 106–7, 110–11, 113, 116, 118–19, 120, 121, 125, 132, 156, 162, 167, 212
Revolution Society, the 92, 214, 219
Revolutionary France, 104, 129, 130, 131, 161, 170, 203, 214
Ricardo, David, 189
Rockingham, 1st Marquess of, 94; Rockingham Whigs, 91
Rolliad, The, 135
Rousseau, Jean Jacques, 182, 254
Russell, House of, 62

Satire and ridicule in rhetoric, 151–53
Satirist; or, Monthly Meteor, the, 64, 134, 136–37, 139, 149, 150, 150–51, 151–52, 167, 266 n. 8
Scott, Sir Walter, 241, 242
Scrivener, Michael, 263 n. 2
Sebberson, David, 45
Shaftesbury, Earl of, 71, 151, 229
Shakespeare, William, 25, 122
Shell, Marc, 189–90
Shelley, Mary: *Frankenstein*, 235, 236, 241–47, 254, 274 n. 34
Shelley, Percy Bysshe, 157, 209, 248, 249; "The Mask of Anarchy," 249, 260–61; "On Life," 266 n. 14; preface to *Frankenstein*, 242; *Prometheus Unbound*, 241, 249,

260; *The Revolt of Islam*, 248–49
Sheridan, Richard Brinsley, 30, 92, 101, 108, 198
Sheridan, Thomas, 40, 41, 43, 58, 60, 69, 70, 71, 92, 183, 231; *British Education*, 31; *A Course of Lectures on Elocution*, 30–34, 35, 54
Smith, Adam, 190; *Lectures on Rhetoric and Belles Lettres*, 34
Smith, E. A., 268 n. 37
Smith, Olivia, 168; 263 n. 2
Socrates, 183, 196
Solon, 85
Somers, Lord, 218, 219, 220
Sophists and Sophism, 85–87
Southey, Robert, 155
Spedding, James, 248
Spenceans, 110
Spencer, House of, 62
Sprat, Thomas, 28
Stevenson, John, 268 n. 37
Sublime, the, 215–16
Swift, Jonathan, 56; *Directions to Servants*, 47, 66

Tacitus, 73
Temple, Sir William, 71
Thurlow, Lord, 164, 256
Tierney, George, 81–82
Times, The, 179
Timmus, 85
Tooke, John Horne, 183, 187
Tories and Toryism, 18, 65, 66, 89, 90, 91, 92, 93, 96, 101, 102, 110, 111, 114, 126, 133, 138, 142, 147, 152, 164, 167, 171, 181, 185, 260
Triennial Bill, the, 76
True Briton, The, 163

Ulman, H. Lewis, 30, 31

Vice Society, 110
Virtù, 66, 67, 68, 99, 102, 104, 127, 129, 170, 203, 204, 227, 228, 231, 233, 239
Voss, Isaac, 53

Wakefield's Reply to the Bishop of Landaff's Address, 143

Walker, John, 30

Walpole, Horace (brother of Robert), 80

Walpole, Sir Robert, 72, 74, 75, 76, 77, 79, 80, 81, 83, 87, 94, 96, 98, 129, 185, 212

Walsingham, Francis, 204

Waterloo, 18, 164, 248

Wentworth, House of, 62

Westminster Review, The, 155, 157, 159

Whale, John, 271 n. 6, 273 n. 11

Whigs and Whiggism, 45, 65, 66, 64, 71, 72, 73, 74, 76, 81, 88–103, 106, 107, 108, 114, 116, 122, 126, 147, 159, 167, 181, 186, 193, 219, 260

Whig History, 136, 138, 155, 201, 212, 213, 217, 257, 261

Whitbread, Samuel, 81, 82, 186

White, Henry: *On the Double Dealings of Mr. Cobbett*, 161, 168

Whitlocke, Bulstrode, 77

Wilberforce, William, 110

Wilkes, John, 54

William III, 205, 218

Wollstonecraft, Mary, 247

Wood, Alderman, 115

Wordsworth, William, 30, 77; *The Borderers*, 225–34, 234, 235, 238, 240, 259; *Lyrical Ballads*, 45; *The Prelude*, 214, 256; "Salisbury Plain," 257